Tied ıN Knots

FUNNY STORIES *from the* WEDDING DAY

Edited by LISA TAGGART *and* SAMANTHA SCHOECH

SEAL PRESS

D0199422

Tied in Knots
FUNNY STORIES FROM THE WEDDING DAY

"Unbridled" by Suz Redfearn was previously published in the *Baltimore Sun* in 2000.

Some photos and illustrations are used by permission and are the property of the original copyright owners.

Published by
Seal Press
An Imprint of Avalon Publishing Group, Incorporated
1400 65th Street, Suite 250
Emeryville, CA 94608

AVALON
publishing group incorporated

ISBN-10 1-58005-175-8
ISBN-13 978-1-58005-175-0

9 8 7 6 5 4 3 2 1

    Library of Congress Cataloging-in-Publication Data
Taggart, Lisa.
Tied in knots : funny stories from the wedding day / Lisa Taggart and Samantha Schoech.
p. cm.
ISBN-13: 978-1-58005-175-0
ISBN-10: 1-58005-175-8
1. Weddings—Humor. I. Schoech, Samantha. II. Title.
PN6231.W37T34 2006
392.502'07—dc22
2005033893

Cover design by Gia Giasullo
Interior design by Domini Dragoone
Printed in the United States of America by Malloy
Distributed by Publishers Group West

To Sarah, Chops, Kloepster,
Karminder, and Alex;
and to Jimbo and Pete.

to Joanna —
I'm so happy to
be working with you +
I look forward to lots of
Sunset stories —
Lis Topol

Contents

Introduction

   HERE'S A STORY for all of the brides-to-be out there—and friends and family helping them—who are in the middle of planning-madness. The best wedding we ever attended was also the most disastrous. It was April in Las Vegas and this really happened:

The day dawned cold—blustery and downright freezing. The judge officiating the ceremony didn't recognize the bride as she stood at the backyard altar because of her red dress. There was a long, awkward silence as the guests shivered and waited for him to begin. Just as he finally started speaking, an off-season rainstorm drenched us all, causing the flowers to droop. A new and untested friend read a twenty-minute poem he'd written for the occasion that consisted of pronunciation variations on the word "love." That was just the ceremony.

Later in the reception tent, space heaters that had been cranked up for the freakishly cold day ignited the best man's new three-piece suit. He wasn't hurt, but two other guests' suits were also charred. The wind blew sand into the buffet. The power went out. The two bathrooms in the couple's home backed up; then the septic tank buried in the backyard overflowed onto the lawn where the reception was taking place. Roto-Rooter showed up to pump just after dinner.

Through it all, however, we ate, drank, and danced around the day's surprising developments. Guests had traveled to the event from India and St. Louis, San Francisco and Los Angeles. We were all ready to make a good time out of whatever came our way. The couple, Karminder and Randy, set this tone: When we were shivering in the storm, Karminder urged everyone to start dancing early. When the power went out, the duo decided it was a nice, quiet moment to cut the cake. When food had run low and cold and Randy was combing the yellow pages for Roto-Rooter, Karminder grabbed a bottle and walked from table to table, asking everyone: "How about a shot of whiskey? All we have now is whiskey. Anyone want some whiskey?"

The story of Randy and Karminder's wedding has become one of our greatest hits; six years later we still get requests for it from friends and coworkers. In the retelling over the years, we've realized that everyone loves a funny wedding story because almost all of us can relate to the heightened drama leading up to the big day. As

Anne Johnson points out in these pages, organizing a wedding is very much like staging your own romantic play. We already know much of the plot points (dress, cake, happy ending) and the characters (over-wrought bride, controlling mother-in-law, overlooked groom). But inevitably the players surprise us, and the unexpected occurs.

In so many ways, weddings are funny. They expose our preten-sions, our inflated visions of self and social roles, our hidden fam-ily tensions and cultural differences. When loving people find them-selves screaming at each other over sun umbrellas or good employees shirk their responsibilities to shop for candles . . . well, it might not be apparent at the time, but this is pretty hilarious.

What we like most about the essays collected in these pages is the writers' willingness to laugh at themselves and the world. Patri-cia Bunin wrestles with her rebellious underwear with wit and zeal in "Knockers Up." In "The Canadian Question," Patty Smith tackles a dilemma of manners the etiquette guides don't broach. Heather Bry-ant and Sarah Gambito take extreme measures when it appears a Republican may infiltrate the family in "My Sister Married a Wiener." Caren Gussoff surprises herself by developing an obsession with wed-ding knickknacks in "Bridal Porn." In these pages women not only share their stories, they admit their doubts, missteps, and maniacal tendencies. In other words, they tell the truth, bypassing sentimen-tality and heading straight for hilarity.

Around 4:00 AM the night of their wedding, Karminder and Randy found themselves in their hot tub, with a number of friends, all still in their party finery. The pair were exhausted, married, and pleased with the raucous celebrating. Despite the sewage and the blackout and the grit in the food, they couldn't have planned a more memorable, enjoyable party.

Getting married has been called tying the knot because of the long-lasting intent of those marital vows. But more than one guest, no doubt, has observed that brides and family members and wedding planners too often get themselves tied up in knots in orchestrating the big day. To all of those in this predicament, we say, *relax.* It's attitude, we've realized, not planning, that makes a celebration. Instead of worrying over tableware, take a break with the stories here. You'll soon understand that whatever it is, you're in good company. And that it could surely be much worse.

— LISA TAGGART AND SAMANTHA SCHOECH

JANUARY 2006

Alive and Well in Texas

JENNIFER CARSEN

⌒ FOR A LONG TIME, I thought Bridezilla was a myth, an urban legend, no more real than the tales of Nessie lurking in Scotland's murky depths. Little did I know that Bridezilla is very much alive and well. She lives in Texas and is now my sister-in-law. Her eighteen-month reign of terror was launched by a sparkly three-karat diamond ring.

The Beginning of the End
Initially, my husband, Tom, and I are happy that his brother has found someone to love. Haylie seems devoted to Brad and his

happiness, and she is very involved in his life. Extremely involved. Maybe a little too involved.

Haylie does not allow Brad to go out with female friends, even in groups. When Brad gets a middle school teaching job, Haylie feng shuis his classroom and insists that his diploma from Princeton be displayed above his desk so that "people know who they're dealing with." She calls him every night before bed from her apartment a mere three blocks away, and demands that Brad not hang up the line if she falls asleep during the conversation (the buzzing sound would disrupt her slumber).

About six months after the googly-eyed lovers' first date, Tom visits Brad in Dallas and notices scale drawings of large diamonds—ring blueprints, really—on his coffee table. He understands that life as we know it will soon draw to a close. After Tom returns home to Chicago and relays this disturbing development to me, we begin to await news of the inevitable.

Eighteen Months Out

The call comes, as we knew it would, setting in motion a flurry of planning and protocol the likes of which have not been seen outside the confines of the Windsor family. It is announced that the wedding will be in Dallas in November, eighteen months hence, for the favorable temperatures and low humidity. Five hundred guests will be invited. Eight attendants will be at Haylie's beck and call. And Tom, poor bastard, will be the best man. My brother, Robert, who hardly knows Brad, is summoned to groomsman duty—one of a small army of men called in to counterbalance the enormous number of female attendants. As future sister-in-law to the bride, I do not make the bridesmaid cut. But thanks to a Southern tradition known as the House Party (commonly used to accommodate sorority sisters, disfavored cousins, and assorted hangers-on), I will nonetheless be included in all the fun of planning and the wedding festivities themselves. Joy.

My specific duties, it is announced ominously, will be determined at a later date.

One Year Out

I open the mailbox to discover a plump, neatly calligraphed envelope addressed to "Mr. and Mrs. Tom Foster" (Haylie has never really accepted the fact that I kept my maiden name). It is too early for an invitation. Too fat for a save-the-date card. Have Haylie and Brad printed a chapbook of original love poems?

It is a stapled booklet printed on heavy cream paper that will soon become known as the Wedding Bible (or, less formally, the WB). On the cover is one of those watery, gauzy photos of two small children dressed to look like elegant grownups, sharing a giggle and a rose. "Brad & Haylie" is embossed above their heads in gold script.

The booklet contains a short primer about the wedding ceremony and the Episcopal faith generally—a sort of abbreviated *Episcopalianism for Dummies*—biographies of all the major players in the wedding party, broken down by category, and a blow-by-blow itinerary of the seventy-two hours leading up to the wedding. Haylie has, I notice, thoughtfully allotted forty minutes of "free time" for everyone on Saturday morning.

We can't get over the bios. At least they answer one nagging question for us—namely, why Brad has recently been calling us with random questions about me and my brother. "Where did Robert go to high school? What are Jen's hobbies?" The WB bios read like a series of personal ads: *Robert Carsen, brother-in-law of the best man and groomsman #7, is a pilot. He likes enchiladas, a good cabernet, and snowboarding at sunset.* . . . The wedding party consists of groomsmen, ushers, bridesmaids, House Party members, and VIPs. The VIPs include a soloist who is currently a Peace Corps volunteer dispatched to Africa to battle both AIDS and malaria, and who might or might not make it back to the States a year hence to sing at the wedding.

The WB also includes our respective duties. Haylie has determined that I am uniquely suited to "helping the groomsmen dress" and "helping the guests find their tables at the reception." It is not clear that either of these groups will in fact require (or desire) my assistance. However, I am exceedingly glad I am not Amy, one of Haylie's intimates *(Amy has known Haylie since nursery school—where she helped Haylie when she was choking on a LEGO!—and is extremely fond of Gummi Bears)*, who is tasked with "bustling Haylie's train" and "maintaining Haylie's hairdo." All in all, the bios run for eight pages.

Six Months Out

The invitation itself is an anticlimax. It is classic, tasteful, and doesn't remotely hint at the craziness emanating from the bride-

and groom-to-be. My friends, devoted fans of the Brad & Haylie Wedding Saga for a year now, are disappointed the envelope doesn't contain something outrageous, like a live dove cooing the love theme from *Titanic*.

The shower invitations, however, are coming fast and furious. There is a coed "Stock-the-Bar" shower (thrown by Haylie's sister—the WB bio notes that she is *mom to the best ring bearer in the whole wide world!)*, a "Kitchen Fun" shower (thrown by the aforementioned train-bustler, Amy), and a "Let's Buy Haylie Lingerie!" shower (thrown by "Haylie's bridesmaids"). Each shower invitation is professionally printed and indicates not only the place and time of the festivities, but the names of the stores where Haylie and Brad are registered.

All the shower invitations look suspiciously similar. I find out after the wedding that Haylie herself had purchased and printed all the invitations, after finding a willing proxy to officially "host" each shower. (Perhaps she should have thrown herself a *Wall Street*–themed "Greed Is Good" shower as well.)

My shock at seeing the registry stores printed on the kitchen and bar invitations, practically screaming "Gimme! Gimme! Gimme!" pales in comparison to my shock at opening the lingerie shower invitation and seeing not a list of stores but Haylie's intimate measurements. And, most shocking, she has actually *lied* about her vital stats. Haylie is built like Janeane Garofalo, but the woman described on the invitation more closely resembles Uma Thurman. If Haylie can squeeze that round bottom of hers into a "small" panty, then I am Kate Moss.

I return home from work one day to find Tom on the phone, desperately trying to calm someone down.

"I'm sure they didn't mean it that way," he is saying. "Look, there must be some sort of misunderstanding."

I don't know who it is, but as the minutes wear on it is clear that the crisis is somehow related to the wedding.

He wraps up with, "Mom, I'll talk to him," hangs up, and turns to me.

"Haylie and Brad aren't allowing Christine and Nora to come to the rehearsal dinner."

"Excuse me?" Tom and Brad's mom, Kathy, had recently married a man named Jim, and they are hosting the rehearsal dinner. Christine is Jim's daughter from his first marriage, and Nora is his granddaughter. Nora is the adorable three-year-old result of a nonmarital fling of Christine's, and everyone in Tom and Brad's family is fine with that. Or so I thought.

"Brad and Haylie said it wouldn't be appropriate to have Christine and Nora there because everyone will be asking Christine where her husband is. They think it will be too awkward."

I am floored. "Why on earth would anyone be asking Christine where her husband is? Your mom and Jim are paying for the rehearsal dinner, right?"

"Yep."

"And Brad and Haylie 'won't allow' Jim's daughter and granddaughter to come?"

True to his word, Tom tries to talk some reason into Brad, but he will not be swayed. Although Christine and Nora will be at the wedding in all their illegitimate, husband-free/father-free glory, Brad and Haylie have decided that this will be acceptable since their presence will be diluted by the hundreds of other guests. At the rehearsal dinner, they'll be more front and center.

Wow. There are just no words.

The Big Buildup

THURSDAY

7:15 PM: Tom and I fly from Chicago to Dallas in time to catch the "welcome dinner," being held at a nondescript bar/restaurant that is about as far as one can get from DFW airport while still being within the Dallas city limits. We make the trek directly from the airport in the lumbering fifteen-person van Tom has rented, as part of his WR mandated duties, for the bachelor party. As soon as we're through the door, Haylie's mom spies us across the room and announces, "Why, it's the Fosters!" I flinch—the inability to get my last name right appears to be a multigenerational problem.

7:30 PM: At dinner, Brad reveals that he will be spending most of the following day catching up with the jeweler. Haylie has already issued a last-minute veto on one wedding ring, and ring number two (which Haylie reports is "somewhat over the top, but it will be fine") doesn't fit Haylie's meaty paw. The jeweler—who I imagine must be regretting his decision to work with this particular couple—has Brad on speed-dial, and Brad, in turn, has procured a beeper (Brad also has a cell phone, but Haylie is taking no chances). The moment the ring is ready, the jeweler will buzz Brad, leap into his Blingmobile, and make the thirty-five-mile trip from Fort Worth to Dallas, where he and Brad plan to rendezvous in a Whataburger parking lot for the drop.

9:00 PM: We depart for our respective events—Tom and Brad and the boys head off to the bachelor party, while I am dragged kicking and screaming to the lingerie shower. On the way out, Brad informs Tom that the bachelor party van will have to make a hotel detour to "say hi to Ben." Ben, apparently, is an usher who has just flown in from Philly and is too pooped to make it to the bachelor party. There is general dissension from all bachelor party participants, as the detour will seriously delay arrival at the strip club (and being too tired to sit and adequately appreciate topless women is just, well, too un-Texan for words).

9:30 PM: The ladies arrive at the home of one of Haylie's friends for the lingerie shower. An enormous "Haylie & Brad Forever!" banner is draped across the living room's large bay window; my guess is that the printing company responsible for the shower invitations gave Haylie a break on it as a result of her loyal and frequent patronage. We watch Haylie unwrap two dozen gifts—all of them too small for her—with nary a "thank you" uttered. Her efficient, goal-oriented unwrapping is interrupted only by a few incoming calls to her cell phone, which she excuses herself to take in another room. I wonder who is calling; how did *that* person manage to escape this lingerie nightmare?

The moment the last pink-ribboned black box has been opened, we all stand up and briskly head for the door. Whoever designed the house has not planned for a mass exodus; we pile against the exit and back off only when it becomes clear that the door swings inward. Over the course of the shower, Haylie's mom twice refers to me as Mrs. Foster.

3:15 AM: Tom arrives home from the bachelor party, rousing me from disturbing dreams of Haylie stuffing herself into a too-tight thong, and reports that a good time was had by all. Brad was accidentally kicked in the chin by a stripper who was executing some sort of handstand, but they successfully managed to stanch the bleeding. Tom reports that he spent much of the night chatting about chowder with a stripper from Boston. Several times during the course of the party, Brad had to be forcibly dragged from the men's room, where he was holed up in a stall calling Haylie on his cell phone. She had asked for hourly updates.

Saying hi to Ben, Tom reports, took less than five minutes but involved an hour's detour from the festivities. Ben has been in Dallas barely six hours and is already persona non grata with the men in the wedding party.

11:30 AM: I arrive at the Neiman Marcus in Plano (read: north suburban Dallas, nowhere remotely near any of the other wedding festivities) for the bridesmaids' luncheon with Kathy, Tom and Brad's mom. Haylie has graciously invited her House Party to join the inner circle. We are told we cannot use our cell phones during lunch because the radio waves will interfere with the signature orange soufflés (I have stopped trying to understand and am now focused on survival, plain and simple). I am inexplicably seated among three other Jennifers, and the conversation is peppered with things like:

Jennifer #1: Who's the parent company of Gucci? I can't remember.

Jennifer #2: You're a Delta Delta? *I'm* a Delta Delta!

Jennifer #3 (to me): So, what's Connecticut like?

Me: I live in Chicago, actually.

Jennifer #3 (twirling her hair): Oh, *Chicago*. I love that movie!

A family friend of Haylie's who happens to be lunching at Neiman's comes by the table and congratulates Haylie on her impending nuptials. She asks Haylie the groom's name. Haylie has to think for a minute but eventually nails it.

1:00 PM: I am desperate to get out of Neiman's—the orange soufflés (high maintenance, but admittedly delicious) are long gone, and I have maybe ten minutes of nice left in me. I tug at Kathy's sleeve but am told that we are waiting for Brad, who has been instructed to entertain Haylie's cousins for the morning and then come out to Plano to collect people and shuttle them back to Dallas. Brad wants to know if Tom and I will have room in our car later to transport Ben and his girlfriend to the rehearsal; for reasons unknown they have not rented a car. Tom has already returned the bachelor party bus to the airport and swapped it out for a tiny Dodge Neon. We tell Brad we have no room.

3:00 PM: Tom and I break away from the scheduled festivities— a serious breach of the WB's itinerary—and head back to the airport to pick up my brother, Robert, and his girlfriend, Emily, who have flown in from Vermont. We cram ourselves into the Neon and head for a bar near the church.

5:00 PM: After a few quick rounds of Shiner Bock (Emily, bless her heart, has offered to drive our soggy selves around town), the four of us head to the rehearsal.

Haylie is deep in conversation with the wedding coordinator when we arrive. Tom and I bring Robert and Emily over for an introduction. Haylie tears herself away just long enough to look us over, declare that "Y'all smell like smoke," and return to her conversation.

We've arrived at the rehearsal ten minutes late but have still managed to beat most of the wedding party there, including the lovely bride's parents—and the groom. Haylie demands that we start immediately. "All the important people are here," she says.

During the rehearsal, the coordinator plays mix-and-match with various permutations of bridesmaids and groomsmen for walking down the aisle post-ceremony. Despite Brad's valiant recruiting efforts, there are still more women than men in the wedding party, and my brother has been given two bridesmaids to escort out—one for each arm. As they reach the back of the church, Haylie's mom hip-checks the near bridesmaid out of the way, grabs Robert's arm (they have not yet officially met), and hisses, "Robert, you're walking *much* too fast." I begin to see where Haylie gets her charming demeanor.

7:00 PM: We depart for the rehearsal dinner. Brad again asks us if we have room for Ben and his S.O. in our car. No, the Neon's capacity has not magically expanded since this afternoon. Tom starts referring to him as the Notorious B.E.N.

The rehearsal dinner is at Maggiano's, which Haylie seems to believe is a delightfully original Dallas institution. She does not want to hear that the chain originated in Chicago and that this is simply one of the many branches that have popped up all over the country. As promised, the event is free of the taint of Christine and Nora. Jim is there and says all the right things, but keeps shooting surreptitious dagger glances across the room at Haylie.

8:10 PM: Brad stands up and gives a long, egregiously sappy speech honoring Haylie. "Light of my life" and "the most beautiful woman in the world" are mentioned without irony. He has a big clump of marinara on his sleeve and a small bruise on his chin.

8:16 PM: Haylie stands up, mentions she will toast Brad later in the evening (which she never does), and announces that "If anyone wants to make a toast honoring us, you don't need to wait for a specific time or course. Anytime is fine." Of the crowd of sixty-five, two take her up on this.

10:30 PM: We are all sent away from the rehearsal dinner with our collectible "Brad and Haylie Wedding Tunes" CD. According to Brad, these are songs from their courtship. We play the CD in the car on the way back to the hotel and it includes, among other things, that weird Alanis Morissette song about washing her hands clean of a creepy affair with an older man. We don't know and we don't ask.

The Big Day

SATURDAY

1:45 PM: We arrive, as directed by the WB, at the church long before the four o'clock ceremony. I go into the "bride's room," and

Haylie is there surrounded by her bridesmaids. Her hair and makeup are half-finished, and she appears completely discombobulated. She blinks at me, zombielike, as if she's never seen me before. In a slow, measured voice, as though addressing a small child or someone who is mentally ill, she tells me I should go "study the seating for the reception." She hands me two lists—one alphabetical, one table by table—and reminds me it's my job to help people understand the seating. Fearful, I take my leave.

1:46 PM: Remembering my other assigned task, I pop into the guys' changing room and brightly announce I'm there to help them dress.

1:47 PM: The groomsmen en masse decline my offer of sartorial assistance and hustle me out the door.

2:00 PM: I successfully dissuade the florist from pinning my corsage into my cleavage, where she thinks "it would look lovely peeking out."

2:15 PM: The groomsmen get pinned with their boutonnieres, which are made up of little red berries. The florist reports they are Saint-John's-wort, a natural antidepressant. We warn Robert that no matter how bad things get during the ceremony, he mustn't gnaw the little berries off. Or at least wait until after the pictures are taken.

3:15 PM: My parents—who, like Robert and Emily, have flown in from Vermont—are summoned to the church for pre-wedding photos. They stand around for fifteen minutes and are then told there is no time. Haylie blows by them a few times without saying hello.

3:45 PM: The pre-ceremony music starts. It's really jarring, a lot of minor chords. Eerily like the film score from *The Bride of Frankenstein*.

5:15 PM: The wedding is over. The House Party has been instructed by the Mussolini-like wedding coordinator not to file out of the first pew where we're sitting; we are to stay put and we will do photos once everyone leaves. We sit back down after the wedding party proceeds out, and everyone, rows and rows behind us, sits back down as well, like a line of falling dominoes. No one is leaving the church. We eventually have to get up and shoo people out. Great idea, Il Duce.

5:45 PM: The pictures at the church are over. Brad once again asks us if we have room for Ben in our car.

6:15 PM: We arrive at the reception. Somehow, miraculously, the guests have found their tables without my assistance. It seems they managed to decipher the complex "numbered tables" system. As I'm chucking my lists, I turn and run smack into Haylie, who demands I retrieve my brother immediately so that he can participate in the wedding party dance. "Am I my brother's keeper?" rises to my lips, but I manage to bite it back in time. Robert is not hard to find—he's at the bar, tie undone, martini in hand. He has floated a few of the berries from his boutonniere in his drink.

7:30 PM: Tom and I are sitting at the head table with Brad and Haylie, the Notorious B.E.N., and Haylie's parents (the other members of the wedding party have vanished—passed out in a corner somewhere, maybe?). Kathy and Jim are sitting at table 47 in the back of the room, behind a pole—Haylie apparently felt that since they weren't paying for the wedding, they didn't deserve preferred seating.

Brad and Haylie get up to do their first dance. Then Haylie dances with her dad, and Brad dances with—what's going on here? Brad leads not his *own* mother onto the dance floor, but *Haylie's* mother.

Even from across the room, I can see the stunned sadness creep across Kathy's face. Tom quickly sprints over, retrieves his mother, and neatly cuts in between Brad and Haylie's mom, handing Kathy off to Brad. Brad later tells us that Haylie felt it would be "rude" for her mother not to get the first dance with the groom.

8:00 PM: I abandon my efforts to chip a bite-size piece off the vulcanized chicken entrée and look down the head table to see if anyone else is having better luck. Haylie's dad is the only other person there. He has speared his chicken with a fork and is holding it like a Popsicle. He also has a large transistor radio glued to his right ear. The wedding was unfortunately scheduled opposite a University of Texas football game.

8:30–9:00 PM: Haylie and Brad flit around the room, trying to say hello to each of their hundreds of guests. Twice I try to intercept them to say congratulations, but both times I am snipped at by Haylie with orders—once to "find Ben" (I never ask why; maybe he needs a ride somewhere?) and once to "check on the seating." I have no idea what she's talking about. Was part of my job to keep guests *in* their assigned seats for the entire reception?

9:00 PM: Tom gives his best man speech and is heckled by a small child calling out "Banana!" over and over. Tom handles it well.

10:00 PM: After being showered with rose petals by their guests (who are perhaps wishing they had been given something a bit more substantial to throw), Brad and Haylie get set to depart in a shiny black carriage pulled by an enormous Clydesdale who looks as if he's more accustomed to towing carts of beer. When the horse takes off, Brad is still in the process of stepping into the carriage, and he clings desperately to its side as they speed out of the portico. Haylie, waving regally to her assembled guests, doesn't appear to notice.

10:01 PM: We receive word from the father of the bride that UT has won the football game. He appears more excited about this than anything else that's happened today.

10:02 PM: Exhausted and cranky, Tom and I abandon the festivities and return to our hotel room. We discover a voice-mail message from Brad: "Haylie and I wanted to know if you could meet us and her folks tomorrow morning at seven for breakfast downstairs. I asked Mom and Jim, but they said they were busy, which is strange. . . . Anyway, let me know. I gotta run."

Tom and I look at each other and know, in one of those synergistic married-couple moments, that each of us is thinking the exact same thing: *Hell, no, we won't go.*

10:15 PM: Tom switches off the light, turns to me, and says, "Let us never speak of this day again." We fall asleep instantly in a haze of booze and bewilderment.

Unbridled

Suz Redfearn

⌐ For many years now, I've worked hard to remain pleasant as my age-mates go through their periods of betrothal. It's been *tough*, though, because those periods invariably involved hours and hours of endless talk about cake toppers, veil lengths, and the harmful diets one must endure in order to don dresses made to fit a drinking straw.

All of that bride stuff made me cringe. Always had. I just couldn't relate. Somehow the supposedly ubiquitous little girl's dream of spending thousands of dollars on flowers and looking like an exploded cotton ball was never baked into me. Oh sure, I hoped I'd find and marry that special human someday, but I pictured a different sort of wedding—a romantic elopement, perhaps, or a ceremony presided over by an Elvis impersonator.

My sentiments about all the usual wedding pomp and circumstance could be summed up by a little ditty I heard my older brother sing a long time ago. It went something like this:

Here comes the bride
all dressed in pink,
open up the window
and let out the stink!

My man, Marty, who just proposed a few months ago, didn't want to elope or go to Las Vegas, so we began to strategize a small, casual, low-budget shindig. Our loose plan was to invite our closest pals and kin to come and stay in a cluster of cool beach houses in remote, coastal Alabama. Guests would be treated to four days of relaxed, formfree communing and general waterfront shenanigans. On the fourth day, Marty and I—minus any bridesmaids or groomsmen, and also minus any shoes—would walk down a sandy aisle demarcated only by shells. My nieces would sing "Happy Together" by the Turtles, and *bam*—Marty and I would be as one.

Much as the crowd might expect such things, there would be no tossing of the bouquet (a hideous tradition that had caused me to hide in the bathroom at many a wedding). There would be no shoving of cake into each other's piehole. There would be no "Hokey Pokey" and, as god is my witness, no "Chicken Dance." My mantra was as follows: *No satin pillows, no prizes under the seats, no unity candles—no way, no how.*

So, to plan the thing, I figured all I had to do was make a few calls to ensure the presence of food. And maybe we'd pick some flowers from a nearby field and stick them on the tables that day. And maybe I'd buy some sort of whitish outfit a few weeks before the big event. But that was as far as I was willing to go. And Marty, a no-frills type of guy, was pleased.

A few days after he and I decided on our über-modest beach wedding, though, I began to feel strange, itchy, like I was walking funny and generally out of sync with myself. Mysteriously, the symptoms also included an achy compulsion to go to Barnes & Noble and flip through the giant hardback *Town & Country Elegant Weddings*. I resisted, chanting, *Must maintain normalcy. Must remain a low-maintenance bride.*

But that afternoon, my friend Babs called and, with one simple question, inadvertently shattered my thin veneer. "So . . . what kind of cake are you going to have?"

"Cake? Uh, I hadn't really thought about that," I sputtered, my head having heretofore been a completely cake-free zone. "*Should* I have a cake? What do those cost? A cake. Well, I don't know. Maybe . . . Yeah, sure! A cake, it is!"

And that was all it took—Babs had kicked me off a tall cliff and I fell, slipping into a deep pit, lined with taffeta and silk and beads, with layers of almond buttercream and handmade pillows and calla lilies to soften my landing. And suddenly, sitting up dazed at the bottom of that pit amid all the pillows, I knew it: The transformation was complete. Then and there, I wanted to learn everything there was to know about wedding cakes—*every freaking thing.*

At that point, a tiny, muffled part of me squealed from the depths: *Don't give in! Forget about the cake. Just serve fruit. Melon balls are awfully nice!* But another part of me savored the fall from grace. Maybe I'd been working too hard to keep my inner Cinderella chained up in a dungeon, covered in dung. Maybe I needed to clean her off and let her out—just a little, to do a few girlie things—and then send her back where she belonged. After all, what harm could come of it?

A changed person, I took a deep breath and got on the Internet to study the suddenly fascinating world of wedding cakes. Just then, Babs called again, this time to tell me about a pastry-chef friend of hers in New York City who I could fly down to design the cake if I wanted. For a moment I actually considered this.

Next, my mom called, wanting to discuss Jordan almonds. It was all happening at once, this nuptial tsunami. I looked at my computer screen as we talked and saw that, without realizing it, I'd changed my desktop art to the image of a funky wedding cake with gold designs crawling up the side of it like evil serpents. I heard a sound, and it was me, yammering about cakes like I was speaking in tongues.

"Enough with the cakes!" my mom said impatiently. "What bra will you wear?"

"Jeez, I don't know, Mom. I don't tend to think about which underwear I'm going to wear six months in advance."

"Well, suit yourself, but I really don't want to see you ruin your big day by wearing a strapless bra."

Wow. The wrong bra could foul up an entire day? I wanted to laugh at my mother, to accuse her of being compulsive and strange. But as much as I hated to admit it, the woman had a point. Surely I didn't want a photo album filled with shots of me tugging at the sides of my boobs and grimacing.

And I realized Mom had a deeper message too: *This wedding stuff,* she seemed to be beaming from her head to mine, *requires that you push through a membrane and access an entirely different lobe of the brain, one that is distinctly feminine and relishes bathing itself in florid details that, pre-engagement, seemed the height of frivolity and stupidity but, post-engagement, make a sort of sick sense.*

And don't be absurd, Mom's head-beam added, *there's no such thing as just picking flowers from a field or buying something sort of whitish for your wedding. . . .*

After that, I didn't fight it anymore; I opened the door and let the fluffy white virus into every cell. It didn't take long before I was stealing about a third of each workday to feverishly plan a wedding that no longer bore any resemblance to my original simple nuptial vision. For most of my waking hours, my head pulsated with large and pressing matters that had once seemed entirely foreign: How many floating candles do we need in the pool? How do I go about making commemorative magnets featuring pictures of Marty and me? Where do I rent those wooden beach chairs that look so Cape Cod-y? And, are Venus flytraps suitable tabletop flora?

Giving in to it all felt *orgasmic.* And on about day six of the illness, a beautiful thought hit me: *I have total control over this thing. Hell, if I want to, I can subject the guests to invasive mariachi musicians, or a puppet show, or a Barbra Streisand impersonator. I can have a little plastic bride and groom strangling each other on top of the cake, or humping. I can play AC/DC's "Dirty Deeds Done Dirt Cheap" when I walk down the aisle. Sure, some people may want to stop me, but they won't be able to because I'm the bride.*

After that, I took to confronting Marty with pressing questions as soon as he got home from work. "Honey? Listen. Should we have lilac-scented hot towels for everyone after they eat, or should the towels smell of gardenia?" He answered with stunned silence, wondering where his woman had gone. Soon he took to spending his evenings hiding in a remote corner of the bedroom.

I knew I'd fallen in the worst way when I gave in and bought a copy of *Modern Bride*. And also *Wedding Style*. I kept the magazines out of sight, so as not to frighten Marty any further. But I relished them, poring over their glossy pages with abandon.

Strangely, married girlfriends started calling and emailing, all aflutter, as if they'd picked up my spastic-bride vibe in the collective unconscious. Babs took it up a notch, ringing every other day; Mom called hourly. They wanted details, and I was more than willing to while away the hours coughing them up. I told them about the Chinese lanterns I wanted to string up and the expensive wedding earrings I'd special-ordered. I spoke of the champagne fountain. I didn't even want to participate in any conversation that wasn't wedding related. The real me was gone.

A few days later, I did the unthinkable: I decided to commit to a strict, unforgiving workout regimen, one that would have me looking like Linda Hamilton in *Terminator 2* by the wedding day. Me, with a long history of mocking others who did such things for their nuptials. Oh, the hypocrisy. But I quickly rationalized that I was different—I was having a four-day beach wedding I had to look like a million bucks for four straight days—in a bikini. At least it wasn't a diet, right? I'd have to draw the line at that.

That night, Marty told me about a wedding where the DJ had regaled the crowd with a horribly goofy trivia contest about the bride and groom. "Hey," I responded, "that's a great idea!" Then I *knew* things were getting out of hand. The former me would have never dreamed of such a thing. But now I was suggesting that Marty and I choreograph an elaborate, gymnastic disco dance to wow the guests. "Let's perform to the Bee Gees' 'You Should Be Dancing'!" I yelped. And I was serious.

The next afternoon, I caught myself calling around to find out where to get a good facial, because *Modern Bride* says to get one every month, starting six months out: "Be nubile! Make sure you have the skin of an eighteen-year-old on your big day!" "Okay!" I responded.

As I dialed the spas, though, I felt an odd tingling. Pretty soon, a deep inner voice was whispering sternly, *Alright, Missy, this has gone too far. Stop it. Stop it right now!*

And then, in a flash, the taunting, cynical inner me—the real me who had been shoved down and silenced by spaz-bride for the past few weeks—emerged. She was disoriented and covered in mucus, but she was here now, alive and free, ready to take back the controls.

And with that, the fever broke. I threw *Modern Bride* facedown on the floor, and, to center myself, I started to chant a true song, a righteous song:

Here comes the bride
all dressed in pink. . . .

Searching for Rabbi Right

STACEY LUFTIG

⟡— PATTY HAD LISTS. And sub-lists, and sub-sub-lists. No detail of her elegant wedding at the Brooklyn Botanic Garden was left to chance. She had even met with the caterers to specify how the napkins should be folded. But there was one thing my best friend had failed to plan for: the possibility that her rabbi—a woman she had befriended, who had been to Patty's apartment for bagels, cream cheese, and home-cured gravlax—would flake out so completely.

Rabbi Melanie Joy never showed up. This was 1996, before cell phones were tucked into every pocket or purse. We had no way to reach her.

I'm not sure how long we waited outside on that warm June day—maybe ninety minutes—before I took it upon myself as maid of honor to march into the garden's office and pick up the yellow pages. The staff quickly took over, and one Rabbi Wasserman, with five-o'clock stubble but otherwise presentable, was there within the hour, as the sun began to set. The restless guests applauded his arrival. Rabbi Wasserman made a few jokes, launched into a *brucha*, and the rest of the wedding went forward without a hitch. Although the bride smiled bravely throughout the unfamiliar ceremony and the fete that followed, she always looked back on her special day with some bitterness.

Eight years later, it would be my turn to plan. Now, I'm no Patty. Her organizational style included color-coded folders and careful timelines; mine was more the find-the-phone-number-in-the-pile-of-junk system. But I was going to be damn sure we found a rabbi we could count on.

Here I should mention that my childhood experience with Judaism had been less than ideal, making any contact with a rabbi a loaded affair. My family never belonged to a synagogue. My father felt it was wrong to have to pay to go to shul—and especially wrong to pay the prohibitively high ticket prices for the High Holy Days. So we would sneak in. The first time, I was six years old. "If they ask you for your ticket," my mother said to me, "tell them you left it home."

"But Mom," I replied, "isn't that stealing? And from God?"

"We're only going for half an hour."

I remember, at the synagogue, the deep frown of a neighbor. He was shrouded in a blue-striped tallis, a garment I thereafter came to associate with authority and disapproval. The foreign Hebrew prayers, chanted by the congregation in one loud, echoing, mumbling voice, were ominous as thunder. From the back rows of the temple, on the cold metal folding chairs, I could just make out the form of the rabbi, also adorned in a prayer shawl. He would place the tallis over his head at certain points in the service, rocking to the rhythm of the prayers, his voice booming and distorted over the ancient sound system. He was both remote and terrifying.

I attended High Holy Day services in this manner—furtively and filled with shame—until I was well into my teens.

Some people feel guilty when they don't go to synagogue. I felt guilty when I did go. Yet when I became an adult, I still felt a perverse pull on the High Holy Days. So in my midtwenties, instead of sneaking in, I started attending the only place where I felt comfortable: New York City's synagogue for gay, lesbian, bisexual, and transgendered Jews. It's not that I fit into any of those categories; it's that it offered what I needed: a pay-what-you-can admission policy.

That's where I discovered Rabbi Susan Mendelbaum. She was a short and sturdy woman, perhaps only ten years older than I. Her sermons were funny and wise. And as a lesbian, she was well acquainted with the way in which shame could be unfairly placed. If the rabbi of my youth seemed to be the disciple of an angry, punishing God, Rabbi Mendelbaum was Adonai's warm, accepting angel.

After many years of attending the gay and lesbian (and bisexual and transgendered) synagogue, I knew that the only person to perform my wedding ceremony was Rabbi Mendelbaum. After two trips to Manhattan's diamond district with Daniel, my boyfriend of six years, I knew I had to act fast; Rabbi Mendelbaum booked up early. So in February of 2004, I dispensed with the usual formality of waiting for the groom to actually propose and called the synagogue. As long as the rabbi was available, any date in 2005 would be fine. But as luck would have it, gay and lesbian weddings, or the lack thereof, were prominent in the news that year. And Rabbi Mendelbaum, being political as well as religious, was busy. Very busy. She was booked for the next two years.

With Rabbi Mendelbaum no longer an option, I decided to wait until Daniel offered me the sparkly vintage ring we'd found before scoping out another rabbi. I would need his help; I knew that Rabbi Mendelbaum's small shoes would be hard to fill.

I had no idea how hard.

Rabbi Number 2 was recommended to us that July by the eccentric German antique collector who owned the electrical-parts-factory-turned-loft where we planned to hold our wedding. "Rabbi Friedman is very nice," she told us. "And so cute!" I was so infatuated with our wedding venue, with its floor-to-ceiling bookcases, its mismatched, shabby-but-beautiful divans and settees, its dilapidated floors beneath crystal chandeliers, that I was inclined to see in a positive light anything its proprietor recommended. Daniel—who, for the record, would have preferred to get married at city hall—agreed to come with me to meet the rabbi after I gently established that he had no choice.

I was soon to learn there are many rabbis in New York City who are not affiliated with any particular synagogue. Without full employment, they often pursue other careers, such as psychotherapy. This was the case with our "cute" rabbi.

Daniel and I took our seats in the Upper East Side waiting room that the doctor/rabbi shared with two other therapists. From there we could see three closed doors, none of which had a nameplate. At ten minutes before the hour, each of the doors opened in succession. Some people entered. Others departed. Therapists exchanged a nod or a few words. Each person glanced at us. Then, all the doors closed. It felt like a scene in a French farce. Daniel and I looked at the doors. We looked at each other. We looked at the doors. After several minutes, one door creaked open, and a head peeked out. "Oh," said a voice. "I didn't realize you were there."

Rabbi Friedman seemed like a regular guy. He was about our age— midforties—wore a sport shirt, shorts, and no yarmulke. He chatted with us about the weather. I hadn't realized at that point just how high my expectations were for our first meeting together with a rabbi, despite my admittedly high regard for Rabbi Mendelbaum. I now understand that I'd entered that room looking for far more than someone to officiate at our wedding; I was looking for a teacher. A guru. A spiritual guide. I was looking for a meaningful connection with the first rabbi with whom I would have a real conversation and a chance to shed some of the guilt that still clung to me like lint.

I think I may have trembled as we sat in the wood-paneled office facing Rabbi Friedman, so eager was I with unconscious desire for transcendence. So when the rabbi asked us, as though he were preparing a grocery list, how much "God-talk" we'd like in our ceremony, the glorious flute and harp music playing in my head screeched to a halt.

He must have sensed that something was wrong. "Am I making you comfortable?" he asked.

"Oh, I'm fine," I said, and nearly meant it. Almost instantly, I decided to think of Rabbi Friedman—our rabbi—as hip, as meta, and was pleased that we could speak in shorthand about our shared spiritual assumptions. Before long, the psychotherapeutic aura of the space, or perhaps of the rabbi, or perhaps my own neuroses, took over, and I found myself recounting the sad tale of my childhood religious experience. As I was filling out the story, wiping away tears, the rabbi's cell phone rang.

"Excuse me just one moment," he said.

Of course I was sympathetic. Didn't rabbis, even those without congregations, have countless souls looking to them for help in a crisis? As we waited—Daniel matter-of-factly, I with a strained smile on my tear-stained face—the rabbi asked the person on the other end how summer camp was going.

"And swimming? Are you putting your face in the water?" He put his hand over the receiver. "She keeps getting water up her nose." Rabbi Friedman discussed the importance of remembering to breathe when the face was turned upward, promised to visit soon, and then ended the conversation with an "I love you" and a smack to signify a kiss. He returned his attention to us.

"That's my niece," he said. "We're very close."

He looked at our stunned faces. "Are you comfortable?" he asked. "Am I making you comfortable?"

Outside the office, I wept with disappointment. Though Daniel didn't appreciate the rabbi's taking the phone call any more than

I did, he didn't think Rabbi Friedman was all that bad. In fact, he liked his unpretentious manner. I cried some more.

The many recommendations we received for Rabbi Number 3 came from strangers: brides on that mother-of-all-wedding-websites, the Knot. I looked up Rabbi Saperstein and read the references I found on *her* website. At first I was bothered by the rabbi's choice to market religious services with hyperlinks, but I supposed that congregation-less rabbis had to make that extra effort to attract new clients. I made peace with it.

Once again we traipsed to the Upper East Side. Once again, our prospective rabbi juggled a second career—this time as an art historian. But the experience of meeting Rabbi Saperstein was very different from our encounter with Rabbi Friedman. This rabbi was older, in her mid- to late sixties, and had gracious European manners and a deep, embracing warmth. She was zaftig, with long, dark ringlets streaked with gray piled on her head in a loose bun. Her large brown eyes, creased deeply with laugh lines, were ringed with smoky eye shadow. She made strong eye contact and shook our hands as though we were reuniting instead of meeting, then ushered us into the living room of a home filled with books, paintings, and sculptures.

Daniel and I sat with the rabbi at a big, friendly table. Responding to her gentle questioning, we began to tell her about our lives. The telephone rang. We stopped speaking. "No, no," said Rabbi Saperstein. "I should have turned the ringer off. The machine will get it." Daniel and I shared a small nod.

We stayed for nearly two hours. The rabbi's focus was mesmerizing. Daniel opened up in a way he hadn't with Rabbi Friedman, describing in detail how he had supervised his mother's care as she struggled with Alzheimer's and talking about her death only a few months earlier. He went on to discuss the traumatic death of his father, when Daniel was just four years old.

We also discussed various ways we might construct our wedding service. Rabbi Saperstein showed us a blank-verse poem she liked to use. It was about the wishes a mother bestows on her daughter and soon-to-be-son-in-law on the morning of their wedding. She read the poem aloud to us. This time it was Daniel's eyes that were wet.

We had told Rabbi Saperstein from the outset that we were interviewing several rabbis. That way, we wouldn't feel pressured to make a decision without consulting each other in private. But we both felt confident by then that we had found our rabbi. As we were preparing to leave, Rabbi Saperstein asked if she could take down some basic information: name, address, phone number, things like that. After filling in the first few blanks, Rabbi Saperstein turned to Daniel and asked, "Are your parents still alive?"

Daniel looked both pale and winded. He managed a one-word answer—"no"—which did not elicit the hoped-for "Of course! How could I ask such a thing?" The rabbi, however, did ask what was wrong. "Nothing," said Daniel, shaking his head as if to clear it. She then turned to me, asking for my first name, which she no longer could recall.

We tried to leave quickly, but as we headed for the elevator, the rabbi followed us. Looking a little too directly at Daniel, her manner changed. She draped herself in the doorway, smiling languidly, and in a husky voice said to him, "You're really forty-five? You look so . . ." and then, noticing I was still there, ". . . you *both* look so . . . young."

I flashed ahead to the final moments of our wedding ceremony. Rabbi Saperstein, smiling coyly, says to Daniel, "You may now kiss . . . *the rabbi*," and yanks him to her tastefully garbed yet heaving bosom.

Mercifully, the elevator arrived.

Clearly, it was time for us to get our rabbi recommendations from people we knew and trusted. I wanted to call Patty. No doubt, she had retained color-coordinated files on any number of candidates. But I feared she might still be sensitive about the subject, and refrained from bringing it up.

We contacted other friends who had been married in recent years; certainly one of their rabbis would work for us. But some rabbis lived too far away, some were unavailable, others were Conservative or Orthodox. A Conservative rabbi would have been fine with us, but only a Reform rabbi, it turned out, would consent to perform our ceremony since the wedding date we'd chosen—May 1—happened to fall that year on the last day of Passover.

The date was particularly acceptable to rabbis who were of a New Age bent. Daniel had met one such rabbi at a recent wedding he'd attended. He wasn't particularly enamored of her (or the fact that she, like Rabbi Friedman, was a therapist) but his newly married friends had liked her. An additional bonus: Rabbi Sheila Osofsky lived just a few blocks away. Most rabbis wanted to meet three or four times to get to know you and to work out the ceremony details. At the very least our meetings would be convenient.

With some trepidation, I called Rabbi Osofsky. She returned my call promptly—a good sign. On the other end of the phone line was a loud, singsong, nasal voice.

"Oh hello, hello, this is Rabbi Sheila. How are you? Congratulations on your engagement!" She was enthusiastic, which was nice. As we chatted, I braced myself against the grating timbre of her voice. I told her we had been looking for rabbis for a while, and that we had met several thus far.

"Oh really!" she said. "And who did you meet with? What were the problems?"

I told Rabbi Sheila I didn't feel comfortable giving her the names of rabbis I hadn't liked.

"Oh sweetheart," she said, "I love all my colleagues! I really do! Now tell me which ones you met with."

Once again, I refrained, and pressed on. "How many times do you like to meet?" I asked. "Three, four, five?"

"Sweetheart, I have to tell you something," she said. "One time is plenty. A wedding ceremony? There really isn't that much to it."

I broke down and called Patty. It turned out she was glad to help. But she did not have a rabbi file. After she, too, had tried and failed to book Rabbi Mendelbaum, the next rabbi she had met with was Rabbi Joy, the one who flaked out. "What about Rabbi Wasserman?" she said.

Of course! The rabbi who had salvaged Patty's wedding was funny and professional—and he definitely had showed up. I called the rabbi, convinced we were at the end of our search. He remembered Patty's wedding—said it was the sort of thing you didn't forget. But as he himself would be out of town on May 1, he recommended a young colleague.

As we rode the subway deep into Brooklyn to meet Rabbi Number 5, Daniel again pitched the merits of employing a justice of the peace.

"We're getting closer," I told him. "I can feel it. Really."

Daniel required something more concrete.

"Look," I said. "This is the last rabbi. Okay? If you like him, we'll use him." Daniel sighed and then nodded, recognizing this was the best deal he was likely to get.

Rabbi Schlimmer had a broad face and a big, open smile, and reminded me of a relative of mine—who was twenty years old. Rabbi Schlimmer was not quite so young himself—but at thirty-two was more than ten years younger than we were. He had co-officiated at a couple of weddings, but he had never led an entire wedding service himself.

While we sat on sofas in the marble-floored lobby of the synagogue—Rabbi Schlimmer was too junior to merit an office of his own—I checked Daniel's expression. He seemed to like the rabbi, and, since a deal's a deal, I decided I liked him too. I hoped Rabbi Schlimmer would have beginner's luck.

"Are you familiar with something called Prepare and Enrich?"

asked the rabbi. I was, but Daniel looked blank. Prepare and Enrich was a personality test that Rabbi Schlimmer matter-of-factly told us we'd have to take. He explained that it was actually invented by a Christian minister and was used across faiths in "marriage prep." We would answer the questions by filling in those little SAT-like bubbles, and the rabbi would send the questionnaire to a software company in the Midwest for "scoring." Once the test was returned to him, the rabbi would discuss with us any issues or conflicts that the test might reveal.

I found the idea sort of amusing. As Daniel and I had already been together for several years, I didn't think we'd find many surprises, but you never know. At any rate, if all it took to finally have a rabbi was a few schleps to Flatbush and some number 2 pencils, I was ready to sign on.

"You're kidding," said Daniel on the subway ride back to Manhattan. "You would actually consider taking a standardized test to determine if we are suitable partners?"

"I think we already decided that for ourselves. But a test might be kind of, I don't know, fun."

"Fun? I'm not going to apply for the right to marry you! I'm not going to send my personal information to some company in Ohio for their evaluation! Do you know how bizarre these tests can be? They can ask questions about your bathroom habits! About your *bowel movements!* And do you know why?"

The other passengers were starting to stare.

"I mean it! Do you know why?"

"Um, no . . ."

"Because some of those questions were originally intended for patients on psych wards, that's why! I am not going to answer questions about my bowel movements to determine whether or not our marriage is a good idea!"

He was clearly more romantic than I'd realized. Nonetheless, this strikeout left us sans rabbi once again. Daniel made another case for Rabbi Number 2—the one with the niece—reminding me that aside from his poor phone etiquette, the rabbi was down-to-earth. I reminded him of the way the guy had pressured us to commit to him right away—ten months early—saying that May 1 (i.e., the last day of Passover) was "a very popular date." His behavior had not made me "feel comfortable." I told Daniel that if he was going to veto Rabbi Schlimmer over the bubble test, then he had to give me one more shot.

I made rounds and rounds of phone calls. I hung up on answering machines of rabbis whose voices sounded cloying or absentminded. I drew lines through the names of rabbis who, when I spoke to them, seemed bored or patronizing. Eventually I was lucky enough to have a long conversation with a Rabbi Schaechter, who seemed compassionate but high-strung. I prepared to take my last shot with him—until he told me he was moving out of the city the following week to preside over a congregation upstate. I was just about ready to call that justice of the peace when Rabbi Schaechter made a recommendation: We should call Rabbi Jeffrey Greenblatt. He said, "I think it would be a good fit."

It was. Rabbi Greenblatt, or Rabbi Jeff, as we called him, was an assistant rabbi at a well-established Reform synagogue (check); he was in Manhattan (check); he was not a psychotherapist (check); he did not require the taking of standardized tests (check). He was young, but not too young. He had been conducting wedding services for eight or nine years.

Best of all, we both liked him. Chatting with us in his office, Rabbi Jeff used the word *invoke* the wrong way in a sentence, and then corrected it to *evoke*, pleasing both Daniel and me (we both make our living as editors). As more than one of the rabbis along the way had offered to show us their complete wedding text for our approval, Daniel asked if he could review and possibly edit Rabbi Jeff's service. Insulted, he refused. He said, "Though I do prepare, I don't write out every word. If we can't establish enough trust that you can feel good about what I might say on that day, then I'm not the right rabbi for you." We were pleased with his integrity, and the fact that Rabbi Jeff took pride in tailoring each service to the desires and personalities of the couple getting married.

We met with Rabbi Jeff a total of five times. Our conversations included not only the details of our wedding and our lives, but politics, philosophy, and, of course, religion. Rabbi Jeff always had popcorn or Hershey's Kisses to nosh on. Our last meeting was just a few days before the wedding.

"I'm going to be out of town the day before your wedding, but I'll be back in plenty of time the night before," he said. "I don't want to worry you—this is standard procedure for me—but just in case, I'm going to give you several phone numbers." I think he gave us about five of them: his cell phone, his home phone, the number of the place he'd be the night before, the synagogue's number, and perhaps a pay phone he'd be passing on the street.

Of course, I found this preponderance of emergency phone numbers enormously reassuring. "I'm a little hyper about making sure you get there," I admitted. "A friend of mine had a bad experience with a rabbi once."

Rabbi Jeff looked at me a little strangely. "I'll tell you a story," he said. "When I was about to conduct my first wedding service, I spoke to the senior rabbi here at the synagogue. I said to him, 'Rabbi—what is the most important thing about performing a wedding ceremony?' And he said to me, 'Show up.'"

Now I looked at Rabbi Jeff a little strangely.

"I thought the rabbi was kidding," he continued. "But he told me that recently there had been another assistant rabbi in this synagogue who never made it to a couple's wedding."

"That happened to my friend!"

"Your friend?"

"I was maid of honor!"

"You were? Was this about nine years ago?"

"Wait a . . . yes! And the rabbi's name . . . wait . . . it was Melanie . . ."

"Melanie Joy?"

"Yes!"

"Oh my God!"

"I can't believe this!"

"You were . . ."

"It was the same . . ."

"Oh my God!"

"I know!"

One of my favorite moments from our wedding day took place near the end of the ceremony. As we stood under the chuppah, the afternoon sun streamed in through the skylight. Rabbi Jeff removed his blue-striped tallis and swaddled both Daniel and me around the shoulders. Then, holding on to us both, he bowed his head. We were surrounded on three sides by friends and family—far from the synagogue of my youth. I held Daniel's hand, and like the rabbi, we bowed our heads. The rabbi's voice, as he chanted the blessing, was so resonant and so close that I could feel the reverberations in my cheekbones. I felt blessed.

Needless to say, Rabbi Jeff had made it to our wedding in plenty of time. This despite the fact that our wedding turned out to share a date with, and intersect with the location of, the largest bicycle marathon in the world. All through the wedding prep and the picture-taking, thousands of traffic-blocking cyclists zoomed by outside. But Rabbi Jeff, who had spent his entire rabbinical career worried about missing a wedding, had of course checked out alternate routes. No one, it turns out, was more prepared on such matters than he. But in any event, we knew we were covered: My friend Mary, who was serving as our cantor, was also legally qualified to marry us.

Just in case.

The Do-It-Yourself Wedding in 314 Easy Steps

SARA BERKELEY

ᴐ— "WE'RE DOING IT in the garden," I chirped. "Under the apple tree! Just a simple thing, no big deal." I can't count the number of times I told people this in the run-up to our wedding. "It's going to be so simple. We're doing it ourselves." For years, I had watched in disbelief as girlfriends and coworkers tore their hair out over how they could make the silverware match the wedding theme and whether they could get away with only five bridesmaids. Not for me the sleepless nights and lists of minutiae. Not for me the wedding planners, wedding consultants, wedding engineers—whatever they are now calling themselves. I was firm: There would be no minutiae surrounding our wedding. Just the basics, the important things. Vows, dress, flowers, food, music. Simple!

I'll let you in on a couple of insights I gained in the months preceding our big day:

1. Just because you are doing it yourself in the garden does not make for a simple wedding.

2. In fact, there is no such thing as a simple wedding.

To be fair, I think we made it look pretty easy, at least in the beginning. Take the engagement ring, for example. I was marrying a shopper. He can outshop me hands down every time. Shortly before he popped the question, I went home to my native Ireland to launch a novel. While I was gone, the man of my dreams spent nearly three weeks researching rings: the stones, the settings, and all jewelers within a fifty-mile radius of our home. When I got back, he asked me to marry him in a rather endearingly unplanned and flustered moment in the garden. He had mud on his jeans, but he did think to remove his gardening gloves. I said yes, a number of times, without pausing for breath.

That weekend, we set off for San Francisco to go Ring Shopping (I feel such a shopping trip deserves capitals). We would start, he had decided, with the Russian jewelers on Union Street. I hadn't known there were any Russian jewelers on Union Street, but then it's not every day I go shopping for engagement rings. The first store we tried had the advantage (to my romantic mind) of being up a rickety staircase. It was small, poky even, with uneven floors and small-paned windows full of antique treasures. We hesitated in front of the first showcase, feeling very new at this. "Um, I like that one," I said, pointing to a really pretty diamond in a slightly raised setting. The ring was from the 1940s. I pictured a war widow wearing the symbol of her dead soldier's love through years of heartache in some wholesome small-town American house with a red door and a porch with a swing. "Let's get it," I said, already feeling mystically connected to this woman. But my fiancé was not quite ready to throw away weeks of research by settling for the first ring we saw.

"Don't you want to look around a bit?" he said. I gazed hungrily at the ring.

"I guess we should," I said.

We then moved on to three or four more establishments, all of which boasted similar old Russian jewelers with eyeglasses and gravelly accents. Each had hundreds of rings, mostly not so beautiful, none that compared to *my* ring. After a decent interval, I turned to my fiancé. "I want the first one," I said. And that's what I got.

We were off to a great start, and Significant Purchase Number Two looked like it was going to be even simpler. Wedding dress shopping is traditionally the domain of the bride and her mother. However, my mother was six thousand miles away. So when I went to buy my dress, my fiancé came too. Being a shopper, he was not about to miss out on this major retail experience. We cut straight to the chase: a small, local vintage dress shop with three racks of wedding dresses. It was a Wednesday afternoon. There was nobody else around. We spent a wonderful hour or so picking out everything from sequined flapper dresses to big, creamy, raw silk Princess Di gowns. I would try something on, then emerge from behind the faded curtain of the dressing room, and he would firmly shake or nod. Yet nothing was quite perfect. Disappointed, we left the store and, on the way back to the car, ducked inside a small boutique that didn't even stock wedding dresses. It specialized in sun hats and upscale sweatsuits. But there, at the back, unassumingly hanging on a rack of vintage jackets and summer skirts, was my dress. It probably wasn't even made to be a wedding dress, but I loved it at once: a fitted, ivory, full-length dress with a skirt that swirled dreamily as I walked. The bodice was covered with fine lacework that hung in delicate droplets over the shoulders and arms. It was reasonably priced (we're talking well under $200) and was *just right.* Dress hunting was an appropriate follow-up to the ring-shopping experience after all.

Then there were the invitations. I didn't want any of those clone-like embossed things with ribbons around the borders and bold type at the bottom listing stern dress codes. We printed ours on our printer on good card stock. "We're getting married!" they read. "Please come to witness, support, and celebrate with us; eat, drink, and be merry; dance your socks off, make music, and have a preposterously good time." The response cards read

We can come! There'll be __ of us, all dressed up and looking fabulous.
We can't come. We are covered in sorrow.

The wording, we felt, reflected the carefree spirit of the whole enterprise. Sadly, so did our omission of a line for listing names on the cards; when the responses came back, we knew how *many* guests to expect but not who they would be.

Once the ring, dress, and invitations were taken care of, we were on a roll. We ordered tables, chairs, china, silverware, and glasses all in one day. We booked a room in a nearby inn for the wedding night, and made reservations for family members at a quirky, historic local hotel, which advertised the "happy clutter" of its dining room. We hired friends' daughters as waitresses and the catering services of a great family-run Italian restaurant where Victor, the proprietor, promised to take care of me like his own daughter.

We were up to late May (D-day, June 4), and we felt just a touch invincible. It was then, four days before our wedding, when I woke up with a swollen face.

I never get swollen faces. I have no allergies, I don't wear makeup, and my skin is about as sensitive as a basketball. Furthermore, and here I will brook no laughter, I really wasn't stressed out about the wedding. Many of the arrangements had been made, and the groom and I were still on speaking terms. Plus when I *do* get stressed, the worst I do is tidy. I never, ever wake up with my face looking like salami. But four days before our wedding, my face closely resembled salty, cured meat. I mean one of those angry, red, tight salamis, not the long, grayish, wizened ones with the kind of whitish floury coating. That would have been better; at least it would have matched my dress.

If you knew me, you would know that I handle large crises quite well. Small inconveniences can send me into a tailspin. Not being able to get the lid off a jar of olives, for example, drives me into a rage of cursing and pan banging. But get me around sudden death, dismemberment, or my face swelling up right before I'm to be married, and I'm pretty cool. So the salami effect did not send me into a panic. Instead, I sank into an eerie calm. The human jigsaw puzzle that was our wedding had already begun to come together. Puzzle pieces had been boarding planes all over the globe. My parents and aunt had arrived from Ireland; my husband's brother and his wife from New York; cousins from Arizona and L.A. I looked like a dermatologist's case study, but I would just have to get on with the nuptials.

Theories about the swelling abounded. I quickly ruled out food. If you have ever organized your own wedding in your back garden, you know that there just isn't time during the preceding week to eat. Unusual skin products? One glance in my bathroom cabinet squashed that theory: some half-congealed moisturizer, two combs, and a crusty container of Q-tips. I just don't really *do* skin products. This is apparently something that endeared me to my husband. When I moved in, I took over every bookshelf in the place, but when I unpacked my stuff in his bathroom, he barely noticed.

Suggestions from family about the root of the facial problems got more outlandish. Perhaps I had been bitten by a snake, suggested a cousin from Ireland, who must have thought California was teeming with venomous wildlife. Maybe it was an allergy to my wedding dress? Champagne cocktails? Too many relatives?

The last began to seem the most plausible, as more family poured in by the hour. My eldest brother arrived from England with his bow tie and his copy of the *Observer.* "Good grief," he said, when I opened the door. Since we hadn't seen each other for over a year, it was not quite the greeting I'd anticipated. Our cousins flew in from Phoenix crowing about how cool it was, at ninety-five degrees, compared to Scottsdale. My aunt, who likes to refer to herself as the Head of the Family (retain capitals when addressing her, please), tripped lightly off her flight from London, looked around, and pronounced The New World sufficiently to her liking. She promptly turned seventy, an event we celebrated with a picnic in a very hot, dry local meadow the next day. Pictures from the event show everyone in fine form, including the groom, who was apparently taking it in stride that he was about to marry Sausage Woman.

What I Learned from Being a Salami for Three Days: If you are reading this in the run-up to *your* wedding and considering treating yourself to a massage to relax before the big day, schedule a trial-run massage a few weeks earlier. That way, if you, like me, prove to be allergic to the detergent your masseuse uses on her linens, you can recover from your allergic reaction in good time and avoid annoying comparisons to bratwurst in the days immediately prior to the event.

The swollen-face thing seemed to start a barely perceptible downward slide in events. My mum, in one of her expansive moments, had offered from the safety of Ireland to make our cake. My mum is a champion wedding cake baker, and to top it all, she really knows how to ice the things. However, she was not on home ground, and she soon discovered that my kitchen was about as well equipped as a garden shed when it came to baking wedding cakes. I had no baking tins large enough, no icing equipment, no cake recipe. Luckily, having known me since birth, she had anticipated some of this and arrived with her own set of somewhat medieval-looking implements: flat knives, tapering, white cloth bags, and an impressive collection of shiny nozzles. (She would have packed her kitchen if she could have.) So all we needed was the tin, which had to be eight inches in diameter and have completely straight, not even slightly sloping, sides (which apparently all my cake tins had). Preferring to leave the mysteries of cake baking unsolved, lest I be expected to someday bake one, I didn't delve too deeply into the rationale for the square-sided cake-tin thing. Instead, I drove her to 743 kitchen supply stores until she found exactly the one she was looking for. It wasn't that square-sided cake tins were so hard to find. It's just that my mother, despite her numerous visits to this country, still had tremendous difficulty with American English. She had a knack for speaking sentences composed almost entirely of British or Irish ways of saying things. "I put the crisps over there between the tea towels and the bin," she'd tell some nonplussed friend of mine. "Now what's for elevenses? Anyone for a biscuit with their tea?" It was very quaint, especially as she really wasn't trying to do it, but it made for very long shopping trips as she struggled to explain to bemused assistants exactly what she wanted. She also managed to get very indignant when people didn't understand her, and generally finished up by hinting that I lived in some kind of barbaric outpost. *How you could live in a country where they don't know what a square-sided cake tin is, I just don't know. . . .*

Once we cleared the hurdle of the tin, however, she was off and running. Actually, she was off and sitting very still. Intense concentration comes easily to my mother when she has an art project in hand, and this cake was definitely a work of art. She spent days hunched over our dining room table, fashioning tiny leaves and petals out of icing. The wedding preparations went on loudly around her, but she was in her own hushed world of whorled rosebuds and spun sugar. Careful not to interrupt, we left plates of food close to her. When it was finished, she opened a small bag and pulled out the pièces de résistance: a tiny wooden piano and matching bookcase, complete with miniature books, that my dad had carved. They were perfect symbols; my husband is a pianist and I am a writer. My mum placed the intricate wood creations side by side on top of the cake. She was done.

I was quite relieved. We now had a spectacular wedding cake, and she was now free to help with the flowers. Despite not knowing a thing about flower arranging, I had somehow thought it a good idea to do all the flower arrangements myself. "It'll be simple!" I had trilled. "We'll do it the day before. All the women. Just like the old days!" I'm not clear which old days I was thinking of exactly, but three days before the wedding we were all sitting around the dinner table and the subject of flowers came up. "We're getting them at the market, right?" I said to my fiancé. He had told me about the San Francisco Flower Mart, how you get there at 5:00 AM, and there are endless stalls of fresh flowers. A sea of flowers. An ocean. But 5:00 AM?

The lunacy of this was now beginning to sink in. Living an hour's drive from there, I would have to rise at . . . 4:00 AM. This did not sound appealing. Then I would have to drive into the city, running into the first wave of commuter traffic, in the dark to a flower market located in an area I only vaguely knew. "So who's coming with me?" I said. Nobody moved a muscle. Everyone was thinking, *4:00 AM? For flowers?* "Right," I said, with sudden new clarity about my wedding flowers. "Plan B. What time is it?" It was 8:20 PM. The local farmer's market closed at 9:00 PM. They had flowers.

My fiancé, my mother, and I scrambled into my car and drove twenty minutes to the farmer's market. We threaded our way through the late shoppers to the biggest flower stall. "How much for everything?" I asked. Everything was $50. We took the lot.

Now all that remained was to transform armloads of flowers into tasteful table displays. Oh, and let's not forget the bridal bouquet. Luckily the flower stall had stunning creamy roses, enough for the bride and all appropriate boutonnieres. Now I was about to get a crash course in bridal flowers. For one thing, boutonnieres need pins, and something to bind the cut end of the flower. Who'd have thought? Secondly, flowers do not arrange themselves, nor do they generally look very good when arranged by someone who has no idea what she's doing. Several of my girlfriends had gallantly risen to the challenge and promised to spend Friday afternoon "doing flowers" with me. Unhappily, none of them knew much more than I did about what "doing flowers" actually entailed. Happily, my mother took charge. What a wonderfully useful person a mother turns out to be when one is knitting one's own wedding and forgets to buy yarn (or a pattern).

By 2:00 PM on Friday, our dining room table was piled with flowers, oases, vases, and cutters, and surrounded by my closest women friends and relatives, all making spectacular table centers under the instruction of my mom. Just like the old days!

Unhappily, my mother is also a worrier. She spent that night agonizing about the boutonnieres. Unable to put her concerns aside, she set to work. When I awoke at six the next morning, I found a box of perfectly bound and pinned boutonnieres and the most perfect bride's bouquet I could have wished for. How my mom got through that day on three hours of sleep was a secret she kept to herself. And there was, not surprisingly, still *plenty* to do.

For example, the rehearsal dinner. In our case, there was no wedding rehearsal, so it had never really occurred to us to have a rehearsal dinner. But suddenly we had twenty-four relatives and close friends in our immediate vicinity, and they all had to be fed. *Simple!* we thought. *Dinner for twenty-four in the garden!* It seemed to be in keeping with the down-home aspect of our wedding. It was not a meal we had put a tremendous amount of thought into, but how hard could it be? Just a few chicken wings, and a couple of bowls of salad . . .

The only space in our garden large enough to seat twenty-four at a table was already taken up by our vegetable patches. "No problem," said my fiancé, always a handy one with a hammer and a few nails. "I'll just relocate the vegetables, take out the two-by-twelves and presto! Rehearsal dinner area."

As with his usual just-a-piece-of-wood-and-a-few-nails projects, his estimates proved woefully optimistic. The vegetable patch relocation took most of the day, and we finished up with giant trays of ailing strawberry plants laid end to end down the side of our house. He lovingly wrapped the roots in damp cloths, but those strawberries never really forgave him. Then there was the problem of tamping down the raised earth once he took the two-by-twelves away. This we took on as a team, pretending we were grape crushers of yore, barefoot on the land, dancing to the lilt of fiddles . . . well, I'm getting a little carried away. Actually we just took off our shoes and jumped about in the potting soil like a pair of maniacs. It's a good thing our garden is surrounded by a thick wall of bamboo. The neighbors might have assumed that wedding nerves had finally sent us over the edge.

The principal disadvantage of rehearsal dinners located on converted vegetable patches can be expressed in a single word: sinkage. The nutritious and fertile soil, while perfect for growing vegetables, was much softer than a regular lawn, and chair legs tend to be pointy.

Furthermore, sinkage occurred in direct relation to body type. Simply put, as the evening wore on, some of us were going down faster than others. My aunt, apart from being the Elder of my clan, is also the Greatest Among Us. At one point, she began singing "Nearer, My God, to Thee" in a tribute to those who went down with the *Titanic*. My brother, six foot six, was delighted to find that his five-foot-two wife finally reached up higher than his ribs. Some people were tipping a little to starboard, others to port. Happily, we finished dinner before anyone disappeared completely, but it certainly gave a new twist to the concept of drinking each other under the table.

I think you must be getting the message by now: If you are throwing your wedding in your back yard, avoid the pitfall of thinking, *But how handy! If we need anything, it will be right there!* This is not strictly true. Particularly if what you happen to need on the day is about three hundred square feet of back yard. We thought we planned everything meticulously, and we still came up short on space. How did this happen? Was it a mathematical error? Was it uninvited guests? Or could it have been because the chairs only arrived the night before, and we never actually placed them all on the lawn until the morning of? No! Surely not!

One of my favorite photos from our wedding day was taken early in the morning. It features a sea of white plastic chairs wedged carefully in rows on our tiny, odd-shaped lawn, with my dad and my husband-to-be sitting forlornly side by side in the last row. Some of the chairs were tilting alarmingly close to rather steep shrubbery and a gravelly patio below. Our lawn is long and narrow, sort of church-shaped if you think about it, with an old apple tree forming the altar. The fact that our septic leach lines run directly under it was not something I thought about until later in the day. At this point, we had laid the chairs out and determined that, yes, seventy of them actually *did* fit, as long as nobody needed to breathe during the ceremony. I snapped the shot of my dad and his nearly son-in-law together in their "pew." Suddenly, the end of our lawn seemed awfully far away, with a vast expanse of empty white chairs in between, and the melancholy thought struck me: What if nobody turned up except the three of us?

I'm sure this would have suited Victor and his caterers. They arrived at our house around eleven that morning. I enthusiastically greeted them, a gang of Italians carrying giant vats of hot food up the thirty steps to our house. "Wer iz the kitchen?" Victor asked, his eyes darting from side to side. "This is the kitchen," I said, gesturing faintly at our rather compact kitchen area. Alright, I'll come clean: Our kitchen is about the size of a lunch box. Plainly, we should have thought to warn Victor. "Wer are the *soorfaces?*" he said, his voice rising a couple of notches. "Wer will we *poot* everything?" I looked at the large Italian cooks blocking out the light in the kitchen/dining area. They were carrying dinner for seventy, and there was a lot of it. *Hmmm.* Where *would* they put it all? My fiancé, my mother, and I scratched our heads. Then, muttering under his breath what I could only assume were complicated Italian curses, Victor and the gang set to work to find enough soorfaces for their goods. Discreetly exiting, we left them to it.

As it happened, I needn't have worried about nobody showing up. Almost everyone we invited turned up, along with a few we didn't. (Who brings along an uninvited friend to a wedding?) The only expected guests who failed to show were two friends, who got the day wrong and showed up begging and pleading an hour into dinner, and our photographer friend, who had promised us his best art for the occasion, but accidentally *forgot to come.* Yes, the friendship survived this rather glaring faux pas, but no, we have never quite let him forget it.

Do-It-Yourself Wedding Tip #4867: Make sure there's a bathroom available for both bride and groom immediately prior to the start of the ceremony. We have two bathrooms, one downstairs, one upstairs. I was in the upstairs bathroom waiting for my triumphant emergence from our upper room. My arrival was supposed to be signaled by Harry, the best man, after he had escorted the groom safely to the back lawn. From the upstairs window, I stared intently at Harry. The wedding song began, and I waited for his sign. And I waited for his sign. And I waited for his sign. Was the groom getting cold feet? Having a last shot of bourbon? Answering email? No, he was waiting for the downstairs bathroom to free up. Trapped inside the house, he could hear the wedding song and was no doubt wondering (a) how long a musician could make one song last, and (b) what the bloody hell my sister-in-law could be doing in the bathroom.

Meanwhile, the pianist, obviously confused by the delay, had valiantly switched to some music that was not quite wedding-entrance stuff but could possibly be construed as such if the groom were suddenly to appear. After a few minutes of this, while the guests shifted in their seats to peer toward the back door, the pianist moved back to the wedding song, perhaps hoping it would jog the groom's memory. At that moment, the back door opened and out came my sister-in-law, all freshened up. She stopped in her tracks like a deer in the headlights. Seventy pairs of eyes looked her up and down. Muttering apologies for not being the bridegroom, she slunk to her seat.

Seconds later, the groom emerged, ready to be married. Harry gave me a discreet thumbs-up, and we were off.

The ceremony passed without a hitch. Everyone fit admirably in our outdoor wedding chapel, and not even one guest tipped down the hill. The toddlers present somehow survived the uniquely un-toddler-friendly aspects of our garden (sudden drops, stone staircases with no railing, sinking vegetable gardens). As we said our vows, a bird began singing in the branches above and kept up his jubilant song until my husband was told he could now kiss his bride.

Afterward, the guests obligingly cleared off the lawn and retired to have champagne on our patio while the rest of the garden was magically transformed from wedding chapel to reception hall. Victor and his team started carrying bruschetta plates out from the tiny kitchen. (We never fully understood where he found enough soorfaces.) Our musician friend sparked the party with some salsa tunes. Absolutely nobody commented on the fact that as we began helping ourselves to the buffet, everything began to smell very faintly of sewage. For those of you unversed in the joys of septic systems, all you really need to know is that our system involves two leach lines. When one fills up (let's not go there), you switch to the other. I'm sure there are scientific ways to calculate when it's time to switch. You could probably even mark it on the calendar. We have always relied on the Nasal Method. Now who would have thought this method would come into play during *our wedding!* It was something so unthinkable that even I pretended it wasn't happening, especially once I had discreetly switched the leach lines and the smell began to go away. What's a bit of odor between friends?

All that remains is to briefly cover an incident that would barely merit a mention except that it involved the near death of a family member. A wedding just isn't a wedding without a near-death experience, don't you think? Ever obliging, my dad saw me and my new husband off to our hotel around eight that evening. When he returned to our house, he walked right through the sliding glass doors to our dining room. Near-death experiences are only funny when they are over, and it wasn't funny to see the giant shards of glass that could have punctured vital arteries. But the spirit of our wedding was somehow hovering over him, and he only sustained a small tear in the knee of his pants. The glass doors fared a little worse. Thanks to my dad, we now have lovely French doors, something we wanted anyway. There's nothing like a wedding in your garden to make all your dreams come true!

So it falls to me to offer the final words of advice to those of you considering the courageous path of the homegrown wedding: *Go for it!* The advantages are legion. You can forever look out your back window at the spot where you took your vows. You can dance to your wedding song on your own patio. You can pee in your own bathroom during the reception. And every time your septic leach lines need switching, the aroma will bring you fondly back to that special day when you and your partner stood under your apple tree, looked into each other's eyes, and said, *I do.*

ʻKnockers ʻUp

Patricia Bunin

꙳— THE SLIDE STARTED while I was dancing at my stepdaughter's wedding. Once it got going, there was no stopping it. One minute I was twirling around my husband, George, the next my body had rearranged itself: The prostheses I'd worn since my double mastectomy were too heavy for my strapless bra. Gravity brought them to my waist. And so, midspin, I suddenly resembled a pregnant kangaroo.

Grabbing my startled husband in what appeared to be a passionate embrace, I whispered to him to dance me off the floor. When he could not hear, because of the music, my whisper grew louder until it turned into a desperate shout.

"Dance me to the ladies' room, damn it!" I demanded, just as the band ended the set and the room went quiet. To his credit, George danced me out into the lobby and over to the ladies' room as gracefully as he could, without ever asking why I kept my body cemented to his, chest to chest.

George stopped me at the restroom door, assuming I was having a tummy upset. As other women walked past, I clung to my husband. Nodding and waving to people we knew, I whispered to him, "Reach your hand under my jacket and unzip my dress."

George's look said, *This is really not the time, and definitely not the place.* But he carefully slipped his hand under my jacket and undid the zipper at the back of my dress. I could see the lightbulb go on in his head. By now, I had managed to turn us around so my back was facing a wall but my body was still tight against his. As though it were a perfectly normal thing to do, George continued to help me undress as he, too, smiled and nodded at wedding guests.

I stopped him when the zipper reached my waist. I had visions of the boobs spilling out, falling onto the floor, and rolling across the hardwood, the most surprising wedding crashers ever: a couple of tiny, round midgets waltzing on the dance floor. People might trip on them, or even worse, step on them. One high heel sticking into the prosthesis would send silicone everywhere. Someone would slip in the greasy puddle. The boobs cost $375 dollars each. Would this kind of a mishap be covered under replacement insurance?

The dark navy sleeveless dress I was wearing had captivated me in the department store. It had a nipped waist that flounced into a flared full-length skirt and a matching mesh jacket that tied in front.

Although I am thin, the prostheses and flared skirt gave me a nice shape. What could be more perfect for the dinner-dance reception, I'd thought, even if my regular mastectomy bra wouldn't work with it? Now I understood too late why no one makes strapless mastectomy bras. But the question was, how was I going to put myself back together? I didn't know many of the guests well. It takes accumulated years of friendship before you're comfortable asking a woman, Would you mind helping me with my boobs?

In the bathroom stall, I slipped off my jacket and carefully peeled down the front of my dress, catching my boobs before they fell into the toilet. The strapless bra, still fastened but limp around my waist, was tough to negotiate; my agility had diminished since my operation and I had trouble reaching my back. I'd discovered that unless the bra was pulled up extremely high on my chest when I first put the boobs in, the weight of the inserts pushed it down, leaving me at high risk for more slip and spill. I had to get the bra at the highest point possible before I stuffed in the boobs.

Dressing for the wedding at home, I'd had George help me. But alone in the stall, I had to be creative. I left the bra fastened, and, because it had nothing in it yet, it was loose enough to loop the back over the purse hook on the stall wall. Lowering myself toward the floor so the hook would pull the bra up high, I prayed I wouldn't accidentally hang myself and be found strangled by my underwear, my falsies at my feet. Finally when the bra was up almost to my chin, I pushed the boobs in to make a nice tight fit.

It worked. Though it might have looked a little strange, this was a case where higher was definitely better than lower. But I couldn't get the zipper of my dress all the way up myself, so I covered my exposed back with the jacket and kept my arms at my side, trying to wash my hands while supporting my bra with my elbows.

Outside, I told George, "All's well, if you'll just give me a little zip." He looked relieved. We returned to the party hand in hand instead of chest to chest. This, however, marked the end of my dancing at that wedding.

But it did prepare me for the battle of the boobs when my own daughter got married two years later. I set out with my longtime best friend (she's BB for best buddy) to find a dress that would, under no circumstances, need a strapless bra. There were, however, a few complications. It was a summer outdoor wedding in Southern California—the kind that speaks to sundresses with light flowing layers, strappy tops with bare shoulders. In other words, everything I couldn't wear.

The high-necked, long-sleeve dresses I tried on were followed by short-sleeve, shapeless dresses with long jackets that made me look old and dowdy. This was my only child's wedding. Dowdy wouldn't do.

Barely three years prior, I didn't think I would live to see Sara get married. But here I was healthy, happy, and fresh from giving a breast cancer survivor's speech. "Thanks to the doctors and staff at this hospital, I am not even thinking about cancer today; I'm thinking about the upcoming wedding of my only child," I had told five hundred patients and survivors at the USC/Norris Comprehensive Cancer Center in Los Angeles. "I'm going to walk her down the aisle next month." And I wanted to look smashing.

Following Jewish tradition, Sara had elected to have both her parents walk her down the aisle, even though her father and I have been divorced for more than twenty-five years. Her groom, whose parents are deceased, had asked George, to whom I've been happily married for fifteen years, to walk with him. Everyone was getting along. George's two daughters were maids of honor. Sara's family and friends and mine were flying in from all over the country. My roommate from my Greenwich Village years, thirty-five years prior, was coming in from England. It was celebration time. I felt great, and, not only did I want to look great, I wanted to look great *and* dance at my daughter's wedding. Without looking like a fertile kangaroo.

BB and I saw the dress at the same time. It was a soft lavender silk, cut just above the knee. My daughter had teased me that I should show off my legs at the wedding because *they* at least were real. The dress was sleeveless with a wide scoop neck and a matching short jacket that I could use for the ceremony and remove for the reception. Perfect. Except it was cut just like the one from my earlier disaster. And it was two sizes too big. But I was in love.

Fortunately, BB is savvy about clothes. She saw immediately how the dress could be altered. "It's perfect," she said. "It's your favorite color and exactly the style you want." Dress in one arm and me on the other, she asked the saleswoman to call the store seamstress on our way to the dressing room.

BB showed me that the dress had two layers on the top; the boobs could be sewn in between them. The seamstress, a small woman with dark hair, arrived. She shook her head sternly, "You cannot do this. And you're so skinny, you don't need pads."

Undaunted, BB knew that the fancy store had several seamstresses on staff and asked for another one.

Seamstress Number 2 showed up in a flower-print turtleneck and a long corduroy skirt. She tried to convince me to buy a different dress in my size, something more "fitting for the mother of the bride," the woman said, pointing to a rack of long, loose Old Lady dresses.

"Is this all there is for me?" I turned to BB, tears starting to roll down my cheeks.

"You are a young-looking, chic woman," BB said firmly. She dabbed at my eyes with the white lace hankie she always carried in her purse. "And that's how you'll look at your daughter's wedding."

I flashed back to the day of my biopsy, three years earlier. I'd been unable to lift my arms to get back into my own clothes. But BB wouldn't let me go home in a hospital gown.

"Give me ten minutes," she told George and ran down to the gift shop; she found a long turquoise dress that looked pretty *and* that I could step into easily. Here she was again, making sure I would look my best under any circumstances.

"Please call the lingerie department and tell them we need a mastectomy specialist," BB told the saleswoman. "And you *must* have a seamstress in this store who can solve this problem. Have her meet us in lingerie."

The next thing I knew we were picking from a selection of breast pads, otherwise known as falsies, with the help of the specialist and Neha, the third seamstress. Neha was sweet and grandmotherly, with a bun on her head and strong, capable hands. "Of course we can make it work," she said in response to my pleas that it was my only child's wedding and I had to look perfect.

Neha worked magic. I got back into the dress, and she stuck pins in it, top to bottom. I felt like a voodoo doll. She transformed the size 6 dress into my size 2. Then she stepped back and said, "Now we do pads." The next minute a straight pin was pointing exactly where my left breast had once been. And then the right. She lifted the dress's upper layer, and using the pins as a guideline for placement, she pinned the pads to the bottom layer. Then she stepped back and smiled. "I know I will get it right the first time."

Five days later we went back for the fitting and it was perfect. I hugged Neha and cried. "How can I ever thank you?" I wanted to tip her generously. She shook her head. "The best thank you you can give me would be to have a wonderful time at the wedding and bring me pictures."

In that dress I felt more beautiful and more comfortable than I had since the mastectomy. As we left, BB handed me a gift wrapped in tissue. "To complete your look," she said. Inside was a delicate pair of lacy lavender panties, the exact color of my new dress. I thanked her. "These are so pretty, it's too bad no one will see them," I said. Back at home, I tucked the panties into the overnight bag I would bring to the hotel, where I was staying with Sara before the wedding.

My daughter, Sara, is a product of my harried days as a single mom. She always lays out her clothes the night before going to work and gets herself organized for the day in advance. Certainly her wedding day was no exception. Sara had arranged to have breakfast brought at 6:00 AM, giving us an hour to linger before our friend Eden arrived to do hair and makeup. Sara's elegant white silk dress hung from the closet door, zipped neatly into its garment bag. Her high-heeled strappy white sandals were placed on the floor below. On the desk was the dramatic faux purple hydrangea she'd selected to wear in her hair instead of a veil. Next to it was the simple gold bracelet, a gift from my godmother, that I was lending to Sara for her "something borrowed." That morning, for a moment, I envisioned her as a third-grader and felt there should be a shiny lunch box on the desk, too.

Sara took my breath away when I saw her dressed and made up, with her silky honey brown hair cascading over her shoulders, the flower pulling her hair just slightly away from the side of her face. She looked confident and capable—her therapist look, the expression I imagined she showed to her clients.

I was proud to be her mother and wanted to make her proud of me. Most of all I didn't want her to worry about me—something she'd done too much of since I'd been diagnosed. Smiling at myself in the bathroom mirror, I admired my for-once perfectly applied mascara and thanked my makeup maven. A moment later my beautiful baby-turned-bride called from the bedroom to say that the photographer was on her way.

I was so excited about the comfort of slipping into my new dress with built-in boobs that the morning's events swirled around me like a blur. "This is Heaven," I thought as I stepped into my dress, minus any agonizing undergarments. Even regular mastectomy bras were not comfortable for me because of the weight and feel of foreign objects where my own body ought to be. The lumps of gel always felt too high or too low, too big or too small. By contrast, the sewn-in pads were weightless and shapely. And in exactly the right spot.

Eden zipped the dress up for me, and we laughed together about my instant shape. Giddy with the glory of the moment, I danced barefoot over to my shoes. Normally I would have worn panty hose, but my fashion-savvy daughter insisted no stockings for a morning outdoor ceremony. So I stepped into my delicate silver sandals and stood with the bridal party for pre-wedding photos.

"It's time to head for the garden," Em, Sara's best friend from college, commanded in her maid of honor voice. I reached for my tiny bow-shaped silver purse (my sister-in-law called it my Vanna White bag). I had carefully packed it the night before with three things: my lipstick, mirror, and a tranquilizer.

Purse clutched in perfectly manicured nails, head held high, I was off. I stopped for a moment to admire myself in the ornate hall mirror of the hotel. I felt so put together. So comfortable.

As we reached the outdoor staircase that led down to the garden, the warm July morning rewarded us with a soft breeze. It blew up my dress and caressed my thighs and everything above. Suddenly my comfort turned to horror. I was not wearing any panties! The bride and her attendants were in long dresses but my above-the-knee lavender ensemble meant the guests already seated in the garden below could see up my dress as I descended the winding stone staircase!

"I need a restroom visit immediately," I whispered urgently to the wedding coordinator. "Give me five minutes." Juliette, who thank God could take orders as well as give them, moved to the top of the stairs and put her hand up to stop the procession. I tried to disappear inconspicuously. As soon as I hit the lobby, I took off my shoes and raced barefoot at top speed to my first-floor room.

BB and I had joked that it was a shame no one would see my panties. Now I was happy for everyone to see them, in contrast to what they had almost seen. No longer calm and cool, but definitely more covered, I sped back barefoot through the lobby, with the thin heels of my sandals hooked onto my Vanna White purse.

Pausing at the door to step back into the shoes, I saw that my feet were sweaty and dirty. I slipped into the ladies' room and dipped one foot at a time into the fancy sinks. I wiped each foot dry with the terry cloth towels. As I left the lobby to return to the garden, panic set in, as I realized I was way over my five-minute break. I turned to Vanna to get my tranquilizer, and it fell out of my hand and rolled down the stone steps, bouncing into oblivion. So much for tranquility.

Back with the bridal party, I forced a weak smile. "Ready to go," Juliette announced in an authoritative voice. Panties on and boobs sewn perfectly in place, I slipped my arm through my daughter's. Her dad took her other arm. "Wonder if he forgot his underpants," I thought.

And then I looked at Sara, who hadn't forgotten anything she was supposed to wear, including the smile on her gorgeous face. Suddenly the fact that I almost walked her down the aisle without any panties on seemed trivial. The sweaty feet didn't matter. Nor did the pill that was now probably calming one of the fish in the garden pond. This moment belonged to Sara. I could feel the sting of tears in my eyes. I was "happy inside," as Sara used to say when she was a little girl.

The music started. I put my shoulders back, chest forward, and took a calming breath. As we neared the garden path, my longtime friend Lou appeared at my side. "Knockers up!" she whispered so only I could hear. I pushed my chest out a little more.

Sara, her dad, and I walked down the winding aisle to her groom, and then I took my seat under the weeping willow tree to do a little weeping of my own. I never stopped dancing at the reception. And, not once did George have to waltz me to the ladies' room.

People Really Like Me

Samantha Schoech

∽ I DID GET TO BE a bridesmaid once. At my best friend Sarah's homespun back yard wedding I got to stand at the altar with her sister and cousin while the bride and groom exchanged vows and then presented his young son from a previous marriage with a new bicycle, sealing the deal with tangible consumer goods. It was an honor, and I was happy standing there holding my spindly Gerber daisies and smile-weeping.

At the reception I made a toast in which I cried in public and managed to work in the word diarrhea. I danced with children. I chatted with the parents of old friends. I ate cake. It was nice.

But, it doesn't really count as a real bridesmaid experience for one major reason. I looked awful. Not just awful in a peach taffeta sort of way. Awful in a character-testing way. Awful in an I-can't-have-fun-when-I-look-like-this kind of way.

This is how awful I looked. The bride, still my best friend, likes to look at the photos of her wedding because I am in some of them, and when she looks at me she has the sort of laughing fit she has been unable to attain since giving up marijuana more than a decade ago. I send her into hysterics. She does that open-mouthed, tear-wiping thing every time.

It's difficult to do it justice in writing, but let me start by saying that I am known in certain circles for my sartorial splendor. I'm no Diane von Furstenberg, but I have a certain knack for pulling it together when I have to, which is why it's so weird that when it came time to buy shoes for the wedding, I chose Montgomery Ward, where my husband and I were replacing our dryer, as my source. My white, faux-leather sandals with a thick, two-inch heel really wouldn't have been so bad if they weren't paired with the dress that my friend had picked out for me, a dress purchased at a patchouli-scented import store, without consultation. A dress that more than met Sarah's desire not to have any of her bridesmaids look better than her on her wedding day.

It's a cliché to complain about bridesmaids' dresses, so I'll just get it over with. It was a beige raw silk sack that strained across my ample bosom and then ballooned out over my hips, hugging the pooch of my belly, before ending in a lopsided hem above the chubby knees I inherited from my mother's side of the family. In an effort to give it shape, I had sewn two ribbons on either side at waist level and tied them together at the small of my back, creating a pouch effect right over my ass. This ensemble was completed with a huge, white sun hat, decorated with a fake rose, and the aforementioned high-fashion sandals. I looked like an overweight special education Texan who had accidentally wandered into a hemp clothing store. I would have given anything for something in peach taffeta.

I realize that bridesmaids are not supposed to complain about the way they look at the wedding. But like holding up a bloody sheet to prove to the villagers that the bride is a virgin, this is a ridiculously outdated notion. Complaining is protected by the First Amendment; and you know what they say—*use it or lose it*. Besides, my ugliness served no purpose. I didn't need to look bad to make Sarah look good. She was stunning in a 1930s clinging gown with a gardenia stuck behind her ear. I sort of hated her for it, but *Oh well*, I thought at the time. There will be other opportunities. I am, I reasoned, very good friends with several women in promising relationships. This first bridesmaid gig was just a warm-up, and I would learn from my mistakes.

That was six years ago.

My ongoing desire for a bridesmaid-do-over is embarrassing for two reasons. First, I like to think of myself as being way too cool and unconventional to want something so predictable and cloyingly feminine. I was raised by a socialist dental hygienist with artistic leanings and a hard-drinking Buddhist. I should be making organic goat cheese in the redwoods, not covetously flipping through *InStyle Weddings*. Second, I'm just way too *old*. I'm thirty-five, well beyond the years when such drippy, girlish fantasies bloom. I'm *married* for Christsakes. Wanting to be a bridesmaid is developmentally stunted. It's as if I were harboring a crush on one of the guys from *The O.C.* or collecting Hello Kitty miniatures. And yet, there it is, a hole in my female experience, an emptiness that can only be filled by a lovely shift, a tasteful bouquet, and the public acknowledgment of my specialness. I want to be a bridesmaid in the same way I wanted to be a cheerleader in the seventh grade. Probably for many of the same reasons.

I know there are women who complain about being bridesmaids. My friend Beth has been a maid something like twelve times. She's forked over thousands of dollars for dresses and airline tickets for the dubious honor of standing up for women she hasn't shared more than a Christmas card with since high school. My sister-in-law has been tapped so often she can do her own chignon in about two minutes without a mirror. I can understand how this would begin to wear on a girl. But, frankly, those who complain about being asked too often to play the role of bridesmaid elicit about as much sympathy from me as women who complain about being too skinny. Deaf ears, my dear.

It smacks of a *Not Biarritz, again* kind of attitude. Either they're showing off or, like some German heiress torturing her stable boy for entertainment, they have become completely cynical and blasé about everything, even the honor of being singled out as a special friend. Being a witness to someone's marriage, literally standing up with her as she makes her vows is, despite Carmen Elektra and Britney Spears and the oft-quoted divorce rate, still a heavy-duty thing. If you do it right, you are more than just arm candy for some frat-boy friend of the groom's; you are backup. And while there are certain drawbacks involved—the ugly dress, the screeching, stressed-out bride, the ridiculous stutter-step walk down the aisle—it's fun. It's like being asked to join an exclusive club—one that encourages drinking champagne at 10:00 AM.

And besides, when I yearn for bridesmaid-dom, it is not to participate in one of those garish, stiff weddings in which troops of women march down the aisle in some sick display of Mitzy's pretend popularity. It's because I want to honor the many women I care about as they make the deep and meaningful step into marriage. And because I like attention. I want a large and obvious display of my own popularity. Getting to be a real bridesmaid is a little badge that unmistakably declares that people really like me.

This really shouldn't have been so difficult. I am lucky to be part of a group of women friends who have known each other since elementary school. We sometimes refer to ourselves collectively as the "Marin Six" for the county north of San Francisco where we grew up. We all returned to the Bay Area after college and started meeting regularly for "girls' night." We have seen each other through broken engagements, parental deaths, joblessness, poverty, grad school, bad jobs, good jobs, sexual experimentation, adultery, drunkenness, fat stages, skinny stages, quarrels, and the *Friends* haircut. But where we really shine is at weddings. Trust me. Nobody knows how to send a girl off into the wifely realm like the Marin Six.

We flutter and fete. We devise elaborate and slightly evil bachelorette parties, some of which have included weekends away at New Age hot springs (nothing makes a girl happy about taking herself out of the dating game like waking up to the sight of naked hippie guys doing the downward dog on the meditation deck). We are there to help transform card rooms and vineyards and back yards into fairytale settings of potted palms and rose petals. We address invitations and throw engagement parties and make great toasts. We are experts on the thong-versus-commando question.

So you'd think I'd have a nice pool from which to glean my brides. You'd think all that friendship and womanly camaraderie would pay off come the big day. But one after another, the Marin Six walked down the aisle without me by their side. I've watched Jewish weddings, Hindu weddings, and drive-thru Las Vegas weddings pass me by. I am never a bridesmaid. Instead I have duties.

I've heard that in more formal parts of the country people with duties have titles. They are called "personal attendants" or "bridal assistants." Where I come from, in lackadaisical Northern California, we are not big on titles, but it's the same thing: all the responsibility of being part of the wedding party, none of the glory.

Having bridal duties at a wedding where there are no bridesmaids is actually okay. It's still not as good as being a bridesmaid, but at least you don't feel like a second-rate friend. There is an inner-sanctum feeling to being with the bride while she gets dressed and has her pre-walk-down-the-aisle belt from your flask. You might not end up in the pictures, but the mother of the bride will call you by name, and at the reception you can bask in the warm glow that comes from knowing that you are one of only three people who knows that the bride is wearing Band-Aids over her nipples and a girdle straight out of the 1959 Sears, Roebuck Catalogue.

At my friend Sadie's recent wedding, I was thrilled to be asked to do her makeup. (In addition to my sartorial sense, I have a strange knack with cosmetics.) Despite the fact that she is the author of a book on bridesmaid etiquette, Sadie, who does not at all seem like the type of person who would write a book on bridesmaid etiquette, went maidless. So in this case, doing the makeup was surely as close as one could come to being a maid. It marked me as a special friend, and it was a big job. While other, lesser friends scuffed the soles of her new shoes out on the sidewalk or washed the breakfast dishes, I sat and chitchatted, waiting for my moment to shine. True, I was not asked to the hair salon to watch her get curled and sprayed, but at least I wasn't the scuffing girl. That was a dupe's job if I ever saw one.

When I arrived at the wedding site I was still flush from my recent proximity to the bride. I had inside information for friends lacking my sort of access. "She seems good," I said to whoever might want to listen. "We had a minor bra incident but she's relaxed and ready to go. She looks beautiful." I delivered my comments with largesse and generosity. What reason did I have to be stingy? This was the big day for one of my very *closest* friends.

But then—and this is why having duties, even at a maidless wedding, is no substitute for the real thing—things started to fall apart. First, I noticed a little swarm of friends from the East Coast knowingly arranging programs and asking people to sign the Quaker witness thingy. One of them leaned over and helped the bride's brother with his boutonniere. A proprietary surge came over me and then a flash of confusion. Without bridesmaids it is nearly impossible to discern among the many out-of-town guests who is really in the inner circle. And now *their* wedding contributions were being witnessed by the guests, while *mine*, although obviously more vital to the proceedings (convincing blemish coverage is every young bride's deepest wish), had taken place behind closed doors. The question ringing in my head, distracting me throughout the vows, was *Who is really Sadie's best friend: the New York girls with their endless program straightening, or me?*

This was answered soon enough. At the reception my husband and I were seated near the busing station, out of sight of most of the other guests, at a table filled with misfits collected from temporary stops along Sadie's life path. There were no childhood or high school or college friends at table 18. There were a few medical school acquaintances of the groom's, and a girl Sadie met on a train in London long ago, and, most horrible of all, her current neighbor, someone who had lent her eggs a couple of times. I was, quite frankly, shocked. It seemed my services as makeup artist had nothing to do with friendship and everything to do with my God-given talents for blending and concealing. It was a grim realization and a painful truth, but in the end I managed to satisfy my need for attention by getting drunk and starting a break dancing circle with other members of table 18.

At Karie's wedding I was assigned to bring her a gin and tonic in her dressing room. I took this very seriously and invested in some frivolously expensive gin for the occasion. My bartending duty was going well until her mother saw me making the drink.

"What's that?" she asked, her lips pursed in undisguised disapproval.

"A gin and tonic," I chirped.

She looked at me as if I had just left a turd on the floor of the bridal suite. "It's 11:00 AM."

I looked at Karie who was frantically shaking her head and drawing a finger back and forth across her neck in the universal gesture meaning "my mother still thinks I'm thirteen, so please don't tell her that I am about to have a completely legitimate gin and tonic before my wedding."

"I'm just so keyed up," I said, gulping the drink like a woman dying of thirst. "It's a big day."

For taking the gin rap I was rewarded by having the mother of the bride veer dramatically out of my way whenever we crossed paths as if I might take her out in my uncontrollable drunken stupor. And I'm not in a single picture. Not one.

I've done makeup at Karminder's wedding. At Lisa's I was invited to hang out with the wedding party beforehand, the only one there not dressed in a beige silk shift the real bridesmaids were wearing. In short, I've come very close but I just never seem to be able to make the leap from good friend to bridesmaid. I'm like one of those nice guys all the girls tell their boy trouble to: trusted, loved, but unable to get laid. So to speak.

And time is running out. I have a lot of already-married friends.

The remaining single women in my life are iffy. It's entirely possible they may choose to not have bridesmaids. As we get older this has become a disturbing but popular trend. For some asinine reason it has achieved a coolness factor. People announce their intentions not to have bridesmaids with the same sort of holier-than-thou pride that should be reserved for trekking across Africa or partying with one of the Wilson brothers.

Which brings me to Alex, a member of the Marin Six and my last promising bride. She has already declared her intention to have a "simple wedding." Read: lots of duties, no bridesmaids. This despite the distinctly unsimple rock the size of a tooth on her finger. But I am dropping hints.

Recently we looked at dresses—strappy, flowing things meant to show off her free spirit and stunning bod. As she stood in front of the mirror, admiring her reflection, I made sure to get in close. I nudged up next to her, hands held primly at my belly button as if carrying a bouquet, and smiled admiringly.

"This looks good," she said.

"Yes," I agreed. "We look great together." And then, recognizing my mistake, I hastened to add, "*You* look amazing!" Flattery is important. Brides eat that shit up.

She grinned, pleased. "You're such a good friend," she said.

I smiled, deflecting. Here it comes, I thought, my heart soaring with uncool anticipation. And then I stood there, waiting like that horny teenage boy for the slim possibility that I might be invited to partake in the wedding equivalent of the finger fuck.

"I think you should do my makeup," she said, squeezing my

hand like she had just generously and unexpectedly written me into her will.

For stalling purposes, I smiled. I am not a good negotiator but there must be something I could do. This was going to be a good wedding—Latin-hipster-beach party with sangria. Not only that, it was my last chance at being a bridesmaid—ever. Alex and I had been friends since third grade. I *deserved* this.

"Can I walk down the aisle?" I asked.

She looked perplexed. "Well, I wasn't . . ."

"Okay," I relented. "Can I be in the program? You know like 'makeup by my dear friend Samantha' and then a little anecdote about our history together?"

"What's a program?" she asked. "People have programs?" Alex is not up on middle class pretensions, but she has other attributes like having a car so filled with crap you can almost always find what you need in a pinch. If you ever pull up at a restaurant and realize you've forgotten your underwear, Alex is your woman.

"What do you want me to wear?"

"You can wear whatever you want," she said, kindly. No taffeta. I sighed.

I was failing at worming my way into being a bridesmaid, and it was also possible that she was getting wise to my intentions. My next move called for subtlety and sensitivity.

"I wanna be a bridesmaid," I whined.

She laughed. She can be a little dense.

"No, seriously. I'd be great. I'll do all the nasty stuff. I'll scuff your shoes and hold your dress while you pee."

She watched me in the mirror as I became increasingly frantic. I was close to getting down on my knees and begging. The saleswoman looked up from straightening the pashminas to see if everything was okay.

"But we're just having our siblings. My sister is going to stand up with me."

"Your sister!" I snorted.

"Look, I want you to be part of my wedding but we've already decided that we're not having bridesmaids," she said.

I closed my eyes and took a deep breath.

"Okay," I said. "I understand."

"I'm glad," Alex smiled. "It's nothing personal."

She turned and took one last look at the back of her dress. I was calming down. It was going to be fine. I would do makeup at Alex's wedding and have a good time. I'd eat and drink and dance. Maybe I'd even make a toast.

I sat on a velvet footstool while Alex went into the dressing room to slip out of the fabulous dress. *Don't panic,* I told myself. *There is still time. Life is long and mysterious and blessings come in many forms.* This might seem like the end of the wedding party road but who knows? I might make new friends. There might be second marriages, or third. True, it might take a while and necessitate a slight reordering of my expectations, but it would happen. I sat up and sized myself up in the giant mirrors. It was clear I was going to have to revise my fantasy. Matron of honor still sounded a little dowdy to me—Mrs. Doubtfire in Montgomery Ward footwear—but it was something I could get used to.

The Sea Witch

ANNE JOHNSON

⌒ THE FOLDING TABLES. That was when we knew we were in trouble. We sat in Mrs. D's office, half stupefied by its reek of perfume, cat boxes, and cats.

Mrs. D spread the contract out on her desk and examined its five pages beadily. "I did not sign this." She flapped page 4 at us, the same page that a week earlier she had amended and initialed, agreeing to include four extra folding tables, gratis, in the cost of our wedding weekend. "This is a forgery."

My fiancé and I looked at each other, then stared down at Mrs. D's shag carpet, feeling strangely guilty.

"You are forgers!" Mrs. D screamed. When she fell into one of her rages, which was often now, the silver-blue wig that was pinned to her head tottered but never quite fell off. "Forgers. Forgers. That's what you are."

We will get married by the sea. Only marriage inspires such firm, declarative sentences, such statements of imperial command. "It is a truth universally acknowledged, that a single man in possession of a good fortune, must be in want of a wife." "I will wear a simple but elegant dress." "We will *not* do The Chicken Dance." And, "We will get married by the sea."

For me and my husband-to-be, the last decision was paramount. We were getting married as grownups; we had to plan and pay for everything ourselves. We knew we would need to scrimp—we would make our own invitations, we would forego a photographer, I would find an inexpensive wedding dress. But we wanted to say our vows within sight and sound of the Pacific Ocean. Peter, my fiancé, had grown up on the beach in Southern California. I had spent my childhood summers at my grandmother's cottage alongside Puget Sound.

One of our first dates had in fact been a beach picnic. We drove along the coast south of San Francisco with a wicker basket filled with cheeses and strawberries and wine: one of those wicker baskets you acquire when you're dating and will never use the rest of your life. We spotted a cove secluded below rocky cliffs and were strolling toward it when a rogue wave rose and smashed over us, knocking us to the rocks. A second wave slammed us back toward the cliffs and, retreating, pulled us out to sea. It was a moment when you think, *This is how I will die.* But we held on to each other and scrambled to safety, more or less intact, minus picnic basket and blankets, and Peter's glasses. Because I can't drive a stick shift, we inched the fifty miles home with Peter in the driver's seat, shifting and steering myopically, while I looked through the windshield, announcing, "The road bends left here."

In retrospect, we might have considered a surfside near-death experience a warning sign. But in retrospect one of our weaknesses as a couple was an inability to recognize warning signs. Instead, we spent January scouring the Northern California coast for a beach resort that still had space for a wedding in mid-June. We scanned bridal websites, read bridal guidebooks, and drove from Santa Cruz to Bolinas, stopping at every hotel with a deck along the hundred-mile stretch of coastline. We considered a seaside schoolhouse near Davenport that smelled of varnish and sweat, and a fading jazz club in Half Moon Bay that smelled of stale marijuana. We looked at tasteful resorts that would have bankrupted us, at affordable motels soggy with mildew and despair.

Then after a month of weekend coastal tours, my fiancé remembered: On business a year earlier he had visited an old resort near Santa Cruz on a bluff above the Pacific. It was a little run-down, he remembered, but it had pretty gardens and wonderful views. It had been called Las Olas, he thought. The Waves. It was owned by an old woman, quite old, really, but still sharp as a tack. "Oh," she had mentioned to him, as if she could foresee his future need, "we do such beautiful weddings here."

We drove down to visit. As we steered through the wrought-iron gates, Las Olas was nothing but lovely. White clapboard cottages, in need of paint but still trim, were set on the bluff above the ocean. Between the cottages, oaks and eucalyptus shaded green lawns and plantings of star jasmine and intense red bottlebrush. From the lawn, a stone walkway led to the cedar deck where weddings were staged: There, saying your vows, you gazed out to the Pacific spreading blue into the southwest horizon.

The price was surprisingly reasonable, too. This may have been because Las Olas had its quirks. Someone had abandoned a dozen old Lincoln Continentals in strange places around the property. You saw them—dented, missing wheels and windshields—nosed against a rickety toolshed, or decaying out by the hot tub, half swallowed by nasturtium vines. And there were cats, too, many cats, thin, furtive, flitting so fast you weren't sure you really had seen them.

Still, after our tour, when Mrs. D asked, "What do you think of Las Olas?" we answered, "It's perfect. We want to get married here."

"And what date were you thinking of?"

"June 25," we said. But we would have accepted any date Las Olas had available.

"Let's go to my office."

Mrs. D led us inside. Coming from Las Olas's jasmine-scented grounds, the transition to Mrs. D's office was a physical blow. What we noticed first was the heat blasting from three space heaters (we would learn Mrs. D kept all three going day and night). Then the smell of heated cat urine and cat boxes and the half dozen cats— fatter kin to the feral cats outside—who idled on overstuffed chairs.

Finally, the decor—Mrs. D's pink shag carpet, her pink velvet couches, the faux French provincial desk where she now examined her registration book.

"Oh, we are in luck," she said. "June 25 is available."

We did not hesitate. "We'll take it."

"Wonderful," she said. While she was assembling paperwork, Mrs. D invited us to look through a large quilted photo album. This, she explained, contained photographs of recent Las Olas weddings. We thumbed through the album. Like Las Olas itself, the photographs were gorgeous. Handsome grooms and radiant brides saying vows, cutting cake, dancing by the sea. How astonishing that so much happiness could be contained in a quilted photo album. How generous that all these couples had given Mrs. D copies of their wedding pictures, out of gratitude for the joy she had provided them. Looking at such happiness, how could we not agree to pay thousands of dollars to Mrs. D to ensure our own joyful wedding as well?

We signed the contract. We paid a deposit. The door to Mrs. D's office opened, letting in fresh air. A pretty woman in a blue maid's uniform carried in the day's mail.

"This is Maria," Mrs. D said. "She will be your wedding consultant." Maria smiled shyly.

A second person appeared, a small, wiry man in a cowboy hat. He looked nearly as old as Mrs. D.

"This is Jorge," Mrs. D said. "He has been my right-hand man for thirty years."

We said hello to Jorge. Jorge smiled.

"Jorge," said Mrs. D, "handles Las Olas's valet parking. Jorge will park all your guests' cars."

At this point I noticed that Jorge's hands were trembling violently, in the way that as a medical social worker for seniors I knew signaled advanced Parkinson's disease.

"Make note," I told myself. "Guests will park their own cars."

How do I describe Mrs. D? Using only her initial lends her the aura of a character from a Victorian novel, and maybe only Trollope or Thackeray could have captured her mix of rage, avarice, and fleeting, steely charm. When we met her she was a short, stout woman in her seventies. She liked tweed suits, L'Air du Temps perfume, and heavy makeup: thick face powder and lipstick that made her mouth look swollen. Her silver-blue wig was so shining and tightly coiled it looked as if she were wearing a salad mold on her head. Still, in her hot, rank office, she displayed a large oil painting of herself at a younger age—forty, perhaps, not beautiful but elegant in a silk blouse, perhaps even seductive in her obvious competence and power. In an era when most women were mere wives, Mrs. D had established her own career, as she was pleased to tell us. Before Las Olas, she had owned a summer camp that catered to the children of wealthy San Franciscans. She had invested successfully in California real estate. Las Olas had been hers for over thirty years. There was never any mention of a Mr. D, but it was clear that Mrs. D did not require one.

As old and eccentric as Mrs. D was, she was still firmly in

charge. Despite the cats and the Lincoln Continentals, Las Olas was a functioning resort. People arrived from Michigan and Arizona to stay there. And Mrs. D had big plans for the future. She was planning a spa and fitness center. She was launching a program of fitness weekends for today's young, female executive—the kind of woman Mrs. D would have been if she had been born fifty years later.

Everything went smoothly at first. We reserved all of Las Olas's forty rooms for two nights in June. We'd fill the entire resort with our family and friends, who would be pleased when they learned how little it would cost to stay at such a beautiful retreat. We would hold our wedding rehearsal Friday afternoon, and the ceremony would start at noon on Saturday. We would rent from Mrs. D folding chairs and tables and table umbrellas, linens and plates and silverware and trash cans.

Maria was a godsend: pleasant, effortlessly efficient. She had recently emigrated from Mérida, Yucatán, and my future husband liked to practice his rusty Spanish on her. *"Me gusta Mérida,"* he said. *"Es una ciudad muy bonita."*

"Si," Maria answered. *"Mérida es muy bonita.* Where will you want to put the bartender's tent?"

As for Jorge, he took the news that he would not be parking our guests' cars with equanimity. He was already busy enough with all the jobs—gardening, sweeping, painting, carpentry—Mrs. D made him do. But Jorge had his own secret passion. One day while we were waiting for Mrs. D in her fetid office, Jorge disappeared into the back room and returned with his own quilted scrapbook.

"Look," Jorge said. We opened the scrapbook, expecting more wedding photographs. We were wrong. This was Jorge's book from the days when Mrs. D owned her summer camp and, we saw, had her little campers stage Broadway musicals among the trees. Here were the faded programs for *South Pacific* and *The Sound of Music*, and faded photographs of ten-year-olds dressed up as Nellie Forbush and Captain von Trapp.

His hands trembling, Jorge opened one of the programs. "See?" he said, pointing to the cast list. There it was, his moment of fame: *Stage Manager—Jorge.*

"That's great," my fiancé said. "*Sound of Music.* 'Edelweiss.' 'Do-Re-Mi.' One of my favorite shows."

"The thing about getting married," our friend Lisa said, "is that you're not just getting married, you have to star as Romeo and Juliet in your own school play."

This is true. A wedding is not just a wedding; it is performance art. There you are in ridiculous clothing, dancing and lifting champagne glasses, and trying not to throw up. As for our own personal performance piece, I was in the throes of finishing graduate school in social work. Most of the organizational tasks fell to my fiancé. Peter designed the invitations, staying late at work so he could surreptitiously copy them on his office's expensive color copier; he compiled the guest list; he found the band.

He was also in charge of finding a site for the rehearsal dinner. He and his best man, Keith, retraced our route down the coast to look for restaurants. They looked at cheap places and expensive places and ended up at a restored historic hotel a little inland from Las Olas.

"We need a place for our rehearsal dinner," my fiancé told the woman at the front desk.

"Congratulations," she said, in what my husband-to-be later recognized was a tone of studied tolerance, unique to Northern California. "These are our banquet packages." Then she turned to Keith and asked, "What kind of cuisine are you considering?" Peter wondered why she kept addressing her questions to his best man.

"You realize," Keith told him on the way home, "that she thought we were marrying each other."

I, meanwhile, was searching for a wedding dress. In our push to cut costs, I knew I couldn't afford any tulle extravaganza. I didn't want one anyway. I wanted simple, elegant, and on sale. I thought I'd found the ideal dress on the sale rack of an expensive San Francisco department store. It was taupe and beaded and $200, marked down from $2,000. It was a steal, and I bought it. Only after I brought it home did I realize it made me look like a wealthy dowager attending the opera.

"What do you think?" I asked my husband-to-be.

"Oh," he said.

I fled to the bedroom to cry. For the next three months, whenever I tried on the dress, I cried. When I stopped trying it on, the sight of it hanging in my closet made me cry.

"Can I come in?" Peter would ask.

"Go away," I screamed. "Go away."

At this point he may have thought, *If I were marrying Keith, we wouldn't be having this problem.*

We also had to deal with premarital counseling. Both Peter and I were lifelong Episcopalians. But even after years of dutiful Communions, we had never been told one little fact: To book an Episcopal priest for your wedding, you had to sign up for premarital counseling. Or, in the preferred church terminology, pre-Cana counseling, named for the wedding at Cana you read about in the Gospel according to John.

Our priest was one of the new generation of Episcopal priests: a woman, ordained as a second career. Even with her clerical collar she had the soignée look of a successful Realtor, with carefully tousled blond hair and a gorgeous manicure. She took her job seriously, though. She gave us the Myers-Briggs personality test; she probed for signs of future marital trouble. Finally she found one. Peter and I did not argue.

"You don't argue?" she said, politely aghast, as if she had found out we had never had sex.

"People who don't argue bottle things up," she continued. "They sandbag."

"Sandbag," we repeated, doubtful.

"When a river floods, the water level rises and people pile sandbags up, higher, higher." As the priest spoke, she gestured to indicate the piling up of the sandbags, and I found myself mesmerized by her beautiful manicure, her elegantly shaped nails a soft, glowing peach color. "But they can't stop the river. The sandbags break and the floodwaters burst through. *Whoosh!"* The beautiful hands flew high to mime this cataclysm.

"Sandbagging never works," she finished.

Both Peter and I noted this in our pre-Cana notebooks. "Sandbagging—*no.*"

With my graduate school exams approaching, a wedding dress that I despised hanging in my closet, and sandbagging to worry about, I was busy, and so was Peter. It took us weeks to notice that all was not perfect with Las Olas, or with Mrs. D.

But, gradually Peter and I began to notice. Maria continued to be a joy. Jorge was at least enthusiastic. But Mrs. D was displaying a disturbing mix of amnesia and greed.

That is another thing about weddings. They invite conflict over matters that at any other time in your life you would laugh at. In our case, over linen napkins, silverware, plastic patio tables, and colorful table umbrellas. For each of these, we tried to confirm precisely how many items we expected to be part of the Las Olas wedding package. For each, Mrs. D assured us that she had not included them at all.

"No, no," she protested. "Linens aren't part of the package. Linens are extra."

"Oh, Mrs. D," we said, attempting to remain calm. "When we signed the contract they were included. See?" We showed her the portion of the contract dealing with linens. She looked grumpy, and we moved on to something else. The table umbrellas—"very expensive, they require a separate deposit"—or the silverware. Very occasionally she relented without a fight. When we realized we would need four more folding tables to hold food, she added these to the contract—which now resembled the Treaty of Versailles in size and complexity—initialed it, and said, "I don't know what else you could possibly want."

Then, ominously, she asked, "What day is your wedding again?"

We began hearing disturbing accounts of Mrs. D from others. The first came from our caterer. Good food was important to us; we had spent years secretly mocking the steam-table chicken and limp vegetables at other weddings. We found a superb caterer, a woman who ran a beloved restaurant in the same coastal town as Las Olas. She was renowned for her artisan breads, sublime pastas, and wedding cakes that glistened in their own chilled display case. She had published two cookbooks, had catered hundreds of weddings, and was considered a consummate pro.

And yet when we told her where she would be catering our wedding, her face clouded.

"Las Olas," she said flatly.

The reaction surprised us. Las Olas was a long-established business only a half mile away. What could be easier?

"We've had trouble catering functions there," she said.

What kind of trouble, we asked.

She did not want to gossip, she did not want to go into details. We insisted. Finally, she allowed, there had been . . . incidents. A number of incidents. The most recent when her catering driver showed up at Las Olas with pans of lasagna for a wedding. "Mrs. D was angry over where Cindi parked the truck," the caterer said. "Mrs. D slugged her."

That was the first warning. We began to hear others. Many people seemed to have Mrs. D stories. It was as if she were like earthquakes or poison oak, a well-known hazard of California life that we had somehow naively ignored. One of Peter's coworkers had friends who had just gotten married at Las Olas. "I don't know what happened," said the coworker. "But they had a lot of problems." Peter left a message for this couple, asking them to please call us as soon as possible. A friend of mine had been involved in a real estate deal with Mrs. D, one that had ended in a lawsuit. Mrs. D had a reputation, said another friend. She was in constant trouble with the city and the county over unpaid taxes and over her swarms of feral cats.

A dark thought crossed my mind—amazingly enough, for the first time. As lovely as Las Olas was, why wasn't it included in any of the where-to-get-married websites or wedding guidebooks? Why in fact did Mrs. D even have space for us on June 25?

Unease spread from Northern California across the nation. We were inviting one hundred and forty people. Many were flying from the East Coast and planned to stay two or three nights at Las Olas. They had booked rooms with Mrs. D; they had selected the Queen with Ocean View or the Family Suite with Garden View. Credit cards had been charged for the rooms, but reservation confirmations had not been sent. Peter's friend John called from Washington, D.C. "I tried to talk to Mrs. D," he said in his calm but firm psychiatrist's voice. "She said she had no record of my reservation." Another friend, Mark, called from New York. He said that when he tried to talk to Mrs. D, she hung up on him.

We tried to straighten things out. Mrs. D did not use computers or email, so we sent cheery notes. "Dear Mrs. D," we wrote, "there seems to be some mix-up with John Hsiao's reservation." When she did not answer, we tried the telephone.

"John Hsiao," Peter yelled into the receiver. Mrs. D had trouble hearing over the phone. "It's pronounced *sh-owww* but written H-S-I-A-O."

"I have no record of him," Mrs. D said.

We got in the car and drove the hour to visit Mrs. D in person. We found her in her office, wearing one of her tweed suits, surrounded by cats. Tentatively we asked if we could check her reservation book ourselves. Grudgingly, she let us examine it—a gigantic, nineteenth-century ledger with hundreds of folded three-by-five cards dangling from it, as if Bartleby the Scrivener had taken up origami.

"Oh look," Peter said. "There he is. John Hsiao. H-S-I-A-O. It's a Chinese name.

"Now," he said, as a few three-by-five cards fell to the carpet, "let's look for Mark Czaja. It's pronounced *zha zha*, kind of like Zsa Zsa Gabor. But it starts with a C. It's a Polish name."

Mrs. D glared at us, obviously annoyed that we had invited only guests with complex foreign-sounding surnames.

"You know," she said. "Your friends have filled up my entire resort. That means I can't rent the rooms to anyone else. And many, many people want them."

After this Mrs. D visit, we had to meet with the priest for the next of our three pre-Cana counseling sessions. Sitting in her rectory, going over our Myers-Briggs scores and talking about how we would manage conflict resolution, it seemed almost gauche to mention the stress we were feeling. Our elegant priest, whose husband was a high-powered attorney who was always flying to Honolulu, would never have dealt with a Mrs. D. Her wedding would have been high Episcopal perfection, with old family china and the sense of well-being that the love of God and a trust fund can confer.

"Remember," she reminded us as we left. "No sandbagging."

After counseling, we walked down to the beach that got us into all this trouble in the first place. We watched the pounding waves, we mused on Mrs. D. Was she evil, or was she sliding into dementia? It was hard to tell. We were still confused about all the cats, about the Lincoln Continentals—a new one had appeared, missing a front fender, parked beneath a eucalyptus at the back of the property. Peter theorized that all of the Lincoln Continentals were actually in fine running order, and that on nights with a full moon Mrs. D would jump into one of them and race around town, scooping up feral cats the way Cruella DeVil scooped up dalmatian puppies. Or, he said, still riffing on Disney movies but staring at the ocean, maybe she was like glamorous, malevolent Ursula in *The Little Mermaid*. A sea witch in silver wig and tweeds.

When Jesus attended the wedding at Cana, the hosts ran out of wine. We learn in 2 John:1–11 that Jesus then located six stone jars holding thirty gallons of water each and, in his first recorded miracle, turned all the water into wine. How convenient, we thought, to land Jesus as a wedding guest. Perhaps if Jesus were attending our wedding he could turn eight linen tablecloths into sixteen, he could turn place settings for seventy into place settings for one hundred and forty. He could turn Mrs. D sane.

It was early June. Everything was falling apart. Peter's job was stressing him out; graduate school was doing the same to me. Mrs. D was now mixing up reservations for people closer to home—my fiancé's father, who was flying up from Southern California, and my father, who was flying south from Portland. Peter and I began to miss our mothers desperately. Both had died a few years earlier. It seemed to us that if they'd been alive they would have made everything right.

We began to doubt ourselves. We were calm, rational people: That was our self-image. We had good senses of humor, we were flexible, we didn't take life too seriously. These traits, we believed, enabled us to deal with difficult people. But our good opinions of ourselves were clearly wrong. We could not deal with anything.

When we drove down to Las Olas, it was swaddled in fog. June is the foggy season on the California coast. We knew that, and yet we had gone ahead and planned our wedding for June. The oaks and eucalyptus were ghosts in the mist; as soon as you stepped out of the car you shivered. This was perfect. We had paid thousands of dollars to get married at a place where nobody would be able to see us.

Mrs. D was in her office, the space heaters turned on high. For once the warmth felt good, or would have if it hadn't been for the stench of cats.

"We have another problem with a reservation," Peter said, not so nicely this time. "Ed Johnson, Portland."

Mrs. D made a production of examining her reservation book. "No. Nothing."

"Yes. It's right there."

Mrs. D stood up, the sudden movement causing one of her cats to leap to the carpet. Her face reddened.

"You know," she said, "this wedding has caused me a lot of trouble. I have half a mind just to cancel it."

She seemed determined to scare us, but we wouldn't be scared.

"Also," I said, "Maria told us there was some problem with the folding tables. We'll need the four extra tables you promised."

"That is not in the contract. The folding tables are separate."

Peter showed her the amended paragraph that included the folding tables. "There," he said. "There it is."

Then the explosion. We had never seen anyone so angry. We looked at Mrs. D, screaming and crying, and thought, *This is what we, as a species, are capable of.* We wondered if Maria and Jorge had to endure these rages. We wondered if she was going to punch us.

I'm not sure how we got out of her office. We got out. The question of the folding tables had not been settled, but that was now the least of our problems. We drove to our last counseling session, and our own rage, suppressed for so many weeks, rose to the surface.

We stepped inside the rectory. As usual, the priest had made tea. As usual, she was wearing an expression of slightly condescending welcome. It didn't matter.

"So," she began. "Our . . ."

"Do you know what she did?" Peter screamed. "She called us forgers. Us! Forgers!"

"She said she'd give us the extra folding tables," I joined in. "But now she says she won't."

"She's insane."

"She's evil."

The priest stood there, stunned in the same way we had been stunned by Mrs. D. Perhaps she felt some amount of guilt. For weeks she had been telling us not to sandbag. Now we had taken her advice, and the results were terrible to behold.

The day before our wedding, we drove to Las Olas, the back seat of our car cushioned by dozens of rolls of toilet paper. We had finally heard from the people who had been married at Las Olas the month before. The groom sounded bruised and tired. Yes, they had many problems with Mrs. D. Yes, she screamed at them, she threatened to cancel their wedding.

My fiancé asked if he had any specific advice.

"Bring lots of toilet paper," the groom said. "When you run out Mrs. D won't give you any more."

We had the rehearsal. The priest arrived in stylish slacks, looking nervously around for Mrs. D who was nowhere to be seen. We practiced our march down the aisle; Peter practiced taking the ring from Keith and slipping it on my finger. We left for the rehearsal dinner. We returned. That night my fiancé stayed awake late under the flowered bedspread in the Las Olas bridal suite, worrying, wondering.

The next day was glorious. We had been worried about fog, but the morning was clear and already hot. The air smelled of ocean and eucalyptus. From the deck you saw the Pacific, deep blue, still, matted with kelp.

There was a lot to do. Friends arrived and helped Maria and Jorge set up tables, other friends left to pick up the crates of local strawberries for the dessert table. People drove around town stapling the ribbon-entwined paper plates we were using for signs: ANNE AND PETER'S WEDDING. A few days before, I had managed to find a second wedding dress, white, with a plunging V-neck; it made me feel as if I was floating as I walked. I got into my new dress and sat with my maid of honor playing a round of Scrabble in which only words about sex could be used. Peter lounged in the hot tub with a couple of his college friends and then put on his wedding suit and stood around taking swigs of scotch from a silver flask. Then it was time.

And it all went . . . perfectly. The sun shone on us, on the priest, on the guests who sat in the folding chairs, on the musical friends we'd convinced to serve as our string quartet.

Peter had attended a beach wedding where he couldn't hear anybody because of the sound of the surf. He was very concerned about that. When it was his turn to say, "I do," he shouted it out like a carnival barker. Everyone laughed.

Then we kissed, and it was over. We were married. We were walking back down the aisle and my husband's high school friend Greg lunged at us with a video camera. Another friend, Richard, a professional photographer, was already busy taking photographs that were beyond beautiful, the best wedding present we received.

We smiled at people in the receiving line, people toasted us and our fathers and our late mothers, we lined up for food, and there was dancing.

That was when I saw her. She had been absent the whole day, and our guests were actually disappointed. They had heard so much about Mrs. D, and they wanted to see her in person. Now there she was among the dancers. She seemed dressed up, perhaps she had been in her office primping all this time. The silver-blue wig had been brushed; she was wearing a new lavender tweed suit and lavender stockings and high heels. She looked, in fact, quite nice.

She cradled something bulky and mechanical in her hands. A Polaroid camera—one of those big clunky models from the 1960s. She pointed the camera at the dancing crowd, clicked it, and the camera spit out a snapshot that Mrs. D slipped into the pocket of her tweed suit. Then she took another.

Of course, I realized. For Mrs. D's album. No one who had survived a wedding at Las Olas would ever have given Mrs. D copies of photographs; they would never have given her anything. So Mrs. D had to take her own.

There were more toasts, and we cut the wedding cake, and there was more dancing, and I saw Mrs. D again. In fact, I heard her. "I'm going to get some of that cake," she said, and waddled on her lavender high heels toward the cake table. She grabbed a large piece. Suddenly, it was time for me to dance with my father-in-law, and I never saw Mrs. D in person again.

We did not spend our honeymoon night at Las Olas. At least we had been that smart. We stayed a mile down the road, at a bed-and-breakfast whose friendly staff and modern rooms seemed all the more luxurious after the weeks we had spent dealing with Mrs. D. The next morning I woke up and realized that this, the day after our wedding, was the happiest day of my life. First, I was married, which was good. Second, I would never have to deal with Mrs. D ever again.

Other people did, though. Many of our friends stayed at Las Olas that night and the night after. The next day, Peter's friend Mark and his family came back from a long afternoon at the beach to find all of Las Olas in the dark. They asked Jorge what was wrong.

"Oh," Jorge said. "We had another wedding here today. Mrs. D thought that the band was too loud. So she just"—here Jorge mimed a knife slitting his throat—"switched off all the power. I guess she hasn't turned it back on yet."

So, it could have been worse.

Las Olas is gone now. It was sold and closed and subdivided a few years after our wedding. We've gone back to look at it, and the last time we could barely recognize where it had once been. Expensive new homes stand where the Lincoln Continentals rusted, where the feral cats roamed, where we said "I do."

Mrs. D is gone, too, a fact that seems strangely hard to believe. We still look at our wedding photographs. In them, our wedding looks beautiful: the jasmine, the lawns, the forgiving ocean light, the people in our lives who had never been gathered together before and would never be gathered together again. We think it is the most beautiful wedding there ever was.

We also own a short videotape of the wedding, taken by my husband's friend Greg. We don't watch it much because it's annoying. Greg was drinking, and most of the video consists of shaky views of people's ankles and ears. Still, my husband likes to watch one part. Greg was near the cake table when Mrs. D approached it. He videotaped her taking a large slice of wedding cake and slapping it on a napkin. She was not happy about being taped. She attempted to run away. Greg followed her.

On the tape, you see Mrs. D pushing her way through the dancing couples and trying to cut across the lawn to the safety of her hot, little office. She steps into a thick row of bottlebrush bushes and gets stuck. Greg continues to tape her. She holds the cake with one hand and bats at branches with the other. She is trapped.

"Smile Mrs. D," Greg shouts. Mrs. D looks as though she wants to vaporize him. The video stops there.

"*Ha, ha, ha,*" my husband laughs when he watches the video. "Look at her." He likes to reverse the tape so that Mrs. D lunges backward out of the bushes, then forward so she is ensnared again.

"Stop it," I say. "That's mean."

"No," he says. "Wait. One more time." Together we sit and watch this happy moment from the second-happiest day of our lives.

A Cynic's Guide to Weddings

DANIELLE deLEON

᠎ I DETEST WEDDINGS. I avoid going to them. I abhor being in them. And even if I don't participate in body, I resent buying gifts for future divorcés. Romance doesn't interest me. I'm a realist. In my world, stories never end in Happily Ever After; they simply end. I'm cynical about ever attaining eternal devotion from a male human being (at least not one who I want to have sex with). But the rest of the world, I understand, is a bit sunnier about it all.

I have two good guy friends. One mercifully eloped; but the other, Josh, went for the whole white shebang, and *(sigh)* he asked me to be a bridesmaid for his wife-to-be, Elizabeth. There was nothing in the world I wanted to do less, except maybe attempt to resolve grievances with my HMO. But I acquiesced. Not only did I owe him for innumerable designated driver rides home from the bar, I've learned not to mess with traditionalists.

I initially found it odd that I should be asked to be in the wedding party at all. I figured that since it was a guy friend getting married, he would pick from a list of his closest male friends to stand beside him, and his soon-to-be wife would pick from her closest female cronies, of which I was not one.

Josh's invite was sincere, but I soon came to understand that I was also a convenience. Josh asked his best friend, Laura, to be in his wedding party and stand with the boys in the Johnny Cash getup he had devised—black shirts, bolo ties, Wranglers, cowboy boots, and hats. Because she would look like one of the guys, she needed someone who looked like one of the girls to accompany her down the aisle. That left me, the only girl in Josh's world open-minded enough to process down the aisle with another woman and not worry about rumors.

Don't get me wrong. Laura's awesome. I've known her since I was a teenager, and I knew she and Josh were great friends. But where did this leave me? While all the other girls linked arms with Josh's cute friends, I completely missed out on the opportunity to get a new phone number. I was there to maintain the boy-girl, boy-girl symmetry, only I was paired with a girl and was thus shit out of luck. Josh meant well, but I felt suckered.

There would be rehearsals, fittings, and weeks of dread. And, of course, I, an ardent tomboy, would have to look like a fluffy bridesmaid, a position solely created to make the bride look radiant in comparison to the tented sows standing next to her. Not that Elizabeth, the bride, needed any help. At five foot seven and one hundred and fifteen pounds, she didn't need our forgettable visages as a springboard. Daylight was her ally. Her blond and boobs were real. She ate chili cheese fries unabashedly. She was the type of person who never tripped. How an average bloke like Josh landed her, I'll never know. It wasn't money, because Princess was also born wealthy. Unfortunately, Elizabeth was also really nice—much too nice for my taste. She was perpetually cheerful and treated everyone—friends and strangers—as if they were her dearest pals. I tried to keep my distance because chirpy people make me itch; but with Elizabeth you didn't have much choice. The instant she saw you, she'd shuffle up in her platform shoes, scuttling like a geisha, and compliment you on whatever you were wearing and on how pretty your hair looked, regardless of the reality. But no matter how many sweet things she said, her skinny presence made you feel as if your ass were expanding like a balloon on a water tap.

Her constant optimism reminded me of my brother's loopy golden retriever, Rosco; when Rosco visited my parents, he would lovingly and unceasingly lick their dog, Quinn, in the face—even while Quinn growled and bared his teeth. Elizabeth was my Rosco, and though I bared my teeth, too, it was behind forced smiles. Elizabeth had never been mean to me—I think she was inherently incapable of it—so I couldn't legitimately say a bad thing about her, but I wanted to. Besides, I'd always been intensely suspicious of anyone who was happy all the time. I needed to know that Elizabeth had an equalizing dark side. Maybe she maintained her size 4 figure with a Tony Montana–like coke habit. Maybe she was a vapid doormat, a soon-to-be-Stepford wife, and was looking forward to a life of merrily Shouting out Josh's skid-marks. Or . . . maybe Elizabeth really was just a healthy, grateful woman who could see the good in everyone, even a snarling brat like me. Maybe she deserved the perfect wedding that she'd undoubtedly get. The upside for me was that her runway bod and Ivory-girl complexion would mercifully take the attention off the horrid bridesmaid dresses we were forced to wear.

Do I even need to complain about the dress? Of course I do. The dress was green. Not a rich, forest green or a retro light lime, but a kelly green on the verge of bright leprechaun. It was fabricated out of some sort of polyester/tarpaulin material that was three inches thick and accentuated every bulge and blob on my normally not-too-shabby body. In addition to the dress came the ugly, dyed-to-match pumps. The whole pile of future Goodwill donations came to $500—a drop in the bucket for the rich, and apparently color-blind, maid of honor who picked them out, but no small tab for me, a struggling writer.

But, I bought the ugly dress. I went to all the rehearsals and shower garbage. (Did I really want to sit for two hours to watch a bunch of women I hardly know giggle over relatively tame lingerie? I did not.) And, most important, I showed up on time on The Special Day.

While milling around before the ceremony, I pretended to be gracious when I received compliments from the guests, who, if they thought I looked good, must have been married to sturgeon. As the wedding guests took their seats, floaty classical music wafted from portable speakers (the wedding took place in the woods), and Laura and I walked arm in arm to the stage. I smiled but avoided eye contact with as many cameras as I could. Pictures are my enemy. I'm a decent-looking woman, but I shape-shift when photographed. My nose doubles in size, bends to the left, and, in all honesty, looks like the head of a penis.

As we all know, the world is a cruel and unpredictable place, and weddings are no exception—if anything, they're the epitome of potentially cruel and unpredictable situations. Cakes don't show up. Bands get sick. Clouds move in. Any number of natural and unnatural disasters can throw a year's worth of agonizing and costly planning down the toilet. Josh and Elizabeth, however, got lucky. Their ceremony went fine, great actually. I cringe to say this, but it was very touching. I watched Josh and his beloved staring glaze-eyed at each other, saying words that I'd never heard any sober man utter, and I was actually happy for them. So happy, in fact, that I started crying. I couldn't help myself. I thought the whole sappy gag-fest was indeed beautiful. Whether they stayed together for the rest of their lives was yet to be seen; but right then, on that platform in the forest, I could tell that they loved each other with every cell of their beings. I've sometimes felt that same adoration toward drivers who use their blinkers.

My small, sentimental crying jag notwithstanding, I'm still never getting married. As I've previously stated, I feel that it is a rare and unnatural event when two people actually stay together for life. We live so much longer these days that I have no clue—since the best relationship I've ever had lasted only a year—how I could stand to live with another human being for twenty, thirty, even forty-plus years. I simply don't have that kind of tolerance for other people's bodily functions and annoying quirks. I can't even stand my own; so as far as I'm concerned, I'm already living with another person. There's the fun, cute, adorable me, and the "other one," who really stinks up the john something awful.

Combining my impatience toward myself with impatience toward another would be an emotional Molotov cocktail. One too many dirty socks on the floor and *kaboom*, we're fighting over who keeps the dog. Besides, even amicable marriages don't seem that fun. Wedding planning is more a portent of aggravation to come than anything else.

Receptions, however, aren't so unpleasant—as long as they have an open bar.

After the "I do's," I ducked into the bathroom, shucked myself out of the AstroTurf smock and donned a more comfortable and flattering flowered dress—one I specifically keep around for wedding receptions and temp jobs. Relieved that the embarrassing part was over, I hit the bar and the buffet with the intensity of Mama Cass. I ate, I drank, I danced, and I tried to find out if any of the cute guys present were single (they weren't). I didn't have a half-bad time, until . . .

I just want to say for the record that I have never cared one iota about a tossed bouquet. If anything, I've run from it as if it were a live grenade. Other women, however, clamor for the thing as if it were Mr. Right himself. I don't really believe in the whole catch-the-bouquet legend; but, just to be sure, I've historically stayed out of the mosh pit. Until Josh's wedding, that is.

I was crocked by bouquet-chucking time, and, for whatever reason—possibly I was still sentimentally hungover from the crying jag—I threw myself into the melee. I shudder as I remember myself and the others milling about excitedly, tittering and teasingly pushing one another away from our tiny land claims on the parquet floor like nervous pioneers.

The whole bouquet craze originated in Europe in the fourteenth century when propertyless women, desperate for a man, would tear at the bride's dress and flowers, hoping that by possessing a small piece of her trashed frock they might experience the same good fortune that landed the bride a breadwinner. The bride, in an effort to save her dress, would fling her bouquet like a flank steak to the pursuing Dobermans and then bolt.

Seven hundred years later, unmarried women are no less desperate, but at least we're a little more civilized. At the moment of climax, Elizabeth turned around and launched the bouquet. It flew as gracefully as a head of cauliflower, flipping end over end through the air as it headed toward the vipers' pit. The entire mass of assembled unmarrieds shrieked and jumped in unison. I was the only one who didn't jump, and momentarily found myself in a hut made of airborne women. But their timing was off; they jumped too soon.

Suddenly the sea of rayon parted, and Elizabeth's bouquet fell on the floor between Josh's nine-year-old cousin, Kristen, and me. Our eyes met and narrowed, and then we dove like Olympic swimmers. Our hands clenched the drooping flowers at the exact same moment;

I figured that because she was small, I could take her. What did she need with a bouquet anyway? But her grip was solidly locked on the prize. We yanked it back and forth. Clearly I had underestimated her. She was a pit bull. I needed a new tactic—something unexpected and possibly ruthless. I was willing to do anything to win this tug-of-war.

So, I bit her on the arm.

Kristen did indeed let go. And while I clogged about the dance floor like Rumpelstiltskin with what was left of the bouquet flapping triumphantly in my upheld arm, she ran off crying.

As I obliviously staggered off the dance floor, a man discreetly pulled me aside and introduced himself as Josh's uncle, Kristen's father. I immediately knew I was in trouble. I'd bitten Kristen as a joke, somehow forgetting that drunken asinine behavior at family functions is not typically well received—especially by someone who won't reach the legal drinking age for another twelve years. Now I had to answer to the little girl's daddy—something I hadn't had to do since I pushed my friend Johanna off a rope swing and broke her arm when I was eight. I knew there was nothing I could say in my defense. I considered vomiting at that point, but I held my stomach and tried to look innocent. His crumpled brow told me that I wasn't fooling anyone.

"That was kind of a crappy thing you did. I really think you should give it back to her."

I felt myself regressing. "She's nine! I need it way more than she does, and, besides, I didn't bite her hard." Despite the quiver in my voice, I refused to cry.

The uncle sighed. "You left marks. Would you like to see?" He nodded toward Kristen, who was tear streaked and pouty lipped, keeping her distance and holding her assaulted arm like I had threatened to take it from her too.

I retreated to a younger, more defensive place in my psyche. "Fine, take it. I didn't want it anyway."

All I wanted now was to time-travel back to the day when Josh asked me to be in the wedding and tell him that I couldn't because I was needed to help break up child-labor farms in Bangladesh, and that it was very important work, and I couldn't possibly participate in the wedding although I was very flattered and wished I could be there. Or I could just shut up and take responsibility for being an idiot. It wouldn't be the first time.

So, Kristen got her way, and I got another several beers. I don't remember much after that, but no one told me later that I'd done anything else that I might not want to remember, so I figured I behaved pretty well. The sun set behind the redwoods, and the day was finally behind me. I could go back to my solitary, non-cannibalistic, jeans-and-a-ball-cap normality.

I've tried to forget that day. For a while, Josh's little brother, Kyle, liked to tease me about biting his cousin. But luckily, since Kyle knocked up his girlfriend and had to drop out of college to become a cashier at Arby's, he doesn't dare mention my minor faux pas. As for me, I've been to many weddings since and I haven't once bitten a child; so I chalk it up to a lesson learned. Neither have I participated in the bouquet-toss, just to be safe.

'Forever Your Girl

MARY O'CONNELL

‿ SISTER AGNES LOOKED like any other pleasant, no-nonsense Iowa woman in her sixties: Her hair was a sprayed gray bubble, and she favored poly-blend blouses with muted wildflower prints paired with casual slacks. She was firm, but kind, too, and she smelled like the AVON Catalog: papery, sweet. But to me she was as scary as any mythical battle-axe in a musty wimple, because Sister Agnes was the sentry, the hierarchical It Girl, the administrator of the multiple-choice tests given to my fiancé and me to judge our readiness and compatibility for marriage in the Catholic Church. Agnes! I see her in my mind's eye as I entered the church office, housed in a sweet cottage across the street from Saint Mary's brick chapel: Her smile encompassing both Steve and me—*you two nutty lovebirds want to get married*, terrific—but accompanied by an ironic eyebrow raise—*How fortunate that no one who marries in the Catholic Church ever divorces! Greetings and welcome to this foolproof endeavor!* She was holding a jumbled stack of folders in her arms, the Lord's paperwork, when she asked us the question every procrastinator dreads: "Shall we get started?" The pope himself had never loomed so large or formidable.

In truth he'd never loomed much at all. My reasons for wanting to marry in the Catholic Church were largely aesthetic: Saint Mary's in Iowa City was a wonder, a red-brick charmer on the outside, a Gothic beauty inside, complete with statuary of the martyred saints, so that your lighthearted love of the Lord—*Alleluia!*—was tempered by all the carved grimaces and moon-marble eyes staring you down.

I had little interest, then, in the actual beliefs and struggles of all the Catholic women who had walked down the aisle before me, but I was crazy for the ambience. I wanted the same lush, solemn ceremony of the black-and-white wedding photos of my parents: my mother, beautiful as the young Sophia Loren, placing a bridal bouquet at the statue of the Virgin Mary; my father, a pensive charmer in his Buddy Holly glasses and classic black tuxedo, placing the ring on my mother's finger.

To marry in a chichi hotel, or a kitschy Vegas chapel, or in a meadow at midnight (Under the stars and black velvet sky! Seeing my beloved in the soft moonlight!) seemed perfectly second rate: not for me the unintentional humor of self-penned vows, the cringe-worthy proclamations about special, special love, the Jesus-freak rants, the impromptu political speeches, the overblown Renaissance sonnets (*Hark! Ode to the general hokum and poor poetry of it all!*). As for my fiancé, he had grown up without religion, and was both a good sport and curious about Catholicism. He liked the idea of the old school wedding. Steve was all in.

And so there we were, sweating it out, sitting across the desk from Agnes in hard-backed wood chairs. I saw the flash of her gold wedding band as she opened a manila folder and puzzled over that until I remembered: Of course—*Duh!*—she's the bride of Christ. She took our names and birth dates, and then,

"What's your address, Mary?"

I easily rattled off "my" address, praying that Steve wouldn't choke when Agnes asked him, because we had opted to start our marriage with a lie. We feared the Catholic Church wouldn't marry us if they knew we were already living together (note to Benedict: *Psych!)* and so we had come up with a fake address and telephone number for Steve. Our friends Helen and Greg had sportingly changed the message on their answering machine—"Helen, Greg, and Steve aren't here right now"—surely making their out-of-town friends wonder what was up with their new arrangement. But if Agnes wondered why a single female graduate student would live in a farmhouse on the edge of town, she mercifully kept it to herself.

When Steve gave Agnes his phony address, he spoke haltingly. He shifted in his chair. Though he had rehearsed it with breezy success, he was now clearly uncomfortable, and so I felt a wild spasm of joy I wished I could share with Agnes—*Check me out! I am marrying a person of integrity who doesn't lie with ease! I waited until I was twenty-nine to marry and I didn't have to settle for some jackassy cheese ball. Can I get a high-five? Anybody?*

The bizarre thirty-minute, short-answer quiz was up next, the SAT of love. Before Agnes passed out the blank bubble sheets and test booklets, she separated us—she put Steve in the library, me at a table in the living room. At first I thought she was worried that we were going to cheat in some way, but when I read the questions, I knew differently: Agnes wanted to minimize the inevitable snickering over the questions. And the test had seemingly endless questions—bubbles upon bubbles to fill in, the pencil lead going wooden and stubby—about value and beliefs, about one's hopes and dreams for marriage.

I had a history of scoring poorly on standardized tests and believed myself at risk of failure. *Are you nervous about your spouse seeing you naked?* What good could possibly come of coloring in the YES bubble? Did the church offer nude therapy? *Go commando for a few days, gradually work your way up to acting in the community theater's double bill of* Hair *and* Oh! Calcutta! As I worked, I tried to memorize all the particularly insane questions so I could laugh about them with Steve later. Occasionally I took a daydreamy ADHD pause to look out the window at Saint Mary's Catholic Church across the street, its gold-capped spires shooting up toward the Iowa clouds. It was so quiet that I could hear Steve breathing, shifting in his chair in the next room. I loved him very much. I

wondered if we were working at the same pace, if he, too, was reading the words: *Are you nervous about starting a sexual relationship
with your spouse?*

Over my head hung an oil painting of Jesus, rendered with his
head tilted to the left and a fey, scolding grin, as if the Son of God
were about to part his pressed, holy lips and say, *You, my child, are a
snob and a big old liar to boot;* this, *this shall be your penance.*

After Steve and I said goodbye to Agnes, we managed to casually
walk halfway down the block before breaking into a madcap run
to the bar. We had to down our first round of gin and tonics before
we felt safe enough, sure that Sister Agnes was not lurking in the
booth behind us, to discuss the questions. Steve said he believed
the Moonies were involved in writing the test, and that he had a
new appreciation for the cultlike attributes of Catholicism, plus a
growing sense of dread and terror. In the smoky bar booth, he made
a series of beeping, robotic noises, and swung his arms stiffly, saying: "Danger, Will Robinson! Danger, Will Robinson!" We laughed
about the hilarious nudity question, the very obvious answers to the
questions in the personal goals category: *Are material goods more
important to you than personal happiness? Do you believe that the only
worthwhile professions are the ones that pay a high salary?* (Say what
you will about the Catholic Church, they do not try to fool you with
tricked-up subtlety; the answer they are looking for is stark black
and white.) And I felt delicious, contented, having a partner, someone to laugh with, someone who would share his last drops of pulpy

lime for my gin and tonic, someone to love. I wondered about Agnes, then, how it felt to have made the choice to be alone with God.

We were back in the church office a week later, thinking the hard part was over, that Sister Agnes would shake our hands—*You passed; Godspeed, kids!*—and move us along to the next stage of our journey to church-sanctioned wedded bliss. After the initial pleasantries— typically Midwestern, with a lengthy discussion of recent weather patterns—we sat down to discuss how we'd fared on the test. Perhaps our smiles revealed a trace of condescension: *Agnes, poor you, having to administer these quaint tests with their obvious answers! What a colossal waste of one's time!*

Sister Agnes smiled right back at us, immune to our smartypants superiority. Predictably, we had answered the questions correctly. And so it was looking like we were very, very compatible, when Sister Agnes ominously cleared her throat and made a mark on the notepad in front of her.

"Steve?"

Steve looked nervous, yet still hopeful, as if there might be some other Steve tucked away in the church office; perhaps Father Steve had appeared behind us in the doorway, ready to hear our confessions.

When it became terrifyingly clear that he was the man in question, Steve smiled bravely and raised his eyebrows: *Sock it to me.*

"Steve, you've indicated that you are nervous about Mary seeing you naked."

And here the scene splintered into a kaleidoscope of terror, shocked disbelief, my fear of sudden death from implosive laughter. The honey brown walls of Sister Agnes's office closed in on us, as if we were trapped in a shrinking acorn; the window air-conditioning unit kicked on with a jet engine *whirrrr.*

I kept my eyes down, fixed my face into a mask of questioning neutrality. *Hmmm . . . interesting. Steve, do tell.*

In my peripheral vision I watched Steve's face redden, as if diseased: A deep pink section appeared at the base of his neck, and rose inch by inch until his face was a blush-burned mask.

Sister Agnes was impossible to read—seemingly neither happy nor amused, not especially wanting to linger over this question. But she waited patiently, her hands folded on her desk.

Steve took a breath. "No," he said. "I . . . I must have made a mistake. I don't feel that way *at all."*

Later I would tease him about that studly *at all.*

Sister Agnes exhaled, her breath holding the ghost of a Wint-O-Green Life Saver. "Alrighty then!"

Sister Agnes continued going over our tests results, but we had checked out, still shocked that Steve, who is decorous and precise by nature, had flubbed the question. In his carelessness, his rush to get past the Catholic premarriage obstacle course, Steve had forced Agnes to use the word "naked": *Oh. My. God.*

But through her very good grace, or perhaps through her simple resignation that there were a great many freaky couples in the world, Agnes gave the go-ahead: We passed! We passed! We were moving on to Phase 2 of our marriage preparations! Phase 2 could be completed either by meeting one-on-one with a "veteran" married couple once a week for six months, or going on a weekend retreat. We decided to take our medicine all at once, and so, Engaged Encounter was *on*.

Three weeks later, Steve and I drove to Cedar Falls, Iowa, seventy-five miles northwest of the city where we lived in sin, to the aptly named American Martyrs Retreat House, where, segregated by gender in spartan dorm rooms, we went whole hog for Jesus: We ate ham for dinner, sausage and eggs for breakfast, and for lunch, a food I did not know existed, porkburgers. There were no vending machines. And so with every cell in my body yearning for Hershey's products or even a green salad that didn't have lime Jell-O as its basic component, the weekend commenced in all its group-topic glory: Values, Finances, In-laws, the dreaded Sexuality, and Wedding Etiquette (do tip the priest; don't forget to invite him to the rehearsal dinner).

Though there was a priest overseeing the proceedings, he rather sensibly left the bulk of the work to the laypeople. (Herewith the requisite *Beavis and Butt-Head* chuckle, the people who *get laid!)* Married couples facilitated the groups, and these men and women were either depressives who seemed a little too willing to share their myriad hardships, to expose marriage as an alternately boring and terrifying commitment *(Here's your gray cardigan; here's your pea soup, dear. Why, yes, it is #@*&% poisoned)* or super-happy Christian marriage cheerleaders. *(Who rules my life in weather stormy or balmy? It's God! It's God! He guided me to my spouse, and now we love being a daddy and mommy! When the kids go to bed we get busy like Pamela and Tommy!)*

Every last one of our instructors seemed sketchy, but perhaps my lack of charity was due to the exhausting premarital regime: Each moment of the weekend was scheduled. The day started at eight and ended at eight. Not counting sleep or the Friday-evening "getting to know you" session, we had a solid twenty-four hours of Engaged Encounter. Time that, as Steve correctly noted—again and again and again—we were never getting back.

Though we were encouraged to spend our time examining our relationships with our future spouses and not be distracted from this primary task by socializing with the other couples (see also: CULT-WATCH), we moved in groups. Even *personal* reflection time was spent as a group, a ring of hopeful pilgrims in folding chairs quietly listening to saccharine pop songs. The lyrics were mimeographed on bright copy paper that bled onto our sweaty hands, giving us impressive candy-colored stigmata. Our task during personal reflection time was to read along with the lyrics, to reflect upon their meaning and individual relevance—an exercise that had all the gravitas of Sunday-morning Top 40 dedications. *(Kasey, would you please play Whitney Houston's "The Greatest Love of All" for all those crazy kids at the American Martyrs Retreat House? Signed, The Lord Jesus Christ, Kingdom of Heaven.)* I thought of Sister Agnes as a comrade then; surely she would find personal reflection time weird, indulgent, and unbearably hokey. I imagined her looking in the window of the American Martyrs Retreat House puzzling out the scene: Twenty couples sitting in folding chairs in a sort of Christly rumpus room—new carpet, a crucifix on the walnut paneling, and bright felt banners with optimistic proclamations (I'M SPECIAL CUZ' GOD DOESN'T MAKE JUNK! FEEL-

INGS ARE NEITHER GOOD NOR BAD, THEY JUST ARE!), a boom box playing "Forever Your Girl." Though the lyrics seemed lame, perhaps they held a deeper meaning, a special meaning: *"Baby don't you know that I love you/And I'd never put nobody above you,"* sang Paula Abdul. *"Just remember I'm forever your girl."*

Did the fine people at Engaged Encounter offer up the Gospel according to Paula as an example of fidelity to the Lord? To one's spouse? Was it possibly an ode to Marian devotion? Agnes would know, and I envisioned her rapping on the windowpane with her short, clean nails, her crucifix wedding band glinting in the glass, mouthing the answer.

Oh, but I most certainly hoped she would turn away for the excruciating portion of the sexuality tutorial, in which a married couple in their late forties offered up the do's and don'ts of married connubial bliss. *(If your spouse has a sexual affair, is this a reason to end your marriage? The answer they were looking for: No. Steve whispered, Par-tay!)*

The man was a beefy extrovert, his wife quiet and predictably mousy. She had come of age post–Gloria Steinem, pre–Carrie Bradshaw, and seemed both puzzled and sensibly horrified—her face pale and moony—by the fact that she was discussing her sex life in public. Nonetheless, in her weak-tea-and-peppermints voice, she was explaining how her sexuality was tied to her emotional well-being—how sh e couldn't have sex unless she and her husband were happy—when her husband raised his palm, cutting her off. He blurted out, "I've got to say . . ." and then took a dramatic pause, in which there was time to reflect: *Define "got," Jackass.* He said it again, giving his bangs a quick finger-fluff, hiking up his brown cords. Then he let loose with a full sentence.

"I've got to say, I like to have sex *all the time.*"

He smiled rakishly: Could he get a shout-out from the Cro-Magnons in the crowd? Why, yes he could. Amidst the hoots and hollers filling the American Martyrs Retreat House, the woman looked at her husband. She squinted her eyes, as if she wasn't quite sure who he was: A flasher in a trench coat? A random pervy stranger lingering over the displays of *Oui* and *Penthouse* at Seven-11? Slowly, slowly, she smiled in recognition, perhaps relief: *Oh, it's you.* And then her smile turned quivery and desolate: *Oh, it's you.* But in a second, she rallied; she pressed her hands together and let out a peal of shrill, horsey laughter.

Occasionally, I could see a priest out the window, smoking a cigarette and walking his standard poodle on the shaggy lawn, where the outdoor stations of the cross offered a kitschy and naturalistic opportunity for prayer. I wondered what Agnes might be doing at that very moment: her laundry, maybe, or working through her crush of paperwork. Was she visiting the sick? Praying for the dismayed and disenchanted? As the church bulletin proved, she had a schedule that would kill off a lesser woman: Agnes was the go-to gal for every charity, need, or problem at the church. Volunteer needed for the rummage sale, contact Sister Agnes. Interested in joining the parish youth group? Please call Sister Agnes. Found: Ladies' Longines silver watch after 5:30 Mass, see Sister Agnes. Not a regular parishioner at Saint Mary's, but hoping to have your wedding in our gorgeous church? Willing to lie on your forms? Contact Sister Agnes.

She was the one doing it all, juggling the Father, Son, and Holy Spirit with her administrative duties. What I admired about Sister Agnes was what I admired about the Catholic Church, her noncorniness factor, her good works, her essential mystery. But it didn't take any theological genius to see that Agnes also highlighted the flaw in the system, because, *come on:* Shouldn't the hardest worker be eligible for the top job? Was it really necessary for a meritocracy to be based on gender?

Now the priest, as Steve pointed out, well, hey, *that* was the gig to have. He jokingly told me that he believed a priest's life to be his personal Paradise Lost: Work one day per week, have someone do your cooking and cleaning, spend hours and hours reading and writing, pondering the Gospels or traversing the outdoor stations of the cross at the American Martyrs Retreat House with your dog, while the laypeople instruct Engaged Encounter.

The priest came to the chapel of the American Martyrs Retreat House Sunday evening to say Mass. He gave a speedy, requisite homily, instructing us to be kind to each other and congratulating us on our upcoming weddings. He thanked the instructors for their time, good-naturedly noting that he didn't have much personal experience being a spouse. After Communion he handed out the certificates that proved we'd endured the weekend and could have our fancy Catholic weddings. He shook our hands and told us to go in peace to love and serve the Lord. Then he put on his windbreaker and went away, back to his Winstons, back to his dog, leaving the rest of us strainers and strivers to our own vocation.

And then Steve and I got married: December in Iowa, sugar snow and red roses, the Lord and a reception with an open bar, and we were happy.

I didn't see Sister Agnes again until early spring, when I was walking into Hy-Vee and noticed her in the parking lot. My heart pounded as if I were seeing an old beau. Agnes was walking by herself, forever her own girl. She appeared to be searching for her car, swiveling her head this way and that, a frown gripped between her eyebrows. Then she nodded briskly, *Yes, of course, there it is,* and took off quickly, fluttering the tails of her wool coat.

I thought of calling out to her, *Don't worry about my husband's fear of nudity thing. You should see him now, vamping around the house like Burt Reynolds in* Playgirl. I imagined she would laugh, but I didn't know for sure. When she got to her car, she paused. Her arms were full of groceries; she was looking at the sky.

My Sister Married a Wiener

HEATHER BRYANT & SARAH GAMBITO

BRIAN WIENER IRONS his underwear. Brian Wiener went to business school. Brian Wiener watches FOX News. Brian Wiener wants to marry my sister.

They met in an Internet chat room for water-sports enthusiasts. Sophia had been on speed dates and eHarmony dates. She had clicked on virtual pictures of men wearing scuba gear or advertisement-crisp suits. Typical Internet fodder: _You should be slim, attractive, and have headlights I can see. I'm spiritual but not religious. The three items I can't live without are my iPod, the_ New York Times _Crossword, and XXL condoms._ Oh God. My sister had entered the world of Internet dating, the domain of spinster teachers in hairnets. We live in New York City. Why the need for such emergency measures? I urged her to rethink her tactics.

"What about going out to a bar? Meeting friends of friends?"

"Oh, yeah right. That's worked so well for you," she retorted.

"I can't help it that I work in the theater," I returned. Two years earlier my best friends from college and I started our own theater company, Women in Theater, or WIT. Not a hotbed of straight men.

I tried to introduce her to people. Miguel, our lighting designer.

"He's gay as Christmas," she said. Damn, I'd forgotten that she'd seen Miguel's spot-on impersonation of Tina Turner.

So off she went into cyberspace to search for her man. I didn't see much of her for a while. My partners and I had just signed a lease on a black-box theater in the Meat-Packing District, and most of my time was tied up working with contractors, making trips to Home Depot, and downing martinis at the nearest bar (gay, of course).

Brian slipped under my radar. My Aunt Rhoda says that Bryant women can see storms coming on a clear blue day. We can warn our husbands five minutes before they're going to belch and embarrass themselves in public. But can we spy a Republican trolling the water-sports network for fresh-from-grad-school sweeties? Can we predict an engagement after four months of dating? Can we smell the Wiener clan from miles away, clamoring their way into our lives in a parade of Mercedes SUVs, Versace culottes, and Jimmy Choo shoes?

Welcome to Sophia's Overstuffed Engagement Party at Daniel, the French restaurant on the Upper East Side that makes the Plaza look like a sad outpost for blue-haired ladies. If I can figure out how to stuff one of the maroon velvet curtains into my bag, I could take it to a seamstress in Queens and have my maid of honor dress in three days. I'm sitting at a table where the silverware alone could pay my rent for a year if I found the right pawnshop. The combination of crystal and candles is like one big diamond, which only serves to remind me that Sophia can barely lift her left hand off the table at the center of the room. Brian is an only child. His parents must have pitched in for the ring, which is more of an anchor than a piece of jewelry.

The tables only seat six, meaning Mom, Larry (my stepdad), Sophia, The Republican, and his parents, the Normy-Norms, are at the head table. I am stuck at an outpost with five aunts, who grill me about my theater company.

"You're staging *Agamemnon?*"

"Yes," I say. "Except, it's going to take place in central China during the time of the T'ang dynasty."

"You are so grassroots!" one aunt says, gripping my hand as if I've just started a new fashion trend she plans to share with her friends.

I use the wrong fork for the lobster, and the waiter has to bring me a new pristine gold tong that I use to skewer the escargot from their gray, greasy shells. Slippery suckers. I glance at Mom, a vegan, who looks lost in the blue dress Sophia gave her to wear to this event.

It's like she is wearing a costume. I refused to color coordinate with the place cards and am wearing a vintage green slip dress with Doc Martens. I regret the shoes when the attendant nearly frisks me at the coat check on my way out. True, I thought about stealing the silverware, but it was only a thought. As I walk up to the Hunter College subway stop after the dinner, the toast of Uncle Friebert still rings in my head: He had held up his glass of champagne and guzzled it all in one gulp. "To the Wieners!"

Before the ring became a sixth appendage on my little sister's hand, back when it was still in a box, I thought she might change her mind. Back then it was still a proposal, not an agreement.

"Brian gave me something," she said when we were unpacking ornaments for the pop-up UNICEF cardboard tree Mom still used every Christmas. Our mother, a social worker with a black belt in guerrilla recycling, didn't believe in Christmas tree farming or unnecessary packaging. Instead of Barbie, I spent my childhood playing with the Sunshine family, little wooden figures with yarn hair that came in reusable cotton sacks. My social life has never quite recovered.

I figured Brian had given her another cable-knit sweater. He'd already given her one in every color—as if one might unravel and leave her horribly naked of preppy garb. Oxford shirts, pearls, tweed. Since Brian arrived on the scene, she was beginning to dress a lot like Marilyn Quayle.

When she handed me the tiny green velvet box, my first impulse was to throw it across the room, which I did. It landed with a nice resounding *thwonk* on the rattan chair. She looked from me to the box and back, but said nothing. I held up a dangling wire ornament made from Coca-Cola bottle caps. Mom was in the kitchen making popcorn to thread and hang around the "tree."

"Did you tell Mom?" I asked. Sophia shook her head. Just a day earlier Mom had confided that she gave the relationship six more weeks. Her precision about the time made me believe her. Sophia and Brian had been dating for four months. I couldn't even say for sure what color his eyes were.

Sophia didn't say, "We're getting married," or "Brian and I are engaged." She never said it out loud, but I knew because sisters know. A link in the chain between us loosened. I hung a paper snowflake on one of the cardboard boughs.

"Will you—?" I didn't say anything more, but she knew what I wanted to ask. Would she invite our dad. She stood up and crossed the room to retrieve the ring, held the soft green box in both hands as if it was a source of safety.

"Brian's family has already ordered the invitations from Kate's Paperie in Soho. They're going to be letterpressed," she said, not answering my question. That was the first time I vowed that I would do anything to stop her from marrying The Republican.

How to End an Engagement in Three Weeks:
a play starring Me, Myself & I

Me: *She's your little sister. She doesn't know anything. She needs to be saved.*

I: *From herself. She hasn't even seen Niagara Falls. Hasn't sung with strange men in front of a piano. Or believed in something so much it kept her up nights.*

ME: *Now that's youth. That's living.*

MYSELF: *Let's make something happen. Let's call someone. Everyone. Ex-boyfriends. People who recycle, for Christ's sake.*

I: *Let's remind her of what she's giving up. Unopened boxes of candy and going out with girlfriends to look for boys. Wearing lovely red blouses and flirting for as long as she can. That's what she should be doing.*

ME: *Let's call someone. Her college boyfriend. What was his name?*

I: *Jonathan.*

MYSELF: *(Silence)*

ME: *The one who played video games all day?*

MYSELF: *(Silence)*

I: *The Pacman impersonator.*

MYSELF: *Better than the Reaganomics-spouting, top-button-buttoned, I-listen-to-Rush-Lim—*

I: *But Jonathan is gross.*

ME: *She's right, you know.*

(Jonathan enters stage left. A musty twentysomething. Eating Fritos. He talks with his mouth full.)

ME: *Jonathan, please. Don't you need a new Sony PlayStation?*

MYSELF: *(Bats eyelashes)*

JONATHAN: *Huh? Dude, my PlayStation's all good. But aren't you forgetting that I dumped her?*

(Pause)

ME: *I didn't think of that.*

JONATHAN: *Buy me the new edition of HALO, and I'll call her up, at least. You know, work a little of the magic-roo on her.*

ME: *Magic-roo?*

JONATHAN: *Yeah, I can just remind her a little of what she's missing in the big bad world. Make her think a little bit.*

I: *Or throw up a little bit.*

JONATHAN: *Whatever.*

(Jonathan exits.)

ME: *We can't let Sophia become a Wiener.*

MYSELF: *I know. Just give me a minute. I'm trying to think. (Paces)*

I: *I've got it!*

ME & MYSELF: *What?*

I: *Ron.*

ME: *The plumber?*

MYSELF: *Utilities technician.*

I: *He was nice.*

ME: *Sophia doesn't want nice.*

MYSELF: *Better than the Exxon-defending, money-mongering, golf-shirt-wearing, "honey-can-you-cook-me-breakfast"—*

I: *He was cute, too.*

ME: *What's his number?*

Ron, as it turned out, was already married, as were Steve, Bill, and Dante. I brought Felix to a fundraiser for Immigration Law where Sophia spoke about issues facing children and families. He ignored my sister and instead picked up a pert paralegal barely out of high school. Otis had moved to San Diego. Ivan gave me the hit-the-highway speech when I showed up at RadioShack to announce that Sophia had gotten over her distaste for men in retail management. Phillip was a sport and came to a potluck my mom organized with her Meals On Wheels friends, but Sophia pushed him aside to get to the dumplings and sangria, which put a dent in my she's-been-pining-for-you-for-months story. That left Richard and Adrian and four days until the wedding. But Richard had moved to Hong Kong; possibly he got wind of my advanced stalking techniques and fled town. Adrian was living out on Long Island, but said he would come to the wedding, and that he was happy for Sophia. I didn't tell him that I planned to push him toward the altar.

My dream wedding goes like this: Sophia is standing in a white smock dress with a ring of nasturtiums, her favorite flower, crowning her head. She is barefoot, and simple bands are kept in a wooden box to one side of the trellis . . . No. She is wearing the tan suit she usually wears in the courtroom, plain, unadorned, except for a tiny perfect bouquet in her hands that I pick from the gardens up by the Cloisters where we used to pluck daisies until they were bare with our wishes for boyfriends. The justice of peace is a heavyset white woman with too much rouge. The man standing next to Sophia is Chris, her friend from college, a gentle Korean American guy with a ponytail who works for an Internet company . . . No. The man standing next to her is Lewis, her former law professor, a soft-spoken New Yorker by way of England and Des Moines . . . No. The man standing next to her can only be described like this: He is her match, the puzzle piece of her heart, her soul's friend, the one who walked a thousand miles to be by her side. She has known him by sixty different names in sixty different lives. He stands in the rain to protest the demolition of community gardens. He takes too much time to order from the menu at a restaurant, because he wants to taste only the best. And he wants that for my sister, the best. Not one pearl. Not one karat of a diamond. The ring is a band of silver found at a flea market. He gives her everything inside himself, and when she comes back for more, he gives again.

Instead. Here we are at the Church of the Heavenly Rest on Ninetieth Street at Fifth Avenue. My baby sister is marrying an Episcopalian in a Brooks Brothers suit. I'm standing next to her before God. Holding too many flowers. No matter how hard I try and concentrate, my bouquet is shaking. She is radiant. There she is, frothing away in dress and breath. I'm wearing a magenta chiffon gown because she has chosen to become a Wiener.

I look over at the rows of families splayed out in church. Brian's side of the church is rigid, respectful. Their carriages couldn't be any more military inspired. Even the children seem oddly poised. Like mini-barristers, with their hot-curled hair and clasped hands. On our side, there is my cousin Meredith who has managed to sneak in a Hershey's chocolate bar. She bends over it nibbling with concentration. My cousins James and Ed, who are nine, squelch their fists under their armpits. The muted flatulence reverberates off the stone floors.

Half of the Bryant clan—my mother's side, imported from Italy—whispers loudly to each other in Italian. The priest raises his voice and looks sharply at a number of the offenders. His glances, of course, go unnoticed. Many of my relatives are none too pleased to attend an Episcopal wedding service in a language they don't understand. Uncle Gennaro and Aunt Elena haven't left Sicily in more than ten years. They don't have the foggiest clue what is going on. They are dressed in black and fanning themselves vigorously, though the church is amply cool. Dad is a no-show. He sent a copy of his latest paper on the impact of Chaucer in Pope's poetry, and regrets, regrets, regrets. My sister tore the paper into tiny pieces. Next Christmas, we can use it to flock the UNICEF tree.

Cousin Meredith pauses from gorging on chocolate to stare down the ten-piece string orchestra that punctuates the ceremony with selections from Pachelbel's Canon. She snorts in disapproval, and it echoes through the Church of the Heavenly Rest. Uncle Mike shoots her a hairy eyeball. At the rehearsal dinner, he had waxed philosophical about the different worlds of the Bryants and the Wieners. "You are hibiscus. We are roses. In the end, we all bloom," he said. *Yes*, I thought to myself. *But some flowers bloom in gated communities. While other flowers can't afford health insurance.*

"Sophia, do you take this man to be your lawfully wedded husband?" the priest asks.

Sophia replies with her sure and curt voice, "I do."

"Do you, Brian, take this woman to be your lawfully wedded husband?"

There is an awkward pause.

Brian says, "I do."

A gun blast of laughter erupts from Uncle Gennaro. Apparently, he understands more than I thought.

"Wrong," Uncle Gennaro admonishes the priest. "You do again."

Another awkward pause. The priest continues.

"Then by the power vested in me, I pronounce you . . ."

"Wrong!" Uncle Gennaro isn't laughing anymore. He is standing up. He is shouting, "Wrong! You do again!"

He's convinced that the priest is giving short shrift to his favorite niece, Sophia. I look over at Brian's parents. Mrs. Normy-Norm has her face buried in her hands. Another awkward silence. Sophia throws her arms around Brian and lands her wedding kiss. The priest closes his book midsentence. The Normy-Norms give each other worried, furtive glances. They wait for a signal or official bugle call. But before the priest can finish the declaration, the Bryant clan has begun excitedly exiting the church, looking forward to the massive banquet they know is awaiting them at the reception in Brooklyn.

At the reception, Adrian is lying on his back at the edge of the imported parquet dance floor, recovering from a failed attempt at the limbo. Sophia hasn't looked at him once. She doesn't recognize her sixth-grade boyfriend, the one she kissed under the monkey bars, but only on the cheek. He's here as my date, but really, he's my last-ditch attempt at a rescue. The priest is in the corner doing shots with Aunt Elena, and I figure getting an annulment out of him later in the evening will be easy.

After six mixed drinks with names that imply compromising sexual positions, I am ready for the challenge of introducing this blast from the past, but first I must make a trip to the bathroom.

The women's bathroom at the Galapagos Art Space has hanging votives and looks like it could double as a medieval torture chamber. I wash my hands twice since my knuckles have been kissed by more Wiener men tonight than I want to remember. Back through the postindustrial steel door, my eyes adjust to the bright lights leading back to the dance floor. I hear a murmur of voices in a room off to the side and figure it's just one of the bridesmaids getting jiggy with a member of the hot catering staff. But then I see Brian's unmistakable gel-assisted bouffant. Figuring I'll catch him red-handed with a cocktail waitress and make my job easier, I lean against the door frame, too drunk to care if anyone notices. I am over my James Bond stealth routine. It's too late to be discreet.

But behind him, already in her plain honeymoon clothes, sits my sister doing that mooning thing with her eyes. "I got something for you," Brian says.

"Really?" she says.

Feeling hazy and belligerent, I'm about to blurt, "What?" when he holds out a box of stacked cards and envelopes. My sister reads from one of the cards.

"Sophia Wiener, oh my god!" It's personalized stationery. On

Crane's 100 percent cotton weave. Trumpeting her new name to the world at large. She starts to cry, and I almost do too. Brian Wiener is my brother-in-law. Still, I find myself laughing out loud at the ridiculous Crane's stationery and at myself for all my planning to stop this wild party, as if my wanting would be enough, as if she would leave Brian for her ex-ex-ex-ex-ex-ex-ex-boyfriend just because I willed it to happen. The girl who was once only my sister, and belonged just to me, hears me and turns around.

"Tell the bartender to put a cap on my sister's tab," she says to nobody in particular.

She catches my eyes, and I see that she is happy to an extent that should be criminal. If the police stopped her on the highway right now, they would make her walk the line, though I know for a fact she hasn't had even one glass of champagne—some tip she read in *Brides* magazine about maintaining wifely composure. But my fun for the night isn't done just yet.

"Sophia, there's someone I want you to meet," I say, hooking her arm and leading her away from The Republican, who is now officially my brother-in-law.

I figure it's worth a try.

$\mathcal{A}$ Lovely Little Springtime Wedding

Sarah K. Inman

꙼ ON A DREARY January night Amy and I ate half orders of ravioli at Angelo's on Federal Hill in Providence, Rhode Island. We had just had our belly buttons pierced at Artistic Tattoo, a brick building on the Hill, the one with a dragon painted on its side.

"I'm thinking about becoming a wedding coordinator," she said.

"Anything's better than telemarketing," I agreed. We'd met at Channel 36. I took a job as the membership coordinator for Rhode Island PBS shortly after finishing college and quickly came to hate it. Amy was the manager for a telemarketing firm out of Toronto called Arts Marketing. Hired to work a nine-month stint, Amy had come down to our little station to follow up with pledge promises and generate new funds through cold calls. At twenty-four, Amy was in charge of hiring and firing people who made those dreaded dinnertime pitches. There was nothing glamorous about it, and on her nights off, she sought desperately to make up for it. Her eyes were clear and blue and looked to me like those of a Kewpie doll. Amy's blond hair hung in tight, natural curls, adding to her doll-like look. She was from Saint Paul, Minnesota, the home of Prince, she liked to remind anyone who doubted the city's coolness.

"And what do you want to be when you grow up?" she asked, spearing the last ravioli.

"I might save up and buy a small place where I can sell coffee, cigarettes, and lottery tickets." I actually hadn't thought much about it, but it was a plan my father assured me would pay off, so I was keeping it in mind.

After supper, Amy and I headed out into the cold night and prepared to walk back to the apartment we shared on the East Side. At the time we had set out to get our navels pierced, the walk seemed a good idea, but now in the darkness of the coldest month of the year, we realized our mistake. Not surprisingly we hadn't really thought things through—an occupational hazard of being in our early twenties, and the reason we'd both decided we were nowhere close to getting married, or even wanting to.

Not that I was tempted with scores of prospects. I was dating a veteran of the first Gulf war. He was from Kentucky, about my age.

He'd moved to Rhode Island on a whim, something he now seemed to regret deeply. He smoked constantly, and it showed in his ashen complexion. His feet smelled bad. If it weren't for his newly acquired German shepherd puppy, I don't think the relationship would have lasted a month.

Our boss, the woman in charge of fundraising at Channel 36, monitored Amy's and my romantic triumphs and failures like a warden. Her name was Leila, and she spoke with a tight jaw, as if she were trying to keep marbles from spilling out of her mouth. Leila had a home in Bristol and a husband with an air-conditioning business. Occasionally, she would remind us that her son graduated from Dartmouth. He and her daughter, both slightly older than Amy and I, were planning to settle down with their chosen mates. Leila could do little for us in the dating department except offer to fix us up with someone from the State House. "I'll introduce you to Patrick Kennedy," she said. "He has a lot of money, you know."

A dry, biting wind whipped through us on our walk home, and we found ourselves navigating around buildings or walking backward to lessen the chill.

"Why wedding coordinator?" I asked Amy.

"There's just something beautiful about bringing two people together, seeing their destinies merge. And I love a party. Don't you? There's champagne and cake, tulle. Don't you just love tulle?"

"What's tulle?"

"You know—the netting that goes on the underside of a bride's dress, the material that gives it its substance, its pouf."

"Like a tutu?"

"Exactly."

I wondered why she knew this shit, but I held my tongue, not wanting to pass judgment.

Later that year, during Channel 36's Spring Auction, Amy was called upon to model a wedding gown.

"Can you imagine what kind of person would buy a wedding gown at an auction?" Leila shook her head in amazement. "People do some crazy things."

In the green room, Leila helped Amy into the long, poufy white dress. I sat while Amy powdered her face and then painted her lips with colored gloss.

"The bride needs a bouquet," Amy said after blotting her mouth with a tissue. She looked wholesome and healthy; she was enjoying herself.

"They want you out there in five minutes," Leila warned.

"Quick, Sarah, find me some flowers." No flowers could be found, so I did the best with what we had. I pulled apart leaves from potted plants in the lobby and cobbled together a lame little bouquet.

"Always a bridesmaid, never a bride," Leila said when I returned. "Tell me you didn't get that from the lobby," she added, seeing the greenery I handed to Amy. I smiled as sweetly as I could and headed to the control room where I watched Amy on the monitor. Her hearty Midwestern bosom filled out the dress in a way that my athletic WASPy figure never could.

"Will you get married some day?" Pablo, one of the program directors, asked. He was from Colombia, and his English was perfect but heavily accented. I shrugged.

"Don't bother," another program director advised. His name was Jim, and he was a recovering alcoholic. Oddly, I found him fun to be around; his misery offered a kind of comfort. "You get married, you get divorced, you think you can do it again, so you do it again, and then one day you find yourself in an empty field of snow. You've had a quart of whiskey already, and it isn't even noon. For some reason you're wearing cross-country skis."

"Wow," I said, not really knowing the proper response to this anecdote.

"My advice is, don't get married." Then he spoke into the microphone to the people working the cameras. "You guys heard that. Don't get married."

A month and a half later Amy was gone, sent by the telemarketing firm to raise funds for the Miami City Ballet. I shelled out a little extra to keep my place on the East Side, lost the ruffian from Kentucky, and in the meantime found a new boyfriend, a man in the Coast Guard. Walter played the guitar and tanned fairly well for an Irishman. He had a skull and crossbones tattooed on his bicep, and whenever possible, he took me along for rides on the cutter in

Narragansett Bay and sometimes on the open ocean. It was summer. We spent time Rollerblading, going to the beach, eating out, and visiting bars. Whenever he drank, Walter filled me with stories of dangerous adventures, of pulling dead people from the water, and of making rescues on rough seas.

About two months after Amy left for Miami, the phone rang late one night. I let it ring for a while before answering.

"Sarah!" Amy screamed as I said hello. She was loaded. "My friend's been arrested, and now we need to have a wedding."

"That doesn't make any sense," I said. Amy launched into a long story about an evening out that began with a bottle of wine, something called "Le Jau Jau de Jau." There were some crackers and cheese, and fruit, but apparently everyone involved was too coked up to eat anything. Then there was the car ride, Amy sitting shotgun with an open bottle of wine, keeping the cups of the driver and the passengers—who they were I wasn't entirely sure—full. I imagined Amy, pale and blond, her hair frizzy from the humidity. She would play the perfect Midwestern hostess to the beautifully tanned Miami hard bodies. The night came to end when the driver, Amy's friend Stephanie, rear-ended a police car at stoplight.

"Have you called a lawyer?" I asked.

"That's a good idea," Amy bellowed.

By September Amy was back at Channel 36 putting ads in the paper for another crew of fresh telemarketers. Her staff consisted mostly of single moms, who worked nights earning money while their children slept, and high school kids looking for after-school jobs.

Amy moved back in, almost as if she'd never left. Some of the apartment's furnishings, as well as most of its knickknacks, were hers—fold-out wooden chairs, the decorative plant holders, and a set of sterling silver spoons so tiny, about the length of my index finger, I wondered why she hadn't just taken them with her.

The night she moved back, I took one of those spoons—the only clean utensil around—and began eating ice cream with it.

"Don't you know what those are?" Amy asked. We sat in the living room, surrounded by her luggage.

I shrugged.

"They're salt spoons. Back before salt shakers, people used spoons to dish out salt. Look at this spoon, Sarah. Isn't it lovely?"

Licking fudge swirl off the spoon, I examined the decorative pattern of its handle. "If they're so lovely, why didn't you take them with you when you left for Miami?"

"So I would be sure to come back," she said.

As always, her logic was fuzzy, but I nodded anyway.

Amy sighed after a few minutes of silent ice cream eating. "I have this wedding to plan. You know Stephanie, right? The woman driving the car that night? Well, she had her license revoked, and she's moving to California, and in California you have to have a car to get around. There's just no way she'll make it without a car, and of course, with a car comes a license, which she doesn't have, and won't have for a while, and I feel like, well, it's my fault we rear-ended that cop. Can you believe it? I mean—my God—they were so mean to Stephanie and me and Adolfo and Raul."

"Who are Adolfo and Raul?"

"Some guys who were working for me. So I have this idea that if I can get Stephanie out here and find her a guy to marry, then she'll change her name and get a new license. Right?" She flashed her winning grin.

"Don't they check into stuff like that?"

"I've heard of this working before. A friend of my cousin's had a DUI, and when she went to the town hall to get her new ID after she got married, they just gave her another license. Just like that. No big deal."

"Can't Stephanie just change her name then?"

Amy shook her head impatiently. "They'll ask why and find out about her record. So I'm thinking springtime," Amy continued. "We'll wait until the spring and have it outside somewhere."

"Why are you doing this?" I asked.

"I got her into this mess, and besides, it's sort of romantic, isn't it? Bringing two people together?"

"What two people?"

She ignored me.

"It'll be a lovely little springtime wedding, somewhere outside. I can put it on my résumé when I become a real wedding planner. What do you think of Roger Williams Park? Too many Puerto Ricans, probably."

"Dominicans," I corrected. "Providence has a large population of Dominicans."

"Whatever," Amy said. Then she continued, "Or one of the beaches—no, that could be pretty cold in April. I have to think. Think! Where can we have this wedding?" As Amy rambled excitedly, plotting this wedding between poor Stephanie and whoever her groom might be, it became clear to me that there was no room for reason or rational thought in her plan. She became childlike, clinging stubbornly to some ridiculous idea of romance and adventure like it was love itself.

"What does Stephanie think of all this?"

"Stephanie likes to party. And she needs a driver's license."

"So they won't live together?"

"Oh, no, nothing like that. She'll get married, have her name changed, and then leave."

"Who's she going to marry?"

"Oh, I don't know yet. I've got to find a groom. We'll have lots to choose from when I start interviewing."

"You're holding groom auditions?"

"No, silly, for Arts Marketing. I've got a week to staff the telemarketers. There are bound to be some prospects. As long as he's over eighteen. That's all that matters. Well, not really, he's got to be a good fit for Stephanie too. She's tall, like you, so he's got to be taller. Who knows? Maybe they'll hit it off, but only if he's taller. She's not crazy about short guys. Have you seen the movie *Peter Ibbetson?*"

I shook my head, and off we went into Amy-land again. "Well, it's an older film, black and white, and it's about these two people who grow up together and fall in love when they're just children. They're destined to be with one another, but the war and his family's financial situation drag them apart, and then he goes on to become this famous architect and she's a countess, and one night they're having dinner, you know, sitting man-woman, man-woman, a nice, formal dinner with a group—this is years later when they're both married to other people—and he says 'krick' and she says 'krack' and it's then they realize they're each other's childhood sweethearts because when they were kids they always did that thing when one of them said 'krick' and the other said 'krack.' Oh my God! I'm going to cry just thinking about it." Amy's monologue degenerated into a Proustian free-jazz session of what romance meant to her. From what I gathered, it had something to do with true love, destiny, and beautiful objects, all the things I didn't really believe in. Her wedding plan had nothing to do with getting Stephanie a driver's license and everything to do with Amy fulfilling her own idea of herself as the conductor of romance.

Within a month, Amy found a groom, a tall, slender high school senior who would turn eighteen by the wedding date. He was a smart, good-looking young man, and for some reason—his parents' recent divorce perhaps—he hadn't yet become cocky, like so many of his peers. His lack of self-confidence made him ripe for manipulation. He was a lanky target in khakis and a button-down.

"Why don't you just ask Pablo if he knows anyone who needs a green card?" I suggested.

"Stephanie doesn't like Spanish men anymore. Miami sort of scarred her."

"Pablo *speaks* Spanish. He's from Colombia," I reminded her.

"Whatever."

"Secondly, they're not really going to live together so it doesn't matter if she likes him or not," I pointed out.

"Stephanie Hernandez, Stephanie Ramirez. No way. The last name would be all wrong—too suspicious. I can't do that."

"What does the groom know about Stephanie?"

"He's seen pictures, and they're supposed to talk on the phone tonight. I think I can reverse the charges to Arts Marketing."

Stephanie bought a plane ticket for the third week in April, just after the Spring Auction. Amy decided on Prospect Park, a patch of greenery on top of a hill on the East Side that overlooked downtown Providence. It was free of charge as far as anyone knew, and it was frequented more often by people walking their dogs than by testosterone-fueled young men driving by with loud sound systems. For $50, she even booked a justice of the peace to officiate. There were still other details to work out—the cake, the dress, the best man. Amy, of course, would be the maid of honor.

"Come shopping with me," Amy urged, and we found ourselves in a bridal boutique in North Providence, home of big hair and IROCs.

"Which one of you is getting married?" the saleswoman asked.

"She is," Amy answered. I was closer in build to the bride. I would have to try on the dresses.

The saleswoman shuffled through a rack of gowns, her plum-colored nail lacquer contrasting against the white. "When's the wedding?"

I looked to Amy who answered, "April 22. It's small, and it's going to be outdoors, so nothing too long. We're thinking tea-length and straight, something she can manage through the park."

"You're cutting it kind of close. We get brides in here who start looking a year ahead of time."

"This is a special situation," Amy said.

The saleswoman nodded and let it go. In a Catholic town, special situations weren't unheard of. "So who's the lucky guy?"

"Steven," I said tentatively, thinking I had the telemarketer-turned-bridegroom's name right. "He's in the Coast Guard." I jazzed up the story with a little of Walter's history. But the very thought of spending the rest of my life with my current boyfriend made me cry. Walter wasn't the only reason for my tears. I had been taking birth control pills on and off since college, and they inspired random emotional overreactions in me. They added pounds to my body and made my breasts ache. Worst of all were the days when I felt like throwing myself through a window or ramming my car into a highway abutment.

"Oh, honey," the saleswoman said, rubbing my arm gently. "Honey, you're doing the right thing." I was sobbing now, and Amy thought it best to leave.

"What's wrong?" Amy asked in the parking lot.

"I can't stand Walter anymore," I confessed. "He's mean. He says I need to grow up. He says you're a bad influence."

"He says *I'm* a bad influence?"

I nodded.

"Well just break up with him then. He's not the one."

My professional life seemed as bleak as my love life. I had been back in Providence for over a year now, and still I hadn't raised the funds to buy my convenience store. To tell the truth, I wasn't really trying anymore. I felt ready to leave Rhode Island. At night while Amy flipped through glossy wedding magazines, I began sorting through catalogs and brochures, preparing applications for graduate school, the one way I knew I could get out of the state.

One night during the March Pledge Drive, about a month after our initial dress-shopping excursion, as I was preparing to make the transition from my desk work to the on-air fundraiser, Amy stopped by my office. A tall, sandy-haired young man stood behind her.

"Sarah, I want you to meet Steven," she said. "He's our top caller, second of course to Cheryl." Cheryl was a staple of the telemarketing team. A mother of two, she left her kids each night, came in to Channel 36, and dominated. She could convince pension-dependent octogenarians to donate their last dimes to public television. "She's psychotic and you can't compete with the psychotic," Amy added quickly so as not to damage Steven's tender ego. "Hey, we're going bowling when we leave here. Wanna come with?"

"I'll be here pretty late," I said.

"Maybe next time. Tim's coming too."

"Who's Tim?"

"Another new hire." Then she whispered, "The best man."

"Congratulations," I said to Steven on his way out. He lowered his head and smiled. It became clear to me then that he was a virgin and understood that palling around with Amy would one way or another relieve him of his burden. He would probably do anything for her.

When she wasn't monitoring the phones, Amy had ample time to work on the wedding, which was now just a month and a half away. After my initial tearful trip, I stopped accompanying Amy on her shopping outings. I was busy making plans of my own, filling out applications, and gathering transcripts. One day she came home with a satin wedding dress she found on the discount rack at Filene's. It was something leftover from last season.

"What do you think?" she asked. It seemed kind of plain to me. "Add a tasteful headpiece and some flowers, and voilà, we have a dress."

"Think Stephanie will like it?"

"I've never seen her wear a dress so I don't know. But I think it's perfect."

"How much did you pay for it?"

"Twenty-five dollars. Oh my God, can you believe it?"

"Walter wants me to chip in to buy his father season tickets to the Patriots," I said, apropos of nothing.

"Tell me you're not doing that."

"I don't even like football."

"Tell me you're not chipping in to buy his father a gift."

"I'm not," I said, glumly. Walter had run out of adventure stories.

By the time the Spring Auction rolled around, I'd met another guy, an Italian. His name was Joe, and he dressed in good suits and worked for the secretary of state. He liked the Red Sox.

One night after dinner he followed me upstairs to our apartment. Amy's car was in the driveway. We found her passed out on the couch in the living room. A young man I recognized as Steven sat on the floor. He was awake, watching TV.

"Hi there," I said.

"I need to go home now," he said, as if waiting for permission.

"You can go," I told him.

"Amy said I have to watch this movie." She stirred at the sound of her name.

"Yes," she mumbled from the couch. "It's *Peter Ibbetson*, and you must see it before the wedding. I've seen it a hundred times."

Steven shrugged and remained seated on the floor. "I guess it's better than doing homework." Clearly, Amy still held sway over him.

Less than a week later, when my Italian lover was busy with me in the kitchen, trying to fuck me on the counter, Amy came home. This time she was with Tim, the best man. They gave us early warning with their loud voices, enough time for us to zip up and act naturally.

"You remember Tim," Amy said, leading the young man into our apartment. More confident than Steven, Tim helped himself to a beer and settled in the living room. "We're going to watch *Peter Ibbetson*. Wanna join us?"

"We were just on our way out," I said.

Word of Amy's plan spread around the station, and as the big day approached, the more real the whole insane event became.

"You know," Leila took me aside one day to say. "I heard Amy's friend with the criminal record is coming to visit."

"She's never been to New England," I offered, innocently.

"Watch out for that girl," Leila hissed. "Don't let her drag you down. You answer to me, you know." I stared back at her icy expression, her clenched jaw. If Leila knew that I knew about the two boys Amy pulled from her staff to star in her show, she'd eat me, or, more likely, fire me. If I didn't get into graduate school and make my big escape from Rhode Island, then what? Jobless in Providence was too grim to consider. I decided to play it safe.

The less I got involved with the wedding, the better. Amy was my friend and I loved her and her crazy ideas, but with Leila pressing the stone to my chest, I had to back down, disassociate myself. I decided not to attend the ceremony—at least not formally.

Stephanie arrived late Friday night. She was about my height but much thinner. Heroin addict came to mind. She had high cheekbones and was the kind of young woman a man might at first dismiss as being plain, but with that good bone structure, she would age well. She went without makeup and wore her hair in what I imagined to be its natural state: long, straight, and brown. I could see what Amy liked about Stephanie as a bride. She was the ideal candidate for a makeover.

"My God," Amy was screaming as she led her girl up the steps. "You lost so much weight. I don't know if this dress is going to fit you. Let's call Steven. I said we'd call as soon as you got in. Then it's bachelorette party time!"

Partying seemed like the last thing Stephanie wanted to do. She appeared sleepy and bored, ambivalent about the whole production. Perhaps she was just tired from her trip. After we had been introduced, Amy told her to get settled in her room. Then Amy went to work in the kitchen, breaking apart psychedelic mushrooms and laying out the bits on a plate as if she were serving appetizers.

Amy offered me some and then picked up the phone and dialed Steven's number. "Hello, may I please speak with Steven Rider?" To us she mouthed, "It's his father."

She handed the phone to Stephanie.

"Hey," Stephanie said into the receiver, lighting a cigarette. We didn't smoke in our apartment, and I waited for Amy to say something, but she never did. With the cordless in one hand and a cigarette in the other, Stephanie strolled into the living room. "No. I don't know where I am, really. Smoking. Out, I think. Right. My last test was totally clean," she said into the phone.

After their brief conversation, Stephanie hung up. We ate some mushrooms and went to a bar on the East Side.

"I want to dance," Amy declared. "Where can we go dancing? Don't you want to go dancing?" Stephanie shrugged and lit another cigarette.

Soon we found ourselves at a nasty metalhead club called J.R.'s Fast Lane. Amy wore a shirt that showed off her belly ring and attracted a lot of attention. To whoever would listen, she told the story of the next day's wedding.

On our way back home, we decided to stop for another drink at a place called the One Up. There, we met with our downstairs neighbors, Mohan and Huessin, Brown computer engineering graduate students. Together, the five of us headed back to our place on East George Street. Amy convinced them to come up for a nightcap.

"We don't have much but vodka, but anything goes well with vodka," Amy said.

"A screwdriver," Mohan said.

"Yes! Screwdrivers. Let's see if we have orange juice. Hey, Sarah, can we drink this orange juice with the vodka?"

"I don't care what you do," I said. I just wanted to sleep.

"You need another mushroom. Have another mushroom. We're going to watch *Peter Ibbetson*."

Late the next morning, I was lounging in bed when the phone rang. I had the feeling I shouldn't answer it, but I was hoping it was my guy calling to tell me what time we'd meet. It was Leila, and through the marbles in her mouth I could hear her anger.

"Where's Amy?"

"I don't know," I said. It was more or less the truth since I could see into Amy's empty bedroom. I suspected she and Stephanie went to get their hair done—something I knew Amy had planned for.

"Where's it going to be?" Leila pressed.

"What?" I faked confused innocence.

"She's in trouble."

I heard Amy and Stephanie come up the stairs. Amy arrived carrying a grocery bag and a cup of Dunkin' Donuts coffee.

"Breakfast!" Amy cried.

"I gotta go," I told Leila, who was still talking. I heard the phone ring as I went into the bathroom to shower. Amy wasn't answering it either.

I tried to stay clear of Prospect Park that day, but when my new boyfriend showed up, I got in his car and told him to drive us to that very spot. I also told him it was important that I not be seen.

It was the kind of day when the sun struggled to push its way through clouds, just warm enough for Stephanie to feel comfortable in the satin dress that hung off her thin body. I made my boyfriend park across the street and I hunched in my seat, peeking out the passenger window like a spy. From the car I could see Steven, handsome but nervous in his rented tuxedo. He picked it up from the same place where he rented one for the prom. The best man was in khakis, a shirt, and tie, and Amy in a simple rose-colored, tea-length dress I had never seen before.

The judge, a tall man with a pockmarked face, took Amy's cash before starting the ceremony. Fifty dollars for a name change, a little romance, and adventure. As I waited for the ceremony to begin I looked around, paranoid. The park was sparsely populated. Some grim-faced dog walkers picked up poop on one end of the park, not wanting to intrude on the ceremony. No gang members that I could see. That would make Amy happy.

"Can we go now?" Joe asked. "If we hurry, we can make it to a movie."

"Just a sec," I said, entranced with the scene. Joe conceded to watch the real-life drama playing out before us.

Moments before the ceremony, Stephanie removed the delicate

silver ring she usually wore on her right hand. Amy made sure to have something for the groom, a thick silver band she picked up at the same flea market where she found the tiny sterling spoons. I have no doubt that Amy covered all bases in terms of getting something old, something new, something borrowed and something blue, but I couldn't make them out from my perch.

The officiant had barely begun when we heard a screech of tires. Disappointment registered in Amy's expression when Steven's beet-faced father hopped out of his idling car. She gasped in terror as her perfect day crumbled.

We couldn't hear but we learned later that Steven's dad threatened to press charges, bring the story to the media, and let them eat it up and spit it back out as they saw fit. Instead he snatched his humiliated son from the park and drove off in a huff, leaving the oddly bedraggled wedding party without their groom. I put my head in my boyfriend's lap as we sped away from the park.

"Stephanie, I am so sorry I failed you," lamented Amy. The three of us sat in the living room later that afternoon, drinking champagne intended for the reception. We were killing time before taking Stephanie to the airport. The wedding dress hung from the door of Amy's bedroom.

Stephanie shrugged. "Maybe Florida records won't make it to California."

"Just find a hot guy to drive you around," Amy said. Then she added, "Poor Steven. Can you imagine having a dad like that?"

"You tried to marry off his only son," I pointed out.

"Oh God, you're right," Amy laughed. The champagne put her in a good mood.

On Monday, Leila tattled to Arts Marketing, and Amy was promptly fired. "I had no choice, really," Leila explained to me in my office. "This is a serious situation. I'm just thankful you stayed out of it."

With her romance spoiled, Amy moved on to adventure. She packed up her things and headed to California to share a place with Stephanie. There, she lived out her twenties in reckless abandon, ingesting the latest drugs and sleeping with burgeoning rock stars. She lived close to the beach with a group of people who kept a nitrous oxide tank in their garage. From what I understand, she had a fantastic time. Shortly after Amy left Providence, I left too, for graduate school in New York City. Years later, when my Italian lover and I decided to get married, I called Amy, who by now had moved back to Minnesota and settled down with a military guy who was a member of Mensa. "That's so romantic!" she cried. "I was there when you first slept together. Tell me," she continued, "have you worked out the details?"

My Man
in Black

MARISA SOLÍS

◦— THE HOT-PINK nail polish on my toes sparkled like rubies in
the sunlight. The three layers of topcoat I had applied two days
ago had obviously paid off: My toes still looked fabulous in spite
of all the sand they had dug into over the last twenty-four hours,
and my hope was that they'd still look salon-fresh in two more
days, when they'd be peering up at me from the $14.99 open-toe
white pleather sandals I bought at Payless.

With my feet propped against the dashboard, my thrift-
store skirt had fallen across my waist, exposing my bare legs to
the warm sun—and to everyone who bothered to check out the

couple in the rented Jeep Wrangler with the top down *and* the sides off. Stripping off its skin was the first thing we did, even before we left the Alamo lot at the airport. We were in Hawaii, damn it, and we were going to ride in style.

In the driver's seat, Jamie was soaking up the rays, too. His shirt off, leaning back in the reclined seat, he was actually driving the speed limit. Unless there was a cop trailing him, this never happened. I watched him steer, riveted by the transformation from intense, hyper, road-rage man to demure Sunday driver. I rested my hand on his thigh and imagined him again in a tuxedo. Before me was a pale, skinny guy with four 12-gauge hoops in his ears, seven tattoos—unbelievably, one of them was my name—cut-off army pants, and worn leather flip-flops. I fingered the scar on his hip, the result of the few dozen minor skateboarding injuries he had endured over the years. I imagined the thin, wavy scar hidden beneath a midnight-black tuxedo tailored perfectly to his six-foot-one frame. I imagined him stalwart and untouchable in his satin cummerbund and patent leather wing tips. He would be my handsome groom wearing the uniform of celebratory love. He would be like the smiling, dreamy guys in the bridal magazines. He would have impeccable manners and perhaps even speak with a British accent. He would take my hand in a chivalrous display of social grace as he invited me to waltz across a polished wooden—

"What are you thinking about, babe?"

"Huh? Oh, nothing."

It was delicious fantasizing about the one thing he detested most in this world: dressing up for other people.

"Are you sure you don't wanna just get married in your bikini?" He poked my boob.

I squinted my eyes at him, pursed my lips.

"I could wear my swim trunks. We say 'I do,' and kiss, and then go swimming. What would be more awesome than that?"

I pinched his hip scar.

"Ow! I'm serious. It'd be so cool. Seriously, don't you think so?"

"I am serious, and no, I don't think so."

He shrugged his shoulders and began whistling "Crosstown Traffic." Even up to the very last minute he was trying to get me to recant my decision that we get married in traditional wedding clothes—and I loved him more for it. I was going to marry a guy who wouldn't give up, and that was what impressed me so much about him from the beginning.

Either side of two-lane Highway 50 was bordered by a mix of flowering hardwoods, creeping red vines, tall ferns, banana plants, and dozens of varieties of palms. Occasionally we'd see a flash of white plumeria, red hibiscus, or yellow heliconia peep out from the mass of green. I was so mesmerized by the lush vegetation that the street sign I was looking for didn't register until after we drove past it.

"Oh shit!"

"What?"

"I think that was it." I bolted upright and checked the address I had folded in my purse.

"Really?" He was obviously as puzzled as I was. The street didn't look any different from the other sleepy ones we had passed that led up to quiet, hidden homes in the hills or down along the water.

"Yeah, that was it. Make a U-turn."

It's not like I expected a huge glowing sign announcing For-mal Wear, neon tiaras blinking in the palm trees, but I guess I did expect the street to be a little more . . . incorporated. But whatever, it was Hawaii, not Hollywood.

Jamie turned onto a narrow lane that was at first residential, but then dipped down to become the city's main street, that is, for all three blocks of it. The place reminded me of the Gold Rush towns I had driven through on camping trips in the Sierra Madre foothills with my family as a kid: dusty, run-down, tired, forgotten. This was a town that had definitely seen brighter days. The odd thing was, ghost town or not, the setting couldn't have been more like paradise.

We pulled into an empty dirt parking space in front of a large storefront with peeling brown paint. I had only been to three tuxedo places in my life. The first time was for Homecoming. The second time was to drive a friend to a groomsman-fitting appointment. The third time was less than a month ago, when we visited our local Siegel's so that Jamie's measurements could be taken and sent to the only store on the entire island of Kaua'i that rented the traditional groom getup. None of those places had been in shabby parts of town. They were in upscale malls or quaint shopping districts—the kinds of places that make you feel good about shelling out a couple hundred bucks to look nice. But this place, despite being on a Hawaiian island, didn't offer much in the way of *ambience*.

My heart sank when I saw bald mannequins wearing tan polyester slacks and plain, white, button-down shirts staring blankly at me from behind the salt-streaked windows. There were child mannequins, too, one wearing a private school uniform, the other a Boy Scouts outfit.

Jamie pushed the heavy glass door and held it open for me. I took a deep breath and walked in. It took my eyes a while to adjust to the darkness; but as I squinted, I could make out a wall of outdated sneakers on the left, a perfume and makeup counter against the right wall, and, in front of me, handwritten SALE signs dangled over round tables heaped with bras only my grandma would wear. The only thing the place was missing was a worn-down soda fountain to complete its 1950s Woolworths look.

"Can I help you kids with something, eh?" asked a voice from between two five-foot-high shelves of panty hose, socks, and belts.

My eyes still squinting, I said, "Um, yeah, we're here to pick up a tuxedo. I had Siegel's in California call over measurements—"

"You kids, lost, eh? Tryin' to get to Waimea Canyon?" The figure that belonged to the voice stepped toward us, a short woman in her sixties wearing navy blue slacks and a cream-colored polyester blouse.

Fearing she might be hard of hearing, I spoke louder and more slowly, "No. We're. Here. To. Pick. Up. A. Tux. E. Doe."

"Hey, whas dat dey sayin'?" groaned a voice from the far back corner of the shop. I could see a slightly hunched figure slowly making his way toward us.

"Oh, dese *keiki* maybe are lost," the woman announced over her shoulder to the approaching man.

"No, we're not lost," I said to the man, realizing that my pupils had finally stopped dilating, but that it was still really dark in there.

Not just dark in contrast to the incredibly bright June day outside, but dark, period. "We're here to pick up a tuxedo. We reserved one."

"Alright then. Come with me," he said and motioned for us to follow him. He stopped us in front of a glass counter filled with fancy-looking things bagged in thin plastic. I couldn't quite make out what they were. Crocheted baby booties? Lacy garters? Handmade doilies? There was an ancient cash register on the counter plastered with Polaroids of smiling customers, mostly children, in brand-new shoes or dresses or sweaters. "What's the name?"

I looked at Jamie, who had the face of a granite cliff: pale, hard, and petrified. I realized he hadn't spoken since we walked in. "O'Shea," I answered.

"O. Shea . . . Shea . . . I don't have anything here for Shea."

"No, the last name is O'Shea. One word. It's Irish."

"Oh," he grinned, displaying an uneven row of teeth, "like McDonald's, eh?"

"Yeah, just like that."

"Oh, look, here it is. OhhhhhShaaaaaay. Got it. Be right back." He disappeared into the back room.

"It smells like mothballs in here," Jamie mumbled behind unmoving lips. "What the hell is this place?"

"I have no idea." Truly, I didn't. I had found it in the yellow pages at our local library. I had learned by calling around that renting a tuxedo for two days from a place on the island was a fraction of the cost of renting one for a week from home. That made sense to me. So I made arrangements with the only place on Kaua'i that rented them. The woman on the phone said all they needed were his measurements. And that seemed perfectly reasonable to me; having grown up in a family that sewed, I understood measurements. I understood the preciseness of inches, the perfection of a well-fitted garment. In measurements, there were no errors.

The man emerged from the back room holding a tuxedo sheathed in a layer of flimsy plastic. The vision of Jamie as my well-groomed, well-mannered man came into my mind again. The man motioned for Jamie to enter the dressing room, a shabby two-stall construction that resembled an outhouse more than anything else. I stood a few feet away, where I could follow Jamie's moves in the two-foot gap between the brown Linoleum floor and the bottom of the dressing room door. I watched his fatigues fall to the floor, watched him step into the dreamy wool pants. For a hot second, I felt a surge of guilt: The groom isn't supposed to see his bride in her wedding dress before the ceremony, but no such rule applies in the opposite scenario. I shrugged off the potential bad luck and continued with my fantasy of seeing for the first time my longish-haired, scrubby rocker boyfriend transformed into, oh, can I say it? A Ken doll.

The wooden door slowly creaked on its hinges. The tuxedo was on, the whole thing, in all its glory. Time, sound, smell, taste—it all froze for me. Even my heartbeat took a break. Before me was something utterly unfathomable: my fiancé in a clown suit. The pants were clearly four sizes too large: The crotch hung almost to the middle of his thighs and the pant legs gathered in huge black puddles over his bare feet. The cummerbund was a satin so dull it resembled sandpaper. The shirt's ruffles were frayed worse than the edges of my cutoff jean skirt. The jacket was a different shade of black than the pants, and the sleeves ended only a few inches past his elbows. But the best part was the bow tie. It was the color and size of a brick.

"Oh, you look so handsome!" yelped the woman who had first greeted us. Jamie stared at the twin pools of fabric around his feet. "What a darling! Lou! Lou, you should get a picture of this one!"

Horrified, I ran to Jamie.

"This is seriously fucked up," he muttered.

I was starting to panic, but clinging desperately to hope. "Well, do you think we could make it work, I mean, do you think we could safety-pin the hem or—"

"I'm *not* wearing this thing in the photos. No fuckin' way!"

The photos we were supposed to take—the only evidence we were bringing back to our friends and families that we had actually gotten married, and in nice clothes to boot—flashed through my mind: the setting sun over the Pacific, on a bluff, me in my full-length, extra-tight gown, looking into his eyes, ready to say "I do," and him, in a *clown suit,* pulling a plastic daisy from his breast pocket to squirt me with a thin spray of water. *No fuckin' way* was right.

"Take it off!" I said, surprising myself. I could sense the shuffling of Lou and the woman, perhaps trying to locate the camera to tack us on the register of shame. "Hurry!" I pleaded as I shoved him back inside the dressing room.

As politely as I could manage, I inquired about my options. Did they have other, smaller bow ties, shirts with fewer ruffles, jackets with longer sleeves, and pants with a thirty-one-inch waist? They said no, that they had ordered the suit from the Big Island, and that this was all they had. I started to get furious. I demanded to know how they could get the measurements wrong. I started telling them how disastrous my photos would be if he wore that . . . that *getup* . . . when Jamie came up behind me.

"You know what?" he said to the couple in his adolescent punk way. "It's just not gonna work out." Then he grabbed my arm and led me out into the blazing sun.

"You didn't let me finish!" I complained as I stepped up into the Jeep. "What the hell are we going to do now? The wedding is in two days and I didn't get to ask if any other place on the island rents tuxedos, though I doubt it because they were the only place listed in the phone book. This is totally fucked!"

Jamie started the car and headed back to the highway.

"It'll be okay," he tried to assure me.

"That's easy for you to say," I snapped. "You never even cared about these damn photos in the first place. All you want to do is get married in your bathing suit and go swimming."

"That's not true. All I care about is you, and I'm with you, and we're getting married, and if we don't have any photos, fuck it, we have each other." He stroked my head. Wisps of my hair were flying wildly about in the open air. I was kicking myself for not bringing a tuxedo from home. Jamie could feel my anger and sense of failure building, and he continued to stroke my head. He was right, of course; all that mattered was that we had each other. But until we reached our hotel room, I remained mad as hell.

I sulked on the balcony watching the small waves crumble across the reef about two hundred feet from the shore. I felt like the water was washing away my entire plan.

Our *original* plan was the elaborate, fairytale kind reserved for starry-eyed romantics too inexperienced to know better. We would get married in Santa Barbara, where we met, at the zoo overlooking the ocean. I would wear an exquisite satin, powder-blue dress and a sweeping veil; he, of course, would wear a tux. With my best friend officiating, we'd say our vows at sunset on the top of the zoo's grassy knoll, which would later be transformed into a banquet area and dance floor. Our favorite restaurant, The Palace, would cater. And a fabulous time would be had by all sixty guests. It didn't seem outrageous or wildly expensive. It seemed very "us" and, we later learned, that was the problem.

Our plan didn't take into account the wishes of "others." There were demands—all from my side of the family—about where we'd be married (in the Catholic Church) and by whom (a priest), who would attend (every single member of my mother's extended family), and the color I'd wear (white). At first I tried to reason, to compromise. But this became frustratingly difficult to do when I was at the mercy of the folks footing a large part of the bill. I was twenty-one and still in college. Our combined annual income was $25,000. I had no leverage at the bargaining table. I was starting to feel myself melt away.

The months following the announcement of our engagement became a tug-of-war between familial obligation and personal determination. Then one day in April, when I was feeling the tattered ends of the rope begin to slip away, Jamie said it. "Fuck 'em all!" This was not news, of course, since that had increasingly become our refrain. "We already have the honeymoon booked, right? Let's just get married there." The shocked look on my face compelled him to keep going. "If people want to tell us how to live, how we should get married, fuck 'em; they can talk to each other about it while we're on the beach getting hitched."

It was brilliant. We mailed out pretty homemade announcement cards inviting people to celebrate our marriage by joining us *in spirit* on the wedding day. We knew my family would be upset (his parents, for the record, were *so* happy their only child, a hyperactive, mega-creative troublemaker, had found someone to spend the rest of his life with that they didn't care *what* we did), but they'd get over it. And over time, they did. Having professional photos taken on our big day was important to us, and standing on that balcony after the tuxedo fiasco, it became the only thing I cared about. The photos would capture a moment in time, cement us in our reckless, naive youth, and reflect our feverish love for all to see. And I wanted to share the moment with others. Photos were the only way I knew how. And now, there would be me in the beautiful dress my aunt had sewn and Jamie in his ratty trunks. It gave me goose bumps.

Not wanting to give up just yet, I scoured the room for a phone book.

"Whaddya doin', hon? Wait, you're not gonna look for another tuxedo? Babe, the wedding is two days away . . ." I looked up "Tuxedo." "I mean, you even said . . ." My eyes scanned the entries. There were two! ". . . that was the only place on the island." I picked up the phone and began to dial. "I know how important this is to you, and

I'm sorry it didn't fit. Really, I wanted to make it work for you. But I couldn't wear that thing. I mean, that jacket was made for a munchkin! I think the photos will look better with just you in—"

"Hello? Hi. Do you rent tuxedos? Uh-huh. Uh-huh. Do you have any in stock? No, I'm in from California. No, I'm not *in* California; I'm in Kaua'i, but that doesn't matter. I'm getting married in two days. Well, it's kind of an emergency. Uh-huh. Uh-huh. Right at the T and then left at the gas station? Okay, thanks." I slammed the phone down. "Let's go. They close in forty-five minutes!"

We jumped in the car and sped to Lihue. I was hopeful and fiercely determined. We'd get a tuxedo if it killed me.

Tropical Wear with a Flair was in a small cluster of upscale tourist shops right off the main street a block from the Marriott. So far, so good. I ran into the store and told the saleswoman, who looked like she was still in high school, my story in minute detail. She nodded and inserted a "Wow, that really sucks" every fifteen seconds or so. I got the feeling she was not going to help me in the least. Luckily, her boss, a woman with more experience in matters of matrimonial mayhem, came over to lend a sympathetic ear to my woeful story and plea for help. She glanced at Jamie, who was fingering expensive bikinis and looking rather forlorn. I was hoping she would take pity on us and help, but part of me worried she'd take us for naive but spoiled teenagers from the mainland who couldn't plan ahead and then demanded recompense when disaster struck. I tried to convince her of the intricate steps I had taken to ensure the perfect day. I was *not* a no-planner. The teenager went off to help a tourist pick out a silk dress with large white hibiscuses on it. I made eye contact with the older woman. She again looked at Jamie, who now had his hands shoved deep in his pockets as he checked himself out in a mirror. He was actually flexing his muscles! Here I was, distraught over the idea of saying my vows next to my half-naked fiancé—and having the moment captured on film—and he was twitching his pectorals. It seriously compromised our air of desperation. I tried my best to look pathetic.

"What time is your wedding?"

"It's at four, but the pictures are at two, at the Kilohana Plantation."

"I'll see what I can do," she said and disappeared.

A fifteen-minute phone call later, she reappeared and smiled, "We'll be cutting it close, but I think we can do it." I wanted to kiss her!

Despite an extremely complicated inter-island shipping system, low stock, and limited styles—hello, it was the end of the day on *Saturday* and we were getting married on *Monday*—we were to return at one on The Day Of; the tux would be waiting for us.

The next day we only did two things related to our wedding: picked up our special-order flourless chocolate wedding cake and my small bouquet of purple orchids. The rest of the time we snorkeled, turned bronze in the sun, and ate grilled *opa* in the open air next a pond filled with splashing koi. It was unbelievably relaxing.

The following morning was not. As we lay in bed, our limbs began to twitch in anticipation of the day's events, our minds tried to grasp the enormity of what we were about to do. But we were ready. We got up, ate French toast, and then separated, promising not to see one another until one o'clock.

At some point, roughly two hours later, after I had applied copious amounts of luxurious pikake lotion all over my freshly shaved legs and the rest of my body, Jamie called to me from the next room. I responded at top volume, "What do you mean you 'don't have the vows'?"

"I mean just what I said: I. Don't. Have. The. Vows."

"How could you forget the most important part of the ceremony?"

"Well, you didn't remember them either!"

"Do I have to remember *and* do everything?" I started to storm out of the bathroom, but turned once I got to the hallway, remembering our pact to not see each other until the last possible second— we were going for maximum surprise potential. "Hey, answer me!" I demanded.

He didn't answer. But I could hear him rooting around. It sounded like he was rifling through my backpack. Then I heard him pull something out, sigh deeply, and plop on to the couch. I couldn't believe it. The most important things we'd say to each other, words that would decree the rest of our lives, would be written impromptu in less than fifteen minutes on the blank pages of my journal.

I went back to the bathroom and continued battling my hair. I hadn't counted on the effects of tropical humidity on my thick, wavy hair. Jamie would later christen it my Island Hair, a disheveled, wild, wiry version of my black hair that, if combed, resembled a gigantic bird's nest. I learned that if I just left it alone, it actually looked decent— and I'd be mistaken for a local. But mere hours before our wedding, I was blow-drying the heck out of it, trying to get it to look shiny and smooth. I pulled my hair as hard as I could without removing the strands from my scalp and held up the dangerously hot blow-dryer to it. I had seen this technique in salons the world over, but I just didn't have the coordination to brush-pull-dry with a result that was sleek and straight. My hair developed the texture of a really bad perm. For a moment I wished my mom were there. I wished she could take charge, work her magic, and transform me into a flawless bride. But no, I was doing this on my own.

Then I had an epiphany. I bolted to the linen closet and pulled the ironing board from its hook on the back of the door. I grabbed the iron and set it to medium. I waited for it to get hot. And then, as gracefully as possible, I bent from the waist, put my cheek on the thinly cushioned surface, brushed my shoulder-length hair out so it stretched across the board, and with my right hand, I carefully guided the iron across my frizzy hair.

It worked like no blow-dryer ever could. I had heard my mom joke about ironing her sisters' hair when they were teenagers, but being a teenager myself, I had doubted just about everything she said, including her strange recollection. Then I smiled, realizing that perhaps, in that desperate moment when I had no idea how to get my hair to behave, I had channeled her, and she came to my rescue. I was grateful. Only once did Jamie interrupt his writing in the next room and blurt out, "Hey what's that awful smell?"

Once my hair had been tamed and flipped at the edges like Ricki Lake in *Hairspray,* I began my makeup. I worked slowly, trying to get the foundation on evenly, the eyeliner on smoothly. I powdered the hell out of my face and neck and chest, trying to prevent the inevitable rivulets of sweat from ruining my look.

Jamie popped his head in the room. "Wow, your hair looks great! You look amazing!"

I smiled at him as he kissed my forehead.

"You know it's one o'clock."

"Huh?" I asked, holding the eyelash curler almost against my eyeball.

"Babe, it's one. Don't we need to go?"

From that moment on, everything was in fast-forward. I squeezed into the Lycra/elastic/nylon one-piece undergarment that promised to shape my body into deliciously proportioned curves. It was like pulling on a wetsuit. With a deep exhalation, I finally got the thing all the way over my boobs. On the other end, it nearly cut off my circulation midthigh. But it worked; I had the shape of an hourglass. I stepped into my dress as delicately as possible. I fastened the veil about thirteen times to my hair before I got it right, then added dendrobiums to it. I finished applying mascara, dabbed on some lipstick, pulled on the white gloves that nearly reached my armpits. I fastened my cheap sandals and admired my hot-pink toenails. I was ready.

When Jamie saw me in my complete outfit, he was speechless. He literally looked me up and down for a good ten seconds before he could move. Then he walked tenderly toward me and went in for some heavy petting.

"We don't have time for messing around! Let's go! Do we have everything? Bring our jackets—it might get cold and I don't know how long we'll be out. Don't forget the keys. Can you bring my purse? Oh my god, we're so late!"

We rushed out the door in a whirlwind of tulle, orchids, and lightweight jackets. "Oh shit! My bouquet!" Jamie ran back into the room and came out with my small bundle of orchids and greens. We got to the end of the hallway. "Shit!" yelled Jamie, who then ran back to the room and returned with my journal: the vows. I rolled my eyes at him, and we raced to the parking garage.

"Wait," I said. "Where's the cake?"

"Shit!" For the third time, Jamie raced back to the room. I watched his shirtless body disappear around the corner, and I felt I loved him more each minute for being such a daring, dashing sport. A large, pasty couple wearing Michigan State T-shirts walked by me, and I pretended that everything was perfectly normal, wedding gown not-withstanding. They mumbled congratulations, and I nodded at them.

Jamie sprinted back holding our cake in its white box. I tried to walk as fast as I could, but despite the long slit up the back, my ankle-length dress gave me limited mobility. Plus, I didn't want to wrinkle it or get it sweaty. Jamie walked ahead of me and threw all our crap on the back seat. He then walked over to the passenger side to help me in, when he suddenly stopped. I did the same. We had forgotten to put the top up and the sides back on the jeep. "Fuck!" we said in unison. Jamie rooted around in the back for the canvas top, which he found covered in sand. He shook it out, and began to frantically attach it. I shyly waved to a couple getting out of their car across from us. I wanted to help him, but I couldn't get my dress dirty. And I was wearing gloves! I watched him struggle. We were racing against time, and putting the top on was obviously a difficult affair. I was getting anxious. "Forget it, Jamie, let's go."

"But your hair, your veil."

"Look, if we don't get you to the tuxedo shop now, we're gonna be late for our own wedding!"

There was no point in arguing. He helped me in. He even fastened my seat belt for me, an act he's never repeated since. He threw the car in reverse and we sped off. Trying to deflect the wind from my body was his goal. But it was useless. It didn't matter if he drove fast or slow or sideways, the wind was everywhere. I gave up on having a wrinkle-free dress and doubled over, clasping my hands together behind my neck, holding my veil and hair in place.

"How you doing there, babe?" asked Jamie.

With my cheek against my knees and the crown of my head dangerously close to the glove compartment, I looked up at his freshly shaven face, his slightly sunburned chest, his blue and gray board shorts. "I'm doing great!"

Twenty minutes later, Jamie parked in front of Tropical Wear with a Flair. I was still in the air raid drill position. "You gonna wait in the car?"

I slowly returned to a normal sitting position. My back ached. "Yes. Hurry!"

He sprinted inside.

I fluctuated between being giddy about legalizing our love in only a few hours and being worried that our photographer would leave when we didn't show up on time; it was now only five minutes until our two o'clock photo shoot was to begin. We were several miles from the plantation and would be at least thirty minutes late. I tried not to think about it, something that was easy to do once I had an audience of locals and tourists eyeballing me. A three-year-old girl caught sight of me and started tugging at her dad's shorts, jumping up and down, shouting, "Cinderella! Cinderella!" Her dad shyly grinned at me. I smiled back. The girl's unflappable jubilations had aroused the curiosity of a sinewy runner, who almost tripped when he saw me, and a middle-aged woman on a shopping spree who shouted, "Congratulations!" from beneath her floppy straw hat. It was all very surreal. I was in a spotlight, under direct two o'clock sun, in an open-air Jeep, wearing a dress so brilliantly white, it deflected the sun's rays for fifteen miles. I had on a veil, I was wearing vintage gloves, and I was suspiciously alone in a gray parking lot in a shopping center.

To make myself look natural, I pulled out the guidebook we had stashed in the door and pretended I was reading a suspenseful novel. I ignored the whispers and stares from the busy sidewalk. I tried not to look up; then suddenly, something caught my eye: A tall figure in black came running out of a store as if he had just stolen something. His brown hair was pulled into a small ponytail; he was carrying a large paper gift bag (cash register money, perhaps?), and he was wearing a very expensive black suit. No, wait: tuxedo. As the man landed in my Jeep in a single bound, I was still in a state of disbelief. Finally, before me, was Jamie in a tux, a sight I thought I'd never get to see. The stunning suit was an amazing fit, a modern, hip style; the fabric was a wool blend, and the jacket, vest, *and* pants matched, everything perfectly proportioned. And best of all, he actually did look like a model in the magazines. "Holy shit!" was all I could say.

I returned to my air raid position as Jamie sped off. With my right cheek once again pressed against my knees and the wind blowing like crazy, I yelled, "So tell me what happened! Was the same lady there? Did she have to adjust anything?"

"Everything was totally straight," he yelled over the wind. "But I think I scared her."

"Who?"

"The lady. She showed me to a dressing room, figuring I'd just wear the thing out, you know? I was going so fast, I didn't bother to close the door, and then I realized that I didn't have any underwear on 'cause, you know, I was wearing my swim trunks, so why the hell would I wear underwear? I let my boys hang loose until I got the tuxedo pants all the way on."

"That's gross!"

"And *then,* I forgot that you're supposed to wear nice shoes, and I didn't bring any socks, so when she handed me the shoes, I just put them on. I have no idea what kind of nasty fungus may be living in these shoes, but maybe she had an idea because she really wrinkled up her nose like she was smelling shit!"

"Or maybe she was still thinking about your sac!"

Thirty minutes late, we came to a screeching stop at the sugarcane plantation. Identified by the huge camera hanging from his neck, Hans was still there, patiently waiting under a banana palm. The grounds were lush and expansive, absolutely perfect for our photos. Grassy lawns, various palm trees, and bright flowering plants surrounded the Tudor-style mansion; beyond were fields of sugarcane as far as we could see. We hopped out of the Jeep and admired each other next to a row of magenta ginger plants.

"I can't believe we almost didn't make it," I said, wrapping my arm around him.

"You didn't have to worry," he said calmly, reaching into the car. "If this tux hadn't worked, I was gonna put my trunks back on." He patted the gift bag and smiled, "I bought you a bikini just in case."

Bridal Porn

CAREN GUSSOFF

ᴏ— THESE DAYS, I KEEP SECRETS.

Like, I can spend two or three hours online—at work, mind you—browsing photos of candles.

Candles.

Click, click, click, I'm mesmerized. It's like porn. Candle porn. I've become a completely batshit bride.

No one expected any of this, least of all me. I am pretty typical of my tattooed, pierced, urban, overeducated, underemployed, postmodern demographic. I held a long-standing and deep-seated mistrust of matrimony. My parents were obviously and profoundly unhappy together. My friends and I were the children of weekend custody and house-key necklaces. When I was little, I didn't play bride or dress-up—my Barbies' faces were often painted with Magic Marker to look like busty Mexican wrestlers, and I had an Indiana Jones costume. In college, I filled my elective credits with courses taught by radical feminists. I read gender theory. Marriage was a tool of the patriarchy, its origins firmly rooted in ensuring the orderly and contractual exchange of goods and services. The whole modern wedding industry existed in symphonic partnership with the weight-loss industry, women's beauty magazines, and the cult of celebrity all sucking away money, time, thought, and any shred of self-esteem from women. I tried to live an unconventional life, moving from city to city, picking up college degrees, writing gigs, and dot-com contract work. I dabbled in uncommon hobbies like burlesque dancing and fetish modeling. I wouldn't get tied down, and anyway, if it ever got to the point where I found someone I wanted to pledge myself to, I certainly wouldn't need a stinking piece of paper to prove my love and commitment. And so forth.

And now, I can spend hours looking at candles, thinking about candles, and don't get me started talking about candles. A few weeks ago, my favorite barista at my favorite coffee shop made the grievous error of asking what I was planning for reception decorations. I immediately launched into a fifteen-minute diatribe, outlining in explicit detail the various virtues and drawbacks of pillar versus taper candles—a subject I never dreamed I'd care so very deeply about.

Days later I realized that suddenly this super-nice woman, her eyes filling with pity and fear, avoids me as if I were a carrier of SARS.

I'd never even gotten around to introducing tea lights into the discussion.

After Baristagate, I began to notice that even loved ones directly involved in my wedding had event-planning saturation levels way lower than mine. I have Tour de France endurance when it comes to comparing fondant to ganache. But even Chris, my husband-elect (I can't say "fiancé" unless I slip into a silk kimono and wave a cigarette holder), would start watching a spot on the wall somewhere over my shoulders after a maximum of twenty minutes debating guest lists and potential ceremony readings—and he really *is* interested and involved with the planning. My maid of honor could brave ten to fifteen minutes of wedding chatter before she tuned out, her eyes turning glassy like a glue addict, and then she'd be off to her happy place.

I care really deeply—agonizingly so—about candles. And place cards. And ring pillows. So, I keep secrets. No one else cares nearly as much . . . unless of course, they are or have, at some point, been a batshit bride. Then I get the nod, the secret handshake known only to others of this cabal (of which none of us are entirely sure how we became members; but, as they say, not knowing how you got into space makes you no less an astronaut). Among ourselves, we trade knowing glances, business cards, good deals, and post obsessively on wedding website message boards (of which there are no fewer than a bazillion).

Online I'm obsessed, but here in the flesh, I keep secrets. When people ask, I keep my answers to a practiced few sentences. "It's going great," I say. "Really excited. Lots to do." They look relieved, really. And I go back to jotting reception playlists and drafting vows. I use the pocket Moleskine notebook I bought to use as my fiction notebook.

By being slightly surreptitious, I can pretend I still participate in the rest of my life. I'm a bit embarrassed by it all—humbled and discomfited and knowingly self-engrossed, reminiscent of when I first grew breasts.

If you'd told me two years ago that I'd be a bride-to-be by choice, I'd have said that joke wasn't funny. Older people occasionally insisted that I would change my mind when I met the right person. I sneered, in my snotty/punk rock/bohemian/cosmopolitan/master's-degreed way.

Then I met Christopher.

He was my best friend's ex-boyfriend's best friend. My best friend and I ran into him at an eighties night at the local gay club. She drank too many $2 doubles and started throwing up under the table. He drove us home.

He was funny and cute. Totally not my type. For the next few weeks, he made a point of showing up where he knew I'd be. At another club one night, aggressively drunk and poetic, I informed him I was through with dating. I waved my arms around. I told him anyone I dated somehow turned out to be a "doorknob." He asked me out anyway, and when he picked me up, he presented me with a beautifully wrapped and beribboned gift box containing a brass doorknob that he'd carefully doodled with a Sharpie caricature of his face.

True love muddles and dilutes convictions. A few months later, we were sitting in the front seat of his car, drinking Slurpees and watching the early September sun sink behind the Seattle skyline. He gave me a perfect "in"—I don't remember the beginning of the conversation, but I was probably recounting some anecdote from my "wild" youth, possibly involving hot tubs or demonstrating against labor inequality or maybe being in a bar fight—and he informed me that nothing I could ever do would surprise him. It was that moment when I pulled out two matching silver bands and asked him if he'd be my husband.

We were getting married. I wanted to marry him. It felt logical. I couldn't explain it any other way. I wanted a piece of paper that bound us together. Marriage had never seemed possible not because of marriage itself (no matter what I claimed), but because I had never been able to imagine anyone I would deem worth marrying. And when I did find someone, I immediately craved some sort of ritual, needed it in a visceral way. To call Chris my "boyfriend" lumped him in with all my doorknobs. He was so completely different.

I'm not sure how we decided to throw a wedding, though. We talked briefly about Vegas (too predictable), Reno (too depressing), and eloping to Europe (too expensive) or the Caribbean (too sunny), or even just going to a justice of the peace (too shotgun). Then we flippantly decided we'd just throw a big, fun party where our friends and family could celebrate with us. There'd be cake. It'd be fun.

The hubris.

I told our families, "No white dress." I said, "No registries or bouquet-toss or fancy invitations." I said, "Maybe we'll do a potluck and have a friend's band play."

I said a lot of things.

I thought I had a strong sense of what I wanted. What I didn't know about who I would become through the process could have filled a reception hall.

I think it must have begun with the bridal show. The Seattle Wedding Show is held in the cavernous Washington State Convention & Trade Center. I attended as a guest of my future mother-in-law, Molly, a travel agent whose business relies on a healthy honeymoon market, so she works a table at the show each year. Thousands of neurotic brides attend, flanked by minions of high-strung mothers and hapless bridesmaids, along with an occasional unlucky, unhappy-looking groom. It's a zoo of vendors with distinct agendas. They want (1) to convince you that their product and/or service is absolutely vital to any successful wedding day, and (2) to harvest as many names and numbers as they can via sweepstakes entry forms. Except no one ever wins. I mean, I didn't, and I filled out so many that at some point the law of averages had to be called into effect.

At the Seattle Wedding Show, I fielded a lot of stares, because I'd dressed for the occasion in a black, pleated miniskirt, a T-shirt with a skull and crossbones, leg warmers, and platform boots. Vendors seemed less interested in me than in other future brides. The only exception to the vendor rule was the string quartet that occupied a booth near Molly's. Grinning, they would break from "Te Deum" and "Jesu, Joy of Man's Desiring" into Black Sabbath's "Iron Man" and a strange Sex Pistols medley when I passed by.

I clomped from table to table, dutifully collected brochures in my complimentary tote bag, and cobbled together a huge lunch of catering samples and a thousand teeny pieces of cake. I watched ten minutes of the fashion show, a loud affair where the models in voluminous dresses shuffled uncomfortably up and down the stage, as male models in tuxedos gyrated around them and announcers barked out designers and numbers. It was horrible. I eventually escaped back into the exhibition hall and managed to get lost . . . in the curtained-off dress room.

Any bridal show worth its salt has a dress room. It's usually the biggest draw, chockablock with brides tearing up the piles of samples, sales, and specially priced gowns, looking for a dream and a deal. Because of the fashion show, the room was completely empty. I figured that since I was already there it couldn't hurt to just take a peek. Besides, I almost considered it my anthropological duty.

Hubris.

I pushed around in the racks, fingered a few of the dresses, the satin deathly cold to the touch and ethereally white. White everywhere. It was heady, creepy, disorienting; dresses were virtually swollen with tulle and trains, sagging with beaded trims and lace and appliqués and rosettes. There was a smell I couldn't quite place. I stopped for a second, holding one particularly puffy number with a bustled train when a saleswoman surfaced from under some crinolines.

"Would you like to try something on?" she asked. Her voice was bright.

I dropped my hands and shoved them in the waistband of my skirt. "No, thanks. Just looking."

"That one's a real beauty," she said. She moved closer to me. Closer. "You won't find any better deals." Closer. "These are specially priced for the show."

"No, thanks," I repeated. I smiled. "I'm not going to wear a white dress."

She was undaunted. "We have some in pearl. Or ivory. Some in bone. A few come in cream."

I shook my head. I looked for the exit. "No, I'm going to wear something simpler. Maybe blue. Something I can wear again."

Her face was suddenly serious. She grasped my arm. "What does your mother think?"

I worked hard to stay polite. "My mother passed away a few years ago." I figured the saleswoman would let me pass, give up on me, the poor, orphaned, friendless bride with a skull and crossbones T-shirt.

Instead, she furrowed her brows, held my arm tighter. Her eyes were full of concern, her voice urgent. "Well, even more then," she said. "You don't want your mother looking down on you on the most special day of your life to see you in something . . . *you could wear again.*"

I flinched. I'd joked with my father quite a few times about how different the wedding would turn out if my mother were alive and had her manicured hands in the planning. My mother had been a woman of, well, extravagant tastes. She would have wanted me in an outfit that looked like it was part wrapping paper, part edible.

Something I would never, ever wear again.

The saleswoman saw me pause and sensed an infinitesimally small flicker of weakness. Before I knew it, she had whipped off the dress's matching veil and plopped it on my head. She turned me toward a full-length mirror. "Now, look at that."

I looked at myself. Oy. "No, thanks. I look like . . ." I searched for the right word. "I look like a beekeeper."

She moved like a bird of prey—determined, feigning just enough sadness for me, the poor, motherless, clueless, goth bride, to keep me there until it was time for the kill. "Try it on," she said. She pulled down the puffy strapless number. She led me to the dressing room. I wrestled myself into the thing. I tripped twice walking out to the bank of mirrors.

But the saleswoman shook her head with lively approval. "You look like a princess!" she exclaimed. "A princess."

It was not "my" dress. I wouldn't buy it. It wasn't flattering; it mashed my boobs down, accentuated my linebacker shoulders, and pushed up multiple rolls of back fat, but damn if I didn't *feel* like a princess. The satin warmed to my body and felt luxurious. The beading caught the fluorescent lights. The sheer extravagance of the gown was staggering. I was a fairytale come to frigging life. I was a princess, had been one all along. Years of kissing frogs and I had finally found my prince: not a doorknob, not a boyfriend, but my husband. I hallucinated my mother grinning broadly at me like Obi-Wan Kenobi at the end of *Return of the Jedi*. I was . . . seduced.

And so it began. My metamorphosis. Only I didn't wake up as a giant cockroach. That might have been easier. Instead, I emerged flustered, desperate, and excited—capable of spending hours considering the most granular details of nuptial knickknacks. I emerged almost unrecognizable, even to myself. And, I learned to keep secrets.

Before the candles, there was the dress. I clicked through a thousand galleries of dresses, from used to couture. I drank tea in bridal salons, had a hundred unbecoming snapshots taken of me in a hundred nauseating dresses. I looked at ball gowns, A-lines, sheaths, empire waists, corset backs, mermaid skirts, beaded embroidery, and portrait necklines. There were the matte silk bateau-necked princess styles, the crepe and faille Basque waists, the strapless gabardine wiggle dresses with miles of detachable georgette train. Each one with a higher price point than I'd ever paid for a car and with potentially more complicated inner mechanisms.

But I clicked. *Click, click, click.* I had to find my dress, the one that was me, the most me, the one that was me and that I would never wear again. And the adrenaline, the heat, and the panic when I found "her" ("her" and "she" like I would refer to the car I could have bought with the money I'd spend), and called the one bridal boutique that distributed the designer and was told "she" would take five months to arrive, so given our wedding date, I'd better come in immediately for a fitting and a down payment. How I sent a slightly frantic email to my boss about leaving early that day, and rushed to my car like a woman given bad news, like a woman off to see someone in the emergency room or in the county jail. I drove half-blind and crazy to the salon, located in the middle of our city's most expensive suburb, in order to paw lovingly at the sample dress and wriggle insistently into it, even though it was a bridal size 12 (an 8 in the real world) and barely closed over my boobs and belly (looking for all the world like the bathrobe of a courtesan). "She" really was beautiful, a halter-necked, tea-length wraparound in pearl white, soft satin: simple and elegant and definitely not something I could even dream of wearing again. I could never create another occasion to which "she" would be appropriate to wear. I wrote the check in a haze and then proceeded to sit in the parking lot outside and cry for fifteen good minutes.

After the dress came more crying. Then an obsession with undergarments, strange Band-Aid–colored body shapers. Then centerpieces, and flowers, and then the wedding favors. Attendant gifts. The specific subject of my batshit bride brain changed as I crossed items off my tidy to-do list. We needed cake cutters. Sparkling wine. Aisle runners. Handkerchiefs. Wedding programs. Candles.

The subjects changed, but the crying remained. A strange, hormonal, sentimental, open-mouth crying. I would get some planning done, sign a contract, mail off save-the-date cards, and begin weeping. I'd see a movie with a wedding scene and start carrying on—even if it was a comedy. Chris forbade me from seeing *Wedding Crashers*, which was playing in theaters at the time, and gently pulled *The Wedding Singer, The Wedding Planner, Father of the Bride, The Philadelphia Story,* and even *Oklahoma!* off our Netflix rental queue. One afternoon, I was passing the Episcopalian church three blocks from my dad's apartment just as a ceremony ended and the bride and groom were climbing into their convertible, their guests halfway clogging the street as they cheered and snapped photos. I burst into tears.

I pulled over and wiped my nose and eyes with a crumpled Taco Bell napkin from the floor of my car. *This is getting ridiculous,* I thought to myself. *Why am I so emotional about this?* And I realized then that it *was* emotional. I was the happiest I'd ever been. I'd come so far in my life, and had found one of the things I had been looking for. By choosing to get married, I was somehow becoming a part of history, participating in traditions that long predated me and would continue long after I'm gone. This was a much larger archetypal experience than I had understood at first. I was tied to the generations of women before me who had, for their own reasons, united themselves with another person. Most important, this wedding I was slaving over was not only for Chris and for me, but for all the people who had ever loved and celebrated and suffered with us in the past. I was the happiest I'd ever been *and* the most afraid. I was leaving parts of myself behind, exchanging them to create a new person, a new family, and a new future.

I didn't wake up as a giant cockroach. That probably would have been easier. Instead, I wound up with a whole new self to contend with: a self as assiduous to candles, etiquette, and frills as to Simone de Beauvoir and stompy boots; a self who shockingly and unpredictably began happily chasing, at first chance, the ignis fatuus of a more conventional femininity than she had ever dreamed possible; a self gathering to her breasts all the accoutrements of a life she had always flat out rejected.

I look at this new self and am ashamed—she is a parody of all I had built, pre-Chris. In moments of solitude, the inside of my head swirls with impossible questions. Am I a fake, a betrayer? Am I a feminist, an individualist, an independent gender-neutral renegade only because I had been afraid to fail at traditional womanhood?

With Chris, however, the chorus is quiet, and the new self is here to stay. My lesson is not in how to creatively and continually berate myself for not being a poster feminist, but instead to remember that nothing is ever black and white. I am, no matter how I cluck, blush, or scold myself, ridiculously happy with my new life. I just have to learn to navigate these strange waters . . . just as I am learning there are secrets to keep and secrets to share.

I settle on our centerpieces and candles the same day my dress arrives at the bridal salon. Plain ivory pillar candles. Nothing fancy, but with an elegant narrowing toward the top. I stand them on every free surface in our living room, some across the floor, and hot-glue indigo tulle bows to their centers. As they dry, I slip the dress from its pink plastic bag and put it on. A bit big in the bust and in need of pressing, but perfect. I spin around to make the skirt flare out, and like a fool self-possessed, I don't even hear Chris come in the room.

"Wow," he says. "You look like a princess."

I look at him in horror. "Go away! You aren't supposed to see me."

He smiles. "Beautiful," he says. "You look beautiful."

"Go into the kitchen. It's bad luck," I say.

"Oh, come on," he says. He looks pleased. He looks at me. "Let me see."

I spin around a bit more. I stick my hip out. I clasp my hands and roll my eyes to the ceiling and try to look virtuous.

"It's totally worth it. All this nuttiness," he says. "All been worth it. My beautiful and totally nutty bride."

My cheeks prickle. Beautiful and nutty bride. I jokingly lunge at him, skirt flapping, candles tumbling and rolling. I throw my arms around him. "We're getting married," I say. I playfully bite his neck.

"Hey, now," he says. "Don't we have to address invitations or something? Fold programs? What are you doing?"

"You're volunteering to do wedding stuff?" I ask, holding him tighter.

"Of course," he says. "I want to . . . help."

I bite his neck again and laugh.

"What are you doing?" He laughs. "That tickles."

"I'm," I say, "I'm going for your conjugular."

Our Bright and Shiny Future

LISA TAGGART

◦— ON JANUARY 1, 1998, the day my boyfriend, Jim, proposed to me on a beach just north of the Golden Gate Bridge,
I had lifetime pretax earnings of $133,297.48. (I got my first
of many low-paying jobs scooping ice cream when I was thirteen.) Of this, I had spent $21,799.50 on cutting, dyeing, high-
lighting, perming, straightening, redyeing, and styling my
hair. To put this in perspective, if the government took the
same percentage (16.4) of the GDP and applied it to, say, education, all sixth-grade public school students across America
would be able to point to Tripoli on an unmarked map, identify

the major players and dates of the Modoc War, and have orchestral proficiency on the French horn.

By that day when I pulled Jim up off his knees in the sand and noticed in his hand a shiny thing so sparkly I thought it must be a toy, I'd had permanent waves, body waves, root curls, and multiple home perms; layers, a razor shag, baby bangs, and spikes; copper, platinum, and magenta highlights; chunky streaks and foil dyes. One mad college night, I went from blond, to red, to brunette, to black. Even when I was in graduate school, living on loans and 50-cent tips, I ponied up $140 every six weeks, plus a $25 gratuity, for a cut and color at Happy Heads with Reggie, the best stylist in Iowa City.

Vanity, it goes without saying, costs.

I knew this. But on the beach as I stopped kissing Jim long enough to breathe out, "Yes, yes, absolutely, yes," at that moment, I began growing out my hair.

It was the impulse of a woman obsessed. It goes way back for me. One of my most anguished preteen memories is of waiting for Gene to finish styling my older sister's hair at FastFix, the salon where my mother had been getting her chestnut waves trimmed for as long as I'd been alive.

Gene had already finished cutting my hair. I'd ended up with the usual, the Fat Girl Bob—straight across two inches below the chin, bangs in a line on my forehead, high and short. Everything about the cut was square edged, accentuating the limp, thin lines of my dust-colored hair. The idea, no doubt, was to create a contrast with my perpetually pink, round face. Round plus square might equal those nice oval faces *Seventeen* featured as ideal in its regular quizzes: What's the right makeup for your face? What shape glasses should you wear? What's the right hairdo for chubby, short, flushed preteen girls?

I hated my haircut, as I hated every haircut I'd ever gotten. I hated how I looked, how my T-shirt stretched tight across my stomach but gapped at my flat chest; how the elastic waistband of my bicolored Dolphin shorts dug into my waist; and how my legs stuck to the squished-down brown vinyl seats in the waiting area of Gene's salon. I hated how all of the faces staring back at me from a dozen or more dog-eared fashion magazines were thinner and prettier and more elegant than I would ever be, and atop each one was a thick, silky, fabulous head of hair.

"Here you go, Jennifer," Gene said to my sister, sweeping off the brown plastic cape he'd draped around her shoulders. He shook it out and tossed it onto a neighboring seat. He pressed his thick fingers into my sister's head, burrowing under her auburn mane, and fluffed. She shook her head, slightly, side to side, watching herself in the mirror. The fat curls running vertically down each side of her face, Farrah-style, bounced. They curled a full four inches, outward first then back.

"My goodness," said Gene, "I think you just about have perfect hair."

My sister was in seventh grade at Red Hill Junior High School, wore a C cup, and had danced on the 40-yard line with the Disco Dolls at Shriner Auditorium during halftime in a blue satin jumpsuit with white fringe down either side. She could feather her hair with a flick of her fingers, but usually did so with her green-handled Unbreakable Pocket Comb. What had happened when it was my turn at the genetic dispenser? This is the best I could do: When Jennifer was in a munificent mood, she would agree to heat up her curling iron, put my hair in mini-pigtails (lending me her rainbow-colored rubber bands), and curl the ends—so that when my friends saw, they said, "Just like Mindy." Of *Mork & Mindy*. What can I say? I was a girl of my time. Back then, that comment left me inordinately pleased.

Women who have perfect hair don't have to adhere to the same standards as the rest of us. Eat too much? With some curls around your shoulders, your hips look five pounds lighter. Pimples? An asymmetrical part and layered bangs cover and distract. Feeling short? One word: updo. Just need attention? Shake it out, baby, bring on the hairspray, and go big.

I'd observed. My sister has perfect hair, thick Irish-red waves: She went from disco dancer to high-powered attorney with a beachside house and two beautiful kids. My best friend from high school has perfect hair, long black tresses: Today, she can identify native birds by their song, and juggles kids and a righteous environment-improving job while growing her own organic produce. My roommate from college has perfect hair, maple colored with highlights from competitive swimming: When we went out to dinner to catch up years later, after she'd finished medical school, a diner across the room reacted to his sushi and she managed to save his life before the ambulance came; her new hunky Nordic husband used the distraction to pay our bill.

I'd been surrounded by perfect-hair types all my life. So is it any wonder I was a little fanatical? That I had one ridiculous, vain wish for my wedding—perfect hair for a day. I knew it was as silly as wanting napkins embossed with my fiancé's silhouette or an Eiffel Tower–shaped balloon arch under which to say our vows. But, c'mon, isn't every bride in some way building a fantasy, an alternate universe where her parents get along and the in-laws think she is worthy of their son?

Perfect hair varies from woman to woman, of course. It's not a simple matter of color and style, but depends on more subtle factors— silkiness, the right thickness in relation to head and face, the balance of body and flounce. It adds poise, confidence, and a certain *that's-her* presence in a room. It was, I knew for certain after much trial and error, unattainable for me. Of course, perfect hair isn't everything; I'm all for intellect and wit, responsibility, kindness, and the handiness of the wash-and-wear cut. It was shamefully frivolous for me to fret so about the dead cells sprouting out of my skull. But perfect hair is so attention getting, so confidence building, I was certain it could have gotten me somewhere. Perfect hair was the ultimate enabler.

I wanted to look for a moment like the woman I might have been—if only. If only I'd had the assurance borne of full curls and golden tones. It was a shameful, secret wish, and I spoke it to no one. No one, that is, except Barbara.

I had absolute confidence in Barbara at Hair Heaven. I had discovered her a year before through a friend's recommendation when I was in a lost, trampy phase, without a significant stylist in my life, flitting from salon to salon—even once popping into a discount walk-in chop shop because I was shaggy and desperate and didn't know where else to go.

Barbara changed all that. She had full, copper-colored, shoulder-length layers, made glass jewelry that she also sold at her station, and wore muscle shirts and miniskirts. Her style rose above the dried flower arrangements and teal walls of her salon.

"I just have to laugh at you trying to walk in those," she said to me as I approached her stylist chair. I was wearing my favorite blue linen sundress and new black platform sandals. I'd learned it's important to dress your best on salon day; you don't want your stylist to get the wrong impression and under-do. "We were wearing those so long ago," Barbara said. She was probably approaching fifty, but looked closer to my age.

The stylist-client relationship can take many forms, omnipotent ruler dictating her customer's appearance to simpering servant obeying her queen. Barbara took a bossy, big-sister approach.

"You look great," I said, changing the subject. "Have you lost weight?"

"What, this?" Barbara stepped back, her arms bent at her sides, one hand clutching a round, black-bristled brush. "I've always had this," she said, nodding at the curve of her chest and the cropped top that exposed a tan, flat stomach and pierced belly button. "It comes easily to me."

I was there for my eight-week trim, the penultimate do. It would set the stage for the wedding adjustments six weeks hence, and the morning-of style and spray. It was a crucial moment in the buildup to the Big Day.

Barbara wanted to know what I had in mind. "A sweep up?" I was a bit timid. "Tendrils?" I was imagining something curly and large. I'd spent months growing my hair to give Barbara material to work with. But I had no specifics on how to make my vision a reality. Just as I'd done when my sister was manning the curling iron, I surrendered control.

Barbara nodded along with my thoughts. She reached her hands to my head and twisted my thin muddy tresses. "More curl," Barbara said. She nodded, and spoke softly, as if she were talking just to herself. "Volume in back. Lots of curl on top." She let go of my hair. "And color, definitely more color. Brighter. Streaks here?" She traced lines down my head. Barbara had a vision. She squinted; I saw her mind make itself it up. She snapped her head in a crisp nod. The bridal blueprint had been set. I was in the hands of a professional.

I was happy to let her have her way. Barbara knew what she was doing. I got a nice cut, base color, and some highlights. The right machinations on the wedding day would be transformational. I skipped out of the salon.

We weren't rushing into anything that spring of our engagement. Jim and I had been dating for seven years. We'd been through joblessness and my parents' divorce; a move to the Midwest, Iowa's worst flood, and some shockingly cold winters; graduate school for each of us; and another move, back to California. We were sure of each other. But it was a trying time; we were out of sync. Jim was finishing his first year of teaching English and history at a Catholic middle school. He'd discovered that his role for the eighth grade was not about illuminating the layers of friendship and jealousy in *A Separate Peace* or opening young eyes to the poignancy of *The Autobiography of Miss Jane Pittman*. It was to maintain order, plain and simple. And the job was a daily dose of indignity.

"Don't you think it's funny that you and Ms. Stanford— [Jim's co-homeroom teacher] both drive such big, old station wagons?" asked Jared Naylor in class the day I was plotting my hair triumph with Barbara. Jim and I had moved back to my hometown, but it had changed while we'd been shivering in the Midwest; with the dot-com boom and a Midas-like real estate market, San Anselmo had bounded up the ladder of socioeconomic indicators. And the most aspiring newcomer families sent their kids to Jim to be taught at the second-most-expensive private school in town.

"It's hilarious," Jim agreed. "It's because we're poor."

He was a teacher; I was a waitress. We had a tight differential between rent and income, but we were fine. Yet there was something particularly painful about working so hard while getting paid so little to teach the children of parents who had so much.

Jared spent the afternoon throwing pencils at fellow students while Jim listed on the blackboard significant events in the buildup to the Civil War. When Jim arranged a parent conference (it wasn't the first, nor the second or third or fourth, time Jared had been a problem), the discussion degenerated into a series of "did not"/"did so" accusations—between Jim and Jared's father.

"My son says he didn't throw pencils," the man insisted.

"I *saw* Jared throwing the pencils," Jim said.

"Your back was turned," the father said.

"Out of my peripheral vision."

"My son doesn't lie."

"There were pencils on the floor. They came from somewhere," Jim pointed out. "I'm the *teacher.*"

At this point, the forty-one-year-old investment manager stood and marched out. *"Why,"* he said, exiting, "should I believe *you?"*

While Jim was working early mornings and late nights with the future criminal rich, I waitressed four days a week at Caterina's small Italian café. I didn't make much—$35 a day in tips was standard—but I had little to worry about. Occasionally, my boss's Italian husband would call me a "fooking eediyat" when I messed up an order. But most days I avoided him and enjoyed his wife's calm presence and generosity—meaning, as many free lattes as I could steam and sip.

So I had lots of leisure time for planning the wedding. I tried to involve Jim, but he was, simply, too tired. Especially for false drama. And, like many nuptials, ours was full of it.

"My mom is making us a spice cake," I announced one evening as he walked in the door. I'd been waiting at the dining table, having long ago finished eating while he was held up at a staff meeting.

Jim shrugged his shoulders and set down his overstuffed bag. We lived in a two-room cottage, recently converted from a two-car garage. The chain for the automatic door-opener hung across our bedroom ceiling. "What's spice cake?"

How could I impress upon him the gravity of the situation? "It's awful. I *hate* spice cake."

"So, why is she making it?" He looked at the table of dirty dishes. "Anything left to eat?"

"You would hate it too," I said. "It's totally foofy." From the skillet, I scooped out the remains of the eggplant risotto I'd simmered all evening.

"My mom says spice cake will be something different. That people are tired of white cake at weddings."

Jim ate the rice, scooping it up in large mouthfuls and washing it down with swigs of Budweiser. "If she's making the cake . . ." he started.

"But it's *our* wedding."

"Then tell her to leave out the spice." His eyelids dipped; he was nearly falling asleep at the table.

"How's Jared?" I asked, then immediately regretted it. In the year he'd been teaching, Jim had developed an odd tic, best described as the tension face-lift. Whenever we discussed school, his face would get whiter and the skin around his temples and cheekbones would stretch back, as if someone were trying to gather his ears into a ponytail. Mentioning Jared's name immediately set off the tension face-lift.

"Forget it," I said. "Who cares?"

Jim sighed. "I should prep for tomorrow."

Another night, when I was sure we had a wedding catastrophe

brewing, I met Jim downtown for dinner so he could go back to the classroom afterward to grade papers.

"My dad's girlfriend says she's not coming." I'd waited until after we'd ordered our Margherita pizza so I could get Jim's full attention. "Because it's at my mom's house. She doesn't want to set foot there."

This news from my father that day over the telephone had made me gasp. He'd been with his girlfriend for a number of years. She and I were not close. But not only was he paying for a huge chunk of the wedding, this seemed a "Sophie's choice" challenge of loyalties to me.

Jim sipped his Coke. "Okay," he said. "So that makes, what? Seventy-four people? Is that right?"

"But—"

Moving the wedding was, basically, unfathomable—like relocating your own spleen. But if we didn't, would we forever label my father and his girlfriend as second-tier? Did Jim not care about the convoluted relationship dynamics here? The spider lines of loyalty and financial obligation, the circles of ramifications that would follow us years into our marriage?

He did not. "If she's not going to have fun, she shouldn't come. We'll still have plenty of people to talk to."

The pizza arrived, piled with melted mozzarella and edged with brick-oven black on the crust. He began detaching a slice. "We can't make everyone happy. Why worry about it?"

I had a practice session with Barbara two weeks before the wedding, with a cut, a test updo, and makeup application; Barbara could do it all. She trimmed, she blew dry, she rubbed in gel and spritzed hair-spray. She used her curling iron to make one perfect arced strand of hair dance at the edge of my collarbone.

Barbara pulled out trays of shadow and foundation and lotion. She powdered my face, dusted my eyelids with Chocolate Love, Taupe Whisper, and Aloha Gold, and outlined my lips with Pert Plum. She unclipped the smock and swept it off my shoulders. "Ta da," she said. "You look fabulous."

And I did. I looked two inches taller, thanks to the piled-on-top do. It made my neck look longer, more graceful, my broad shoulders more feminine. I looked skinnier too, thanks to the voluminous shape, the suggestion of curls and body at the back of my head. My new red and gold highlights glimmered, giving my skin a fresh sparkle; the powder and liner added depth to my eyes. I sorta even had cheekbones. Damn it if I didn't look smarter too. Funnier. More capable. *Better.*

"Ohhh," I was captivated by my reflection in the huge mirror. "Thank you. I feel great. This is better than I've ever looked."

Barbara nodded smartly. "No problem, kiddo. And you'll look this good on your wedding day, too."

I paid Barbara a small fortune, tipped her the rest of the balance in my checking account, and drove off to surprise Jim.

It was the last week of school. And Saint Anselm's ended with a bang: parties, concerts, speeches. The night before, they'd had their spring carnival complete with a carousel, the Zipper, cotton candy, and caramel apples. And a student-led theft of the ticket booth, Jim had reported to me that morning with a goodbye kiss. A champion snoozer, I'd absorbed only the faintest of details before nodding off again.

Students, parents, and teachers were pouring out of the church when I drove up that afternoon. Organ music trailed them. Jim was at the base of the steps to the rough-cut stone chapel, talking with the principal and two parents. A young man with shaggy, dark curls, who must have been the couple's son, stood nearby, outside the conversation circle, shifting his weight from foot to foot. I wandered into the sea of people separating me from Jim with the new confidence of a woman with Nice Hair.

I figured my hairdo's presence was all the announcement needed. The parents looked at me with quickly flashed, quickly gone smiles; clearly they were too caught up in some drama with their son to acknowledge my emergence as a swan.

I waited. After a few minutes, I tugged at Jim's arm. What a professional he was; not even this level of beauty could distract him from concern over a young man's future.

"Hi," Jim said, smiling and turning back to the couple. It was a nice-to-see-you, one-sec smile. Not a Oh-My-God-You-Are-Beautiful smile.

I stepped to the side and waited, shifting my weight foot to foot much like the thirteen-year-old a few feet away. I could hear a bit of what the principal was saying. "If Jared writes an apology note . . ." She was a stout woman in a red blazer, and spoke with her hands clasped together in front of her breastbone, like some kind of Zen Catholic. ". . . And returns the money, then he will receive his diploma. But no walking through graduation. And we will discuss summer school."

Aha, the famous Jared. I glared at the little rat. I edged closer to Jim, trying to catch his eye. So the kid stole some cash. So they were graduating kleptos. So his folks were concerned about their child's morality, their own abilities at parenting, and, most especially, what everyone else was going to think about sticky-fingered Jared attending summer school instead of running off to soccer camp. But . . . *what about my hair?*

I could tell the parents were dying to get away from there. The woman had inched over to the road's edge. Her whole body was arched toward their black Lexus. Jim had the tension face-lift going as tight as ever. Finally, after too much more mumbling and negotiating, they shook hands and dispersed.

I batted my eyes. "Hi."

Jim sighed. "That was a long day."

"Yeah." I shook my head side to side. "Notice anything?"

"Oh." He looked at me, then reached out a hand but kept it cupped several inches above my head in the air—as if those swirls of gold and auburn were coils of radiant heat. "You got your hair done."

I waited. "And?"

He looked at me.

"What do you think?"

"It's—" He paused to find the right word. "Big."

"Big?"

He's no dummy. He knew immediately that wasn't right. "I mean nice," he said. "Just bigger than usual."

"Big?"

"It's just so fancy looking." The tension face-lift pulled at the tip of his nose. "Fancy is good. It's big and fancy."

Okay, so he wasn't so good with the adjectives. "I thought we could go out," I tried. I waggled my head. "I got my makeup done too. Don't want to waste looking good, you know . . ."

"Ohh " He dropped his shoulders. "I've got so much to do before the last day of school."

My smoky charcoal liner and taupe and gold powder did a good job of emphasizing the tears rising up in my eyes. I knew I was being selfish and ridiculous but I couldn't stop.

"Fine," I said. "I'll let you finish up here." I stomped off. At the edge of the parking lot, I turned back. I could see him through the clusters of students and parents. "I made an appointment for you with Barbara on Saturday," I yelled. He was sitting on the stone steps, his head resting on his hands, looking defeated.

Saturdays were busy at Caterina's café. I walked home that evening worn out, with a quart of Swiss chard and another of penne with mozzarella and tomatoes. Caterina was generous with the leftovers.

I crossed through the little courtyard we shared with the tenants in the main house, past the fountain, and opened our wood front door. "I brought dinner," I called out.

The fountain murmured.

"Hello?" I called.

Jim came out of the bathroom—the only place we had a mirror—rubbing his forehead.

"How'd it go with Barbara?" I asked. His hands covered the front of his head, but I could see he had a nice trim on the sides. Barbara had told me she'd give him the "handsome groom cut."

"It looks good, I think," I said.

Jim slumped into one of the dining chairs.

"What's wrong?" I asked.

"She tried to sell me products," he said.

"They *always* do that," I told him. He'd never been to a hair salon in his life. He'd gone to a barber shop as a kid; in college, he cut his own hair with a trimmer. The salon style, I'd thought, would be a kind of wedding gift to Jim.

"You don't have to buy it," I said. "You didn't buy products, did you?" I couldn't believe Jim would be suckered into Walnut-Scented Hempseed Oil Volumizer or Ginger Cocoa Soy Silkening Creme; sure, I'd probably at one time or another bought every possible scent and application combination from every hair-product line on the globe. But Jim thought brand-name Q-tips were a personal-care splurge.

"That stuff is totally expensive. But Barbara is persuasive. I'm sorry, I should have warned you."

He didn't say anything.

"We can probably take it back."

"I didn't buy anything." His voice was glum.

"So what's the problem?" I dished the pasta and greens into bowls and stuck them in the microwave.

"She said she had products for me. She was rubbing my head, right here." He patted his crown. "And she said she had special products for me to deal with this." He let his fingers rest on top, where his forehead was steadily creeping across his skull. Though he had surely noticed as well as I had the growing skin-to-hair ratio there, we had never discussed it.

"Oh," I said.

He nodded, his lips pressed together. His ears flared back, the tension face-lift again.

"She said it's too bad I didn't go see her earlier because she really could have made a difference a year ago. She said there are pills you can take. And if treated early, there's a wider variety of products you can use."

I sat down across from him.

"She just kept rubbing my head, talking about products." He shook his head side to side. "Rubbing my head and talking about products. Rubbing my head. Mentioning products. Special products."

"You didn't buy the products?" I asked gently.

"I don't *want* any products," he roared.

We sat at the table and ate. As Jim scooped up the pasta—which was delicious, Caterina really could cook—he kept rubbing the top of his head, lightly, with his fingertips. When he was done eating, he put both hands on the table.

"Does it look bad to you?"

"It looks great," I said. I knew a thing or two about delivering hairdo compliments. I stood up. "Nice and tight on the sides. Very clean on the back of your neck." I was circling him. "That looks super."

"And on top?"

I stood above him. "It looks, it looks good."

"Really?" He raised his eyebrows.

"It looks a little sparse," I admitted.

His eyes went wide. "Sparse?"

It looked, honestly, like a newly seeded soccer field. Just on the first half of his head. That would not be a good thing to say, I thought, right after I said, "It looks like a newly seeded soccer field."

He closed his eyes.

"With more established fields on the side," I went on.

He exhaled; opened his eyes but didn't look at me.

I tried peppy. When I'd complained to my father as a preteen that it was so *unfair* that Jennifer got all the looks in the family, he'd cheerily pointed out that I could beat my sister at arm wrestling. *Every* time. "But it's nice you have this sagital crest." I traced the slight ridge at the very top of his skull, a Cro-Magnon anachronism made all the more visible in recent years. "It looks brutish and manly."

The arm wrestling thing hadn't worked for me either.

We had lots to do in the final week's countdown to the wedding. There were appointments nearly every day, favors to wrap, and lots of last-minute calls from and to guests, my mother, and the caterer. "I've got to go," I yelled to Jim on Tuesday. I was standing in the little alcove that was our kitchen, out front of the closed bathroom door. "I have to meet the caterer."

Jim murmured from inside.

"Do you want to come? I'm tasting the romesco sauce."

"No thanks." I heard water running.

I knocked again. "Can I come in? I want to brush my teeth."

It took a minute. He was flushed. "What are you doing?" I asked.

"Nothing," he said. "Why?"

The next morning I waited at our front door. "Time to go," I called. We were to review our vows with our rabbi; he was unconventional, a former journalist and a hippie, because who else would wed a Catholic and a Jew on a Saturday afternoon? "We're running late."

Jim said something from the bathroom. I went out to the courtyard and sat by the fountain. Fluffy papyrus stalks poked out of the water. Jim emerged a full five minutes later, the front of his head suspiciously shiny. He saw me looking.

"I was trying your hair gel," he confessed. "But it was too sticky so then I had to wash it out."

After my last dinner shift before the wedding, I came home to find the cottage dark. It was late, after eleven. Jim had finished up school and decided, with both reluctance and relief, not to return. His parents were arriving from Connecticut the next day; my grandmother was coming from Michigan. Our windowless bedroom was so black it took a moment to confirm—nobody in the bed. "Jim?" I called.

A line of light peeked out from under the bathroom door.

"Jim?"

He was startled when I pushed the door open. He jumped back, nearly falling off the chair he was standing on, and pulled his hands from his scalp. "You're home early," he said.

I shook my head. "It's 11:30. What are you doing?"

His amber eyes looked side to side; he caught his own reflection in the mirror, then blushed and looked at me. "Nothing."

He had one of my eye shadow compacts in one hand, opened to the small mirror. His other hand held my black comb. "I was just combing my hair."

I nodded. He was standing on a dining room chair in front of the mirror in our bathroom in the middle of the night combing his hair. He towered over me in the hot, tiled room.

"I was just wondering . . ." he said, climbing down. I backed out of the doorway to make room, ". . . if you could see through it when I combed it up."

He sat down in the chair he'd just moved. "The angle of the light," he explained, "seemed better from above." I put some water on for tea. I pulled down two mugs. He fiddled with the edge of the woven place mat on the table. I stood behind him, looking at the closely cropped dark hair on the back of his head.

He sighed and turned around to face me. "Should I buy products?" he asked. "Do you want me to buy products?"

We had two days to go before the wedding, before we would commit our futures to each other in front of our families and all our friends. But I had already given him a part of myself—a bad part. I'd wanted Jim to be involved in wedding planning and had instead taken my life's insecurities and planted them in that thinly covered skull of his.

It was clear I'd be sharing a porch someday with Jim and his shiny, bare sagital crest. *That* I wanted like I wanted nothing else. But who wants to spend her days with a vain neurotic? Jim held up a mirror to my own obsessions, by now totaling more than $22,000 worth, and it wasn't pretty. I had turned him into me, and I wanted to take it back.

Jim was facing a steep cliff, and there was nothing to do but jump. In the last year, he had turned thirty and launched a career only to discover it made him miserable. In thirty-six hours he would pledge to be with one woman for the rest of his life. And now he was having to say goodbye to his hair.

I didn't want a chemically altered husband sprouting hair from his elbows and the bottoms of his feet. We were about to join hands and march off into the future together, so why try to be someone else? The only things ahead of us for sure were aging and changing in hundreds of unknowable ways.

I saw then that I could take my understanding of hair neuroses and use it for a greater good. That maybe all those peroxide nights and sulphur-stink perms had not been in vain, but had brought me to a wise, gentle place where I could help the man I loved.

I tried to put all of my admiration for him and our many shared jokes and gratitude for a million small kindnesses into my voice. I thought of the time he baked a birthday cake for my mother when I'd fallen asleep instead of doing it myself. I thought of how he agreed to move to Iowa with me when neither of us had money or a job, and we had never set foot in the state. I thought of how, when he's spooning up cereal in the mornings, he sometimes forgets himself and hums a happy-eater tune. I tried to sound like I was speaking to the sexiest man in the world because, really, I was. "I don't want you to buy products," I said.

I slept the night before the wedding at my mother's house, in the bedroom I'd had as a teenager. In the morning my sister brought me a Jamba juice and then we headed over to Barbara's. She did everything she'd done before, on our practice day; but she was a little rushed. She had my mom and my sister and my mother-in-law and Jim's aunt on her agenda too. I think she didn't put in as much hairspray. And, honestly, I was a little distracted. My sister whipped out her new cell phone, a tiny little thing made only of wires, unlike anything I'd ever seen before; dialing and popping it into my ear, I pulled out a few strands of Barbara's arrangements. I rushed anxiously back to the house, though everything was on schedule, and the wind in the car tousled my do a little more. Dressing upstairs in my mom's bedroom, I had a beer with my bridesmaids. I smeared my makeup, tangled my bracelet in my curls, and tried to fix it all in a flurry of giddiness. Then when I was helping my mother put the final rose petals on the white cake she'd agreed to make for us (with orange caramel cream between the layers, it was delicious), I knocked off my veil and had to jam it back in to get it to stay.

I walked down a grass aisle in the back yard with my mother on one side of me and my father on the other. Everyone stood and looked at me: There was Mary from grad school—oh hey! And the Shrive, and lifelong friends Marsha and Michael. Caterina was there, in a gray pantsuit, beaming. And Karen, my dad's girlfriend, showed up after all in a pale straw hat.

And then I remembered to look ahead. At the end of the path was

Jim. He had on his new dark suit and a white shirt, cuffed with the ribbon studs it'd been packaged with; we'd forgotten about links. The sun shone down on him, on his lightly flushed face, his beige silk tie, and on the pink skin visible between the dark hairs on the top of his head. We looked at each other. His expression was nervous and full of joy. It was the best moment of a wonderful day.

It never occurred to me, then or during the party afterward, to think about my hair. My crazy obsession, my raison d'être for the previous six months, had flaked away like so much dried-out leave-in conditioner.

Shortly after we got married, Jim and I moved to a new town. We both got new jobs. And Jim shaved his head. The first time we went to visit his parents in Connecticut after that, Jim's mother didn't recognize him getting out of the rental car.

But he has made his peace with it.

And I have made my own, too. Near our new home one day, I stumbled upon a small salon. It had exposed brick walls, a line of five chairs. The owner, James, believes in working within the limits of the raw materials at hand. He insisted on a short cut; he just shook his head at my mention of razor edges or bleach. He produced a high-angle bob with volumizing base layers and talked me into a subtle all-over red. It suits me. I've kept the same style for years.

Now I think back on my time with Barbara, and the many stylists before her, with amazement. And wistfulness. I'm amazed at how lost I was, how willing to try anything in my struggle to find my self. And

I am wistful realizing that no longer do I think anything is possible. Never will I have a blond waist-length shag or a sleek Lucy Liu do. No sassy pink Gwen Stefani for me.

There's no going back. I see this, sitting in my back yard with Jim at our patio table. He sips coffee and reads the newspaper. The sun gleams off his tanned scalp. When he stops to turn the page, he touches my hand and refills both our mugs. And how wonderful it is, I think, to be sure of the choices you've made.

A First-Class Affair

Jennifer Li Shotz

 Barbara wouldn't stop calling. She was relentless. She called from her office and from her cell phone. She called in the evening, in the morning, and sometimes around lunchtime. She called me from the mall, where she was shopping with her daughter. She called from the car, but we got cut off as she drove under a concrete overpass. I was grateful for concrete.

Barbara worked for Entertainment Specialists, a Boston-based company that represents wedding bands. I'd found her number on a wedding-planning website and thought she might be a good place to begin investigating music options for our reception.

My fiancé, Brian, and I were getting married on Cape Cod, where his family lives, but we were planning our wedding from our home in New York City. We had only six months—which in wedding years is like the blink of an eye—and we had to make important choices fast and from a distance. Though deciding to get married in the first place was really the only decision that truly mattered (in a grand scheme sort of way), finding the right band was pretty high on the list if we were bothering to have a wedding at all. No one would ever notice if our napkins weren't just the right shade of red, but everyone—from our parents to the wait staff to my thirteen-year-old cousin, Cory—would suffer if we had a musical misfire.

Brian and I were working hard to have a lovely, festive wedding that had as little to do with banquet halls and unity candles as possible. We were both firmly in our thirties and paying for everything ourselves, so there were no misty-eyed parents dusting off Grandma Esther's crystal vase and insisting we blend sand in it. This was Brian's second wedding (the first had involved a two-hour Catholic Mass, a ten-member wedding party, a very tall tiara, and a not-so-surprising divorce just two years later), and I had extremely divorced parents and no illusions about the correlation between a "perfect" wedding and a strong marriage. Brian is an Irish Italian recovering Catholic, and I am half Chinese, half Eastern European, with a formerly Southern Baptist mother from Mississippi and a Jewish father; needless to say, we were not attached to any particular tradition. Together, we were nonreligious, totally pragmatic, and looking for a good time that reflected the fun we had together—not some wedding-planning book's vision of our Big Day.

So, in modern-day wedding terms, we were going the relatively simple route. We were getting married on a farm by a pond, and the reception would be held in the "dance barn." We had paid as much to rent the entire property for a week (which included a grand old house that slept twenty) as we would have paid a restaurant or other facility for six hours. There would be no wedding party, just our siblings standing up with us. My mother and grandmother would walk me down the aisle, and we didn't dare include the traditional father/daughter dance or my mother might have thrown rice in my father's eyes—except we weren't having any rice throwing, either. The ceremony itself would be short and funny, not too formal, with no staid officiant. Brian's lifelong best friend, a comedy writer, had applied for the one-day authority to marry us, and, for better or worse (and apparently without checking references), the governor of Massachusetts had complied.

We also had strict entertainment parameters: nothing cheesy—if anyone even tapped out the first few notes of "I Will Always Love You," they wouldn't get paid; lots of horns; plenty of R&B classics and jazz standards and no lame contemporary covers; no matching outfits; and absolutely no team dancing by the band. We wanted the music to appeal to every demographic—from the octogenarians on down. And we were firm in our desire for a band. We wanted *real* music. Plus, the last time we'd been to a function with a DJ, there were flashing colored lights and a dance contest.

During our first conversation, Barbara listened patiently as I enumerated our requirements; then she said, "No problem. We've got the best. Why don't you go to our website and see some of our bands. There are song samples and videos there, too. But you'd better hurry—June 14 is right around the corner."

It was true—according to conventional wisdom, we should have had our band booked and the deposit check cashed weeks earlier. The pressure was on.

Though I had introduced myself as Jennifer, Barbara called me Jen as we were saying goodbye, as if we were old pals on the quest for our perfect band together. I took this to be a good sign. She understood me; we were on the same wavelength.

Brian and I logged on to the Entertainment Specialists website, our hopes high. After all, Barbara had said she had the best. "The best," as it turned out, was a long list of bands with names like First Class, Night Rhythm, Moonglow, Rare Form, Mirage, Search Party, Majic, Mystique, Intrigue, Hip Pocket Orchestra, and The Touch— names you would expect to find on knock-off perfumes you can only buy at T.J. Maxx. I tried to keep a straight face and not judge a band by its schlocky name, but I couldn't keep from wondering who could celebrate their lifetime union to the musical stylings of Mystique.

"Maybe," I said to Brian, "Search Party should head out by Moonglow to find Intrigue and Majic at the Mirage."

"If we hired The Touch," he replied, "do you think I'd find them in my Hip Pocket, looking for a little Night Rhythm?"

We clicked on the links to some of the bands. One group, Mirror Image, consisted of a frizzy-haired, middle-aged blond woman flanked by two mustachioed, middle-aged, pale men—both playing keyboard. In their promotional video, the woman stood downstage center, with one man on either side behind her, plunking away on matching Roland Synthesizers (the only musical instruments in sight). I guessed the men were supposed to be mirror images, though they looked more like a kinky electronic love sandwich to me. Other bands, such as Hip Pocket Orchestra, performed flashy synchronized dance moves, with the male vocalist shimmying his hips and flashing a broad smile à la Color Me Badd while the female singer did her best Belinda Carlisle, flipping her head (and hair) from side to side and clapping vigorously.

From what we could tell, most bands in the Entertainment Specialists stable had two vocalists—one male, one female—and one of them (but only one) was almost always black. If the male vocalist was black, the female vocalist was white, and vice versa (in case someone requests "Ebony and Ivory," perhaps?). Each band's song list was practically identical, with a selection of America's most vaunted classics: Bette Midler's "Wind Beneath My Wings," Bonnie Tyler's "Total Eclipse of the Heart," Celine Dion's "Because You Loved Me," Shania Twain's "You're Still the One," The Commodores' "Brick House," Wild Cherry's ubiquitous (and magically race neutral) "Play That Funky Music (White Boy)," and "The Chicken Dance," for which someone had the sense not to claim credit, and which was categorized only as "Ethnic."

Brian and I were speechless. Either these bands were reflective of a subset of our peers that we had never met and would not want to trade iPods with, or the musicians had never looked up from their sequined gowns and polyester tuxes long enough to take stock of the evolution of musical styles over the past two decades. Perhaps the most startling revelation of all, however, was that this kind of star power didn't come cheap—Entertainment Specialists' bands ranged in price from $3,000 to $6,000 for a four-hour gig (overtime could be arranged for an additional fee). If we were going to pay that much, why couldn't we just get Wild Cherry to reunite for a few hours? They could probably use the cash.

Horrified, we did a quick search for other band-booking companies, thinking we would find one with a higher cut of musicians, or at least one with some groups that didn't look like their last gig was my prom. Our horror deepened to terror as we discovered that all the Boston-area companies represented the *same bands*—there was Majic, there was Night Rhythm. We were trapped in a hall of mirrors, the high-pitched squeals of Whitney Houston covers ricocheting off the walls around us.

Barbara, the lean, hungry sound in her voice, called the next day to tell us that First Class was available. "It's amazing," she said. "They're always booked solid, but they had a cancellation. You are so lucky. The lead singer, Concetta, has got an incredible voice. She's so soulful—she can really belt it. She's like Aretha. She can really engage the crowd, get people up dancing."

I told Barbara we would check out First Class. We downloaded the short video of Concetta and her cohorts from the website, thinking maybe we were jumping to conclusions about these bands; maybe some of them really did sound great. We wouldn't mind a little Queen of Soul at our wedding.

The first strains of a ballad began to pipe through our computer speakers. We held our breath. Concetta appeared on our monitor; sure enough, she looked a bit like a young Aretha. We smiled at each other.

Maybe this was the band for us, we said with our eyes. And then she began to sing. Concetta sounded like she was whispering the lyrics to "Because You Loved Me" through a long, narrow plastic tube, and as she sang the first three bars, she stood motionless, her eyes focused closely on a single spot just in front of her microphone. She looked and sounded terrified—like a Star Search contestant performing outside her living room for the first time. We had told Barbara we wanted a lot of horns. Indeed, the horns in First Class were multiple— as many as the synthesizer could simulate all at once. Concetta and the band—all six of them—wore matching gold-embroidered vests, and one fellow strummed passionately on a double-neck guitar, the likes of which I hadn't seen since Def Leppard's '83 "Pyromania Tour." The ballad faded out and the medley continued with Concetta and First Class pouring their hearts into a rousing rendition of Will Smith's "Gettin' Jiggy Wit It," complete with synchronized side-to-side dance steps. They looked like my Uncle Carl learning the Electric Slide at my cousin's bar mitzvah.

When Barbara called the next day, we told her that we didn't think First Class was right for us. We wanted something a little hipper, we said, a little less "wedding band-y."

"Yes, of course," Barbara replied. "Nothing wedding-y. Got it. Let me see who else I can find who's available for your date. June 14 is right around the corner, you know. Most of our bands are booked— it's a miracle that First Class is even available. These guys are huge, you know. But I'll see who else I can find."

The next morning, the phone rang. "Jen, it's Barbara." She had long ago stopped saying "Barbara from Entertainment Specialists."

"Listen, I spoke with Concetta last night and you know, I told her that 'this girl who is getting married is worried that you guys are too wedding-y,' and she just laughed and said, 'Barbara, we play at *colleges!*'" Barbara laughed too.

I tried to interrupt her, but she was on a tear.

"They play at colleges, Jen. These guys are hip! They're great! Why don't you call Concetta and speak with her directly? Why don't you talk to her yourself and she'll tell you what they're capable of."

"Barbara, thank you so much," I said. "But they're really not for us. But thanks for calling."

"Okay, well, I'll let Concetta know you'll think about it. And I'll see who else I can come up with."

The next day, Barbara called to tell us that First Class was going to be snatched up any second by one of the other agents in the office. Brides had been calling by the dozens to book them, but they were fending them off while waiting for our yes or no. We'd been saying no; but, like a bad boyfriend, Barbara didn't seem to like to listen as much as she liked to talk. How, I began to wonder, would we ever break up with her?

Brian and I continued to search for alternatives, trying to track down independent bands and higher-end booking companies, but with no luck. All the wedding bands we found fell into the same category, and we began to wonder if maybe we were the misguided ones. Maybe we were the ones who were trying to buck the system for no good reason, when the system worked for thousands of brides and grooms every weekend around the country. Maybe a little slow dancing to "Lady in Red" really was the recipe for a huge hit of a wedding that everyone would be talking about for years to come. Our desperation was growing.

Two days later, Barbara left another message, this time with a recommendation for a band called Uptown Sound. She told us to check out their website and get back to her ASAP, as they too were going to get "snatched up" any second. When she left messages on our machine, Barbara's voice was mildly plaintive, and she hit a high note at the end of each sentence. Somehow I found this more grating than if she were just plain whiny.

We couldn't turn down any possibility, so we dutifully went to Uptown Sound's website, tried to ignore the photograph of four middle-aged white men forming a half circle around one middle-aged black man (all in matching long-sleeved black shirts, though the black guy wore a leather jacket and shades, to set him apart), and suffered through the band's tinny but heartfelt version of "Disco Inferno," complete with suggestive growls and drum machine. Brian put his head in his hands. I turned away from the screen, like I did when we watched reality TV.

I did not call Barbara back after this recommendation. But like clockwork, she called again the next day, leaving a message to ask if I'd had the chance to check out the site. She also slipped in the suggestion that if we didn't like Uptown Sound, First Class was still available. Funny, since all those brides had been clamoring for First Class for close to a week.

We listened to Barbara's message, and almost before she was through talking, Brian hit DELETE. We just couldn't do it. We just couldn't stomach one of Barbara's bands. This was getting ridiculous—

if we were going to have the kind of marriage we wanted, then surely we could manage to have the kind of wedding we wanted.

We had to take matters into our own hands. I sat at the keyboard while Brian paced the room behind me. He shouted out keywords and I typed quickly, punching in as many phrases as we could think of to describe what we wanted—"funk," "blues," "soul," "horns," "drummer," "club," "bar," "dance," you name it. In an inspired moment, we decided there was one crucial word we would leave out: "wedding." Sure enough, that did the trick. Within hours, we found them—the Evan Goodrow Band, a funk, blues, and soul group with five great musicians and a male and female vocalist. Evan Goodrow is a formally trained jazz and blues guitar player. He writes his own music, but the band's song list is also filled with Al Green, Stevie Wonder, BB King, Marvin Gaye, James Brown, and Otis Redding numbers; they play Duke Ellington, Cole Porter, Glenn Miller, and even Rodgers and Hart songs. The band looks cool. Their outfits don't match. They don't have a single Mariah Carey song on their playlist. They cost less than the cheapest one-man band Barbara could ever drum up. And Holly, the woman who booked them for us, dropped us an occasional email, called once or twice, and understood that we wanted real horns that require actual musicians to blow into them.

The thing is, Holly is the exception. Barbara isn't alone out there. There are dozens of companies just like Entertainment Specialists that specialize in peddling the schmaltziest crap known to mankind to "dozens of brides" just like me. But perhaps the worst part is that *someone must be buying it.* Someone must be getting strong-armed into booking these bands, someone is being bullied into believing that this is what they're supposed to want, just like we almost did. Someone is shaking a groove thang to the Night Rhythms of the world into the wee hours in the hotel function room of their wedding dreams—or there would be no Barbara and there would be no First Class. There are a whole lot of Barbaras in the wedding industry selling you on the idea that your wedding should be *just like this,* and bucking the rules is a scary row to hoe. But I know there are plenty of other couples out there *just like us* who want to do something a little different, a little nicer, a little more contemporary. Why celebrate your specific love with the most generic wedding possible?

We waited until the weekend to call Barbara back, so we could leave a polite—and final—thanks-but-no-thanks message on her office voice mail. I tried to sound friendly but firm, and I felt relieved when I hung up the phone. Maybe, I thought as Brian high-fived me and I smiled back, it was possible that Barbara was right: Maybe we should have jumped at the chance to snatch up First Class. Maybe First Class was the Frank Sinatra of wedding bands, and maybe—like hippies passing on tickets to Woodstock—we were fools to let them slip through our snobbish fingers. We would never know.

Barbara would call again—that we were sure of. But we would keep screening our calls, just in case she didn't get the message.

Shotgun Wedding

SOPHIA RADAY

⌒ I LIKED THE IDEA of going out with a cop. Liberal Girl infiltrates the Establishment. I enjoyed the way Barrett called me "ma'am," the small gifts or flowers he always arrived with, and the secret knowledge of the handgun on his hip. Barrett was fun to date, but it was nothing serious. I took him to the Boys Choir of Harlem. He took me shooting. I figured it'd be over in a few months.

It used to amuse me to imagine us getting married. I pictured the assembly—blue-uniformed policemen on the groom's side, barefoot, tie-dyed flower children on the bride's. Maybe the flower children would carry signs, MAKE LOVE NOT WAR, and maybe the policemen would too, something like MAKE LOVE *AND* WAR.

A few months passed and we were still together. Friends became worried—was this getting serious? My housemate, Jamie, worried the most. We had met in college, and she had shared my Berkeley cottage for nearly three years. We always said that when I found the right guy, and she found the right gal, we would all live together. She wanted to build a solar cabin somewhere off the grid. I was hoping for a rambling house with a view in the Berkeley hills.

At first Jamie got a kick out of me dating a cop. We played Barrett's early phone messages over and over, trying to capture the authoritative voice and the police lingo. She liked to ask, "Is Mr. B-Bravo, A-Alpha, R-Romeo coming over tonight?" The whole thing was a lark, something to laugh about. Until I found myself crying. There I was—a lover of Gandhi, a former activist, a feminist—falling for a soldier, a policeman, a Republican. I didn't see how it could possibly work out. Jamie cried too, because what if it did?

Before dating Barrett, I liked to wear a button that said BAD COP, NO DONUT. Once I'd climbed over the barbed-wire fence at Moffett Naval Air Station to spray paint WORK FOR PEACE under the BE ALL YOU CAN BE slogan on a recruiting billboard. In college I was a peace activist, a follower of the principles of nonviolence, and someone who really believed Mondale had a chance in 1984. After getting my master's in public policy, I trained low-income women to start businesses and oversaw loans for development in poor communities.

I loved to garden, go to poetry readings, and eat salads of assorted organic heirloom tomatoes with fine balsamic vinegar. I wore hemp and had been known to smoke its cousin. On my nightstand were Anne Carson's *The Beauty of the Husband, Fine Gardening,* and a book of Sappho's poetry.

Barrett subscribed to a magazine about wound ballistics. He had his hair cut at least once every two weeks, "high and tight." When his haircut particularly pleased him, he'd exhort me to feel the needle points of his scalp, rolling his head around in my hand and crowing, "I had them use the number 1 blade!" He wore pants with cargo pockets, exclusively, long before they were fashionable.

Barrett believed in always being prepared to defend oneself. (Hence the bulletproof vest and gas mask tucked under the beach toys in my trunk.) He was the lead firearms instructor at a major metropolitan police department, where he was also on the SWAT team. He was a lieutenant colonel in the Army Reserve. He knew what Numbers 1 through 5 were at McDonald's, Wendy's, and Burger King, in addition to which were best for eating while driving, and which were best for carrying if you were ordering for you and your coworkers. On his nightstand were Theodore Roosevelt's *Outdoor Pastimes of an American Hunter, American Rifleman,* and four alarm clocks.

I can't tell you any specific moment when I started thinking more seriously about Barrett. There was the time I called him crying, because I saw a dead dog on the side of the highway. I knew that a random dead dog didn't mean squat to him. In fact, he'd had to shoot several himself. But I needed to talk to someone, and I needed to talk right then. He was on duty, and I heard the crackle of the police radio in the background. I felt stupid for bothering him at work. And then I heard his voice, clear through the static. He said simply, "I'm pulling over."

There was the time, one of many, when I decided to break up with him. I asked him to meet me at a waterfront park on a sunny afternoon. We sat together on a concrete bench, my bare leg touching his cargo pants. Through tears I delivered the message Jamie had helped me prepare: What we were doing was a waste of time; we should get the breakup over with; it would never work. He held my hand and listened. I talked and talked in circles. You and I have nothing in common. We don't believe in the same things. We aren't interested in the same things. People who are meant to be together shouldn't have doubts like this.

Then we just sat a good while holding hands. I started to feel the pebbles in the bench making indents in my thighs.

Finally he said, "So, are we breaking up?"

"Don't you think we should?" I said.

He replied, "I don't care if you like the same things I do, or think the same way I do. I like being with you."

What tempestuous heart could resist such calm?

Over the next year or so, we settled into a routine. Barrett would arrive at my place in the early afternoon of his day off, and we'd retire directly to the bedroom. For dinner we'd order in Thai or Chinese, right around the time Jamie would get home from work. She'd notice his Blazer out front, and walk in with her hands in the air, yelling, "Hold your fire!" Then she would scrunch up her nose at the smell of Barrett's mu shu pork and mutter something about dead animals.

Barrett tried to be friends with her. He brought her a name tag for her coveralls, let her try on his shoulder holster, asked how often she changed the oil in her truck. But she was still chilly. I remember the day I told Barrett that I planned to always live with Jamie. "So what do you think? Could we get a bigger place and all live together?"

Barrett looked at me. He started to speak, stopped. Then he just started laughing.

"C'mon," I said. "I know it's been a little rocky, but maybe after a little time, I mean, you both like trucks, the outdoors—her dad was in the foreign service like your dad. I mean, really, you have a lot in common."

Barrett said, "Babe, if we were in combat, I'd worry that she was going to shoot me in the back."

In the first year and a half, Barrett and I did the regular steady-couple things: established our favorite restaurants, took care of each other's dogs, saw a couples therapist. After a while, we started getting tired of commuting the forty-five minutes between our houses.

Jamie, in the meantime, got really interested in a local group called Copwatch. They had a website on which they posted pictures of cops accused of brutality. One night Jamie invited me to a girl-band benefit concert for them. I thought about going, but I had a feeling it would piss me off. I tried to explain to Jamie that I understood the police perspective better now, but she got mad. "You just aren't the same person anymore. You've completely changed for some guy!"

"You know," I said, feeling my cheek muscles tense, "you don't even make an effort to understand why I like Barrett. *You're* the one with the whole agenda about who I should be."

"That's not true. I just think you're making a mistake."

"The thing is, as different as Barrett and I are, I still get to be me. *He* doesn't put pressure on me to be anyone else. *You're* the one who's always disappointed."

She shook her head. "I just don't get it. I never will."

"Well, that sucks because I want him to move in."

She exhaled slowly, pushed her chair back and lifted her palms toward me. "Alright, it's your life," she said. "But I'm out."

Barrett moved in with me. Jamie moved into a big rambling house with a view in the Berkeley hills with three other single women and wouldn't return my calls. I lost my best friend. Barrett sold his three-bedroom/two-bath house. I figured we were virtually engaged.

I anticipated he'd pop the question and we'd make it official within a few months. But my August birthday came and went with no proposal. So did our diving vacation to the Bay Islands of Honduras. So did Christmas. And Valentine's Day.

The day after Valentine's Day we were driving to Tahoe. We had lots of time to talk. I asked him as casually as I could, "So . . . how are you feeling about getting married?"

"Getting married? Well . . . I don't know . . . I mean, I'd hate for it not to work out . . . It's a real drag getting a divorce."

I was determined to use the active-listening techniques we learned in therapy. I nodded and rephrased. "So what I'm hearing is that you're nervous because you've been divorced before."

"I mean . . . Not that it's not going well," he said. "It's just that, I guess getting married just gives me the habeas creepus."

"Uh-huh. I understand. Say more about that."

I tried but couldn't keep the tears from sliding out from under my sunglasses.

"Babe, what is it?" he asked, and touched my knee.

"I'm sorry. I know I'm not supposed to react," I snuffled, "but this just so hurts my feelings. This is so unromantic. Why aren't you excited about getting married to me?"

He returned his hands to the ten- and two-o'clock position, but kept glancing over at me, while I sniffed and snorted. Finally he said, "Well, I guess it wouldn't hurt to start looking at rings."

I'd already picked one. In fact I'd had my perfect wedding mapped out since long before I'd ever met Barrett. There would be a long weekend of festivities. There would be moments when we celebrated the children, moments when we remembered the dead. There would be a hip officiant who would weave together varied rituals into a personal and modern ceremony. And naturally, there would be a groom who shared my enthusiasm and vision.

The experts say pick your invitations first. I asked Barrett, "Which do you think is most casual-yet-elegant: the Petras Script or the Fusion Engraved?"

He looked wistful and said, "You know, Walker and his wife eloped."

I said, "Walker? Okay, I know he's your best friend on the force, but are we modeling our life after Walker now? The guy who refers to himself in the third person all the time? Who calls himself 'The Walk-Man'? Who named his own biceps 'The Guns of Walkerone'?"

I started to resent his lack of participation in the wedding-planning frenzy. The level of detail was oppressive. I was shouldering it all.

"I need to talk to you about the wedding," I told him after a long day of trying on dresses in tiny hot rooms with my mother and sister-in-law.

Barrett was doing dry-fire drills with his automatic rifle, dropping to one knee, pulling the butt to his shoulder, and aiming at the kitchen sink. When I spoke, he lowered the nose of the weapon and stood up. "Sure, babe, what's up?"

I exhaled slowly, trying to relieve the pressure in my temples. "The lady at Nordstrom thinks all the bridesmaids' dresses should be the same material or the photos won't look good."

"Don't worry about it. I'm sure she's wrong." Obviously he did not recognize the gravity of this issue.

"No! You're *not* listening! What if she's *not* wrong?"

He shook his head and spoke slowly. "Babe, you have to keep this all under control. Don't you realize that this whole darn wedding is a self-inflicted wound?"

It was hopeless. He would no more join in my tizzy about fonts and matching weaves than I would take an interest in dry-fire drills. I was the one with the long-held wedding vision, not him. I decided not to bog down on details. Plus, his hands-off attitude gave me freedom to do just what I wanted. Or so I thought.

I worked on the ceremony. Ever since attending friends' Jewish ceremony, I'd imagined adopting the ritual they'd had, where the men in the audience sang one melody while the women sang another. I explained to Barrett that the audience became part of the event, that the bittersweet male tenor and the soaring female soprano captured the sacrifice and joy of marriage. It was postmodern, yet ancient and lovely. It was perfect. Barrett said, "Walker will *leave*. He will stand up and walk out."

There was one point we agreed on. We'd have a bagpiper. I loved the drama of it and the way it evoked Barrett's Scottish heritage. He liked it because cops generally have bagpipes at ceremonies, and to him it felt official. One of Barrett's favorite CDs—second only to his military cadences—was the Royal Scots Dragoon Guards. It was his duty to get a recommendation from the Police Officers Association for a good bagpiper. But when he got it, he lost enthusiasm. "Sharon Wright. She lives in Sacramento," he said, looking at the ground.

"She sounds great. So, what's wrong?"

"I know you're not going to like this. But—"

"What?"

He looked up, sheepish yet defiant. "I want a male bagpiper. It's just traditional, and it's what I imagined, and, well, it feels more martial."

Oh great. We're having a martial wedding. Just what I'd always dreamed of.

I'd planned for a celebration at a rustic ranch in the California wine country. Guests would arrive Thursday afternoon and stay through Sunday morning, with the actual wedding on Saturday. One day while driving home from a meeting with the caterer, Barrett said he thought we should provide additional activities for Friday.

"How about sporting clays?" he proposed.

"Sporting who?"

"Sporting clays. It's like skeet shooting. There's a gun club about fifteen minutes away from the ranch."

I noticed he was speaking quickly, and he was bouncing his non-driving hand up and down while counting, "I've got the Benelli, the Remington, the Ithaca, and the Winchester. That's four shotguns. Walker could bring a few, and your brother still has your dad's double-barrel, I'm sure. We could go recon the gun club later today."

There comes a moment in all wedding planning when the bride loses it. That moment when her back is to the wall, and her vision, her dream of perfection, is slipping away.

"There will be no shotguns at my wedding!" I yelled.

He was still leaning forward in his seat, shoulders and eyebrows raised in anticipation, and I watched the eyebrows settle back in his face, watched the shoulders slump.

"Oh right. Of course. Never mind, sweetie. Forget it."

My skull pressed inward. The base of my tongue was suddenly thick. My God, what am I getting myself into? How can I be marrying this person? This warrior?

I should be marrying someone like Mark Burkhardt from college. Although that would've been tough considering I could never get him to actually notice me. He was so cool, with his FREE NELSON MANDELA pin and the ribbon below it that said STOP POLICE BRUTALITY. Once I sidled up to him at a party, saying "Hello, remember me from the Stanford Out of South Africa meeting?"

"Oh yeah, right . . ." he'd said, looking confused. "So . . . done anything political lately?"

How do you answer that? I'd stuttered, crumpled.

Or how about my last boyfriend Nate, the sensitive New Age guy? Why did Nate dump me? Supposedly because I was too tall and my garden was too messy. But surely he'd used "I" messages. He'd been to Lifespring, seen a shaman, drummed naked in the woods, read Robert Bly. Surely he'd said *I feel* you are too tall and *I feel* your garden is too messy.

I noticed a small gold object rolling from side to side in the foot well of Barrett's Blazer when we went around a corner. I picked it up. It was a bullet. A round tin of Skoal slid across the console and came to a rest next to my Grateful Dead bootleg.

"You okay?" Barrett asked, taking my hand.

It was hard whenever I looked at Barrett through someone else's eyes, when I just thought of him as a bunch of labels: cop, gun nut, right-winger. When I imagined him that way, our relationship became something I should be ashamed of, that tarnished my own character. Sometimes I was scared that the Jamie worldview was right, and that I was a fool, a great joke everyone was laughing at.

It was easier when I thought of him and all his individual quirks. Like that he chews tobacco to stay awake on dogwatch. Also that his mom died when he was twelve. That his dad married five times, once to their seventeen-year-old Irish housecleaner. That he joined the army because he needed somewhere to belong, some kind of family.

I turned to Barrett. "You ever heard of Jimmy Cliff?"

He shook his head, so I told him about riding in the back of a police car on my way to the Elmwood county jail in Milpitas, California, after being arrested for protesting Stanford's investments in South Africa. How the police car smelled of stale bodies and cigarettes. About the mosaic of grime in the tan vinyl seat.

"No kiddin'. I'd never set foot in the back seat of my car."

I told Barrett how cold I was, wearing only shorts and a T-shirt. About moving my legs up and down and listening to the sucking sound as the plastic peeled away from my skin. How I learned later that if you think you might get arrested you should have a support team in place, ensure that you are not alone in jail (I was the only woman), and probably cancel your plans for an evening at the theater with your mom (I thought we'd be cited and released).

"Wow," said Barrett after a while, "but I'm confused."

"What about?"

"What's this got to do with Jimmy Smits?"

"Jimmy Cliff."

I told Barrett how I sang Jimmy Cliff's song, "Peace Officer," to the policeman driving me to jail. I told him about wanting to reach out and help the officer rethink his role in an oppressive society. How through the mesh barrier, I could see only the ruff of his blue utility jacket, the pink of his balding pate, and an occasional flash of his glasses in the rearview mirror. I told Barrett about how I realized that the cop was amused and how that really annoyed me.

"So let's hear it," Barrett said.

What the heck. I think it was Adrienne Rich who said, "my heart expands to accommodate my contradictions?" So I sang to a different policeman, this one the man I was going to marry. It made him laugh too, but this time I laughed along.

The mirth loosened the tethers to my wedding vision. Maybe perfection wasn't about capturing exactly what you've always imagined. Maybe perfection could include spontaneity, unexpectedness. Maybe sporting clays were hilarious, memorable, perfect in their own way.

"You know what? Sporting clays will be fine," I said.

Like I'd planned, the wedding was a multiday affair. On Thursday morning Barrett went ahead to the ranch with Walker and his wife. I stayed behind to get a manicure and pedicure. Later, as I drove up alone, each moment felt electric. I turned into the driveway, my tires crunching the gravel. There was no one around. I saw Walker's silver truck, my mom's Audi, numerous rental cars. I looked for Jamie's beat-up Forerunner. No sign of it. I had sent her an invitation with a handwritten note, "Please be a part of this." She hadn't responded. I looked at the little wooden gate that led to the courtyard where forty of my family members and friends were gathering. I hung back, enjoying a final still moment.

The gate creaked when I opened it. My brother and his kids were throwing a beach ball back and forth in the pool. My mom was sitting at a table on the deck with my aunt. A group of women stood in the shadow of the adobe. Standing with her arm around a femmy redhead in strappy sandals was Jamie. She saw me coming and stepped away from the group.

"I'm glad to see you don't have big hair," she said. "I was worried."

I laughed. "I know you were."

"Well," she sighed, scuffing her toe in the dust, "I guess you two really *are* going to stay together."

"That's the idea," I said and hugged her.

That night my women friends sent me into my next phase of life with sage burning, hula dancing, and arm wrestling. The men drank port and smoked cigars by the pool.

The next day—Activity Day—the water went out in most of the cabins. The cops headed out to the Knaack boxes on their trucks for their tools and were surprised to find several women had gotten to their own pipe wrenches first. A four-year-old, mad at his mom, climbed a twenty-foot tree and got stuck. Luckily one of Barrett's guests, the department's hostage negotiator, talked him down.

Despite the variety of activities we offered—wine tasting, bicycling, hiking, massages—the sporting clays were the biggest hit. Barrett and Walker enjoyed themselves, but perhaps not as much as Jamie and my other lesbian friends, who were particularly enamored of yelling "pull" before each shot. At the rehearsal dinner the women jostled one another, trying to demonstrate who had the most badass bruises on her shoulder.

On the day of the wedding I got up early to do sun salutations. Then I was scheduled for a massage. Next: hairdresser, makeup artist, getting dressed. Jamie ran into my husband-to-be about the time I was settling into the hairdresser's chair. She asked him how he was doing. "I've cleaned all the shotguns. I've checked all the fluids in my truck. And it's only noon. I'm ready," he said.

During the ceremony I looked out at the gathered crowd of well-wishers and noticed that many of the audience members—male and female—had the same flattop haircut, the front stuck up with gel. I was reflecting on this when it came time for the exchange of promises.

I said,

Barrett, you are my friend and soon, my husband.
My morning shall dawn because of you.
My feet shall dance because of you.
My dusk falls gently because of you.

And Barrett responded,

Sophia, you are my friend and soon, my wife.
My courage is bolstered because of you.
My toes curl because of you.
And my dog, Oscar, gets fed because of you.

At the very end of the ceremony Barrett and I jumped a broom. This symbolized passing from one phase of life to another and, specifically, crossing the threshold of domesticity. A photo shows me leaping over, both white sandals at least sixteen inches off the ground. Barrett, holding my hand, is crossing with a formal march step.

Barrett had picked the menu for the wedding dinner: prime rib, jambalaya, coleslaw, and corn bread. I'd added a vegetarian alternative, then put Jack Daniel's in the wedding cake as a consolation. When Walker made his best-man toast, he said, "Congratulations Sophia, you have impressed not only The Walk-Man but certainly everyone here with your accomplishment. You found yourself a real man, which ain't easy to do here in California." Barrett's military friends yelled "Hoo-ah." A couple of my friends exchanged the finger-down-the-throat sign.

Aunts, uncles, children, friends waltzed to the zydeco band. Luminarias twinkled, the moon came up. Tattooed former marines danced among tattooed lesbians in the soft midsummer evening.

When we finally crawled into our bed late that night, I told Barrett the memory that was most crystalline. He stood with his two brothers below me on the hillside. The six-foot-three bagpiper in full Scottish dress led them to the ceremony. The music, aching and joyful, was somehow a part of my skin, my cells. My breath caught, and I began my walk toward him.

He kissed me, then whispered, "See, it was good we had a male bagpiper."

I smiled and kissed his prickly head. Then I mumbled sleepily, happily, "Good cop, big donut."

Solid Gold

MIMI TOWLE

⌒ IT'S BEEN TEN YEARS and I wonder if they remember. Does Ellie Bennet know that I was carried out of her wedding after doing a solo performance of the hustle and stealing handfuls of mints from the powder room? Does Lauren Kelly remember that it was I who got tangled up in her wedding dress while she danced with her father?

Unfortunately my true *Solid Gold* moment, when I boogied down at my friend Jane's wedding like some spastic disco queen, can never be forgotten since it remains forever in that historical document known as the wedding video.

But, after my year of celebrating stupidly, I have come to terms with what happened. As part of my personal recovery I now live one-wedding-at-a-time.

I chalk up 1995, my year as the Worst Wedding Guest Ever, to unrealized dreams of stardom, garden-variety insecurity, and an abundance of cool, golden alcoholic beverages. It would be nice to be able to say I was a teenager at the time and use youth as an alibi, but I must admit to pushing thirty like a locomotive. It took me longer than most to understand the concept of personal alcohol limits, so this is where I place the blame. That, and the fear of bad breath. In college I worked for a caterer and learned to be wary of appetizers containing seafood, garlic, or cheese. Later, as a party guest, I passed up halitosis-inducing treats—and instead had a cocktail.

The pioneers of my peer group started to get married when I was in my late twenties. Around this time, I was lucky enough to find Peter, the man who took me for better or worse (and I certainly made sure he saw some worse). Together we explored the world of nuptial events.

We weren't an entirely likely pair. We came from different backgrounds: He was a fifth-generation San Franciscan, with city sophistication. His mother and grandmother instilled in him a sense of decorum as well as a sense of confidence and belonging. I, as Pete likes to say, "grew up on a farm." What he really means is that he thinks I am a bit rough around the edges. As an only child living on a ranch on the Big Island of Hawai'i, I counted among my friends abandoned baby sheep, pigs, and my horses—none of whom challenged my social skills. I won't say my family neglected teaching me manners; but after "Mable, Mable, strong and able, keep your elbows off the table," the lessons were done. Besides, I tell Pete, while he was busy at his Teddy Bear Tea, I was roping cattle. I'd choose my upbringing over his in a heartbeat.

Not surprisingly, he was a few steps ahead of me when it came to wedding etiquette. The first occasion caught me completely off guard. Peter's childhood friend, a girl I'd gone to college with, was throwing an intimate wedding for five hundred in San Francisco. I wasn't invited.

"I'll just go with you, and we can leave early if we're not having fun," I told him. "Then we can stop by Annie's house party. I promised we'd be there." It was a great plan.

Peter took a deep breath. "You don't just show up at someone's wedding. And you don't just leave a sit-down dinner." He got up and pulled the invitation off the refrigerator.

"Easy," I responded. "Just don't go, and we'll both go to Annie's instead."

He spoke slowly. "I've already RSVP'd. I'll call Ellie and see if I can bring you."

Turns out the bride remembered me from our sorority days and graciously gave him the green light to bring me as a last-minute guest. My concern was not over what to wear to the wedding, but what to tell Annie. Since I had promised to help with her party, I feared her wrath if I didn't at least make an appearance. At the time, a postcollegiate house party sounded more happening than a wedding.

But I hadn't imagined such a sumptuous wedding. The ceremony took place in Gothic Grace Cathedral atop Nob Hill, the city's old, elite neighborhood. As we entered the church's marble foyer, I was mesmerized by the thousands of white stargazer lilies, their sweet scent filling the space up to its forty-foot vaulted ceiling. Pete wanted to look at the fountain his Uncle Ed had donated in the garden, but we didn't have time.

"How did Ellie get to have her wedding here?" I asked, as we sidestepped to our seats in a long wooden pew. Pete only shushed me. Soon the ceremony began. When the minister spoke the couple's names, I giggled, "Elinor? I never realized that was her real name." Pete shushed me again. "Don't shush me," I scowled, "I'm just saying . . ." I felt his strong grip on my shoulder.

Afterward, we walked a half block from the church to the hulking Pacific Union Club, past stately structures built for the shipping and railroad barons of the nineteenth century. The tuxedoed and gowned crowd was elegant in a way I'd never encountered before. I was humbled. I realized that I had weaseled my way into this couple's moment. I had crashed their wedding. My only distinction in this endless sea of formal wear was that I was the very last person who'd been invited. That, I supposed, was something.

A string of gardenias swirled around the stair railings at the entrance to the club. I thought about how much just one gardenia cost at the florist near my house. Inside, Pete spun off to the restroom and got swept up in conversation with old friends across the hall. I was left alone. I smiled at a short, stocky girl I recognized from English class a few years back, but she turned away just as I started to say hello. I saw a tall blond woman I thought I knew, but her long legs carried her up the stairs way ahead of me.

"Welcome," said an elderly man in a tux at the top of the stairs. He extended a glistening silver tray. "A glass of champagne?"

"Thank you," I said. I looked him in the eyes with gratitude. I don't usually drink champagne, but I needed something to hold as a prop. Around me, other women gushed over new shoes. I searched for Pete. I kept walking. I sipped my drink. I walked some more; I sipped some more. The elegant flute was my one friend.

I switched to chardonnay at table 24, and was well into my second "Oh please no more refills" glass when I overheard the man across from me on his cell phone (an uncommon device in those days) talking to what must have been the social columnist at the *Chronicle*. "I'm sitting at the table with Bebe Snow wearing Oscar de la Renta, Henry Russell the third, the newlyweds Geoff and Diana Crowley . . . and an unknown."

I didn't look up, but I knew he was talking about me. I turned red; I squirmed. I kept my eyes averted from the others at the table who seemed to be enjoying the game of who's-who-and-what-they're-wearing.

"I'm not wearing Oscar de la Renta," screeched Bebe.

"She only shops at Ross," laughed her date.

I reached for the free-flowing, and might I add lovely, chardonnay. Perhaps this is what sent me to the dance floor. Or maybe it was the growl of The Commodores calling me home.

By the time I was on the edge of the parquet, "She's a brick house" thumped through my veins. "She's the one, the only one . . ." I threw my arms up and sang along. Although I am definitely *not* built like an Amazon, I was mighty, mighty and letting it all hang out. I dropped my left shoulder followed by the right, shimmied and shook. My form-fitting, floor-length gown didn't let me fully express my inner diva (I'd borrowed it from my roommate, without asking, so I didn't want to rip the seams). Nonetheless, I kicked my leg out from the thigh-high slit and waggled my ass for The People. I was finally having fun. I looked around and everyone at the party now seemed a friend. They all *wanted* me to dance for them.

I learned later that Annie's party, the one we missed, suffered from our no-show. She hissed at me a few weeks later, as we taxied from our friend Lauren Kelly's wedding ceremony to the reception hall, "I heard you were quite the dancer at Ellie's."

"I saw an opportunity to burn some calories and I took it," I said. "Again, I'm sorry we didn't come by; you wouldn't have wanted us at your party anyway—I sorta overserved myself."

"Sorta? I heard you were bossing people around on the dance floor."

"Who told you that?" I scoured my list of friends for the likely mole.

I hadn't told Annie that Pete had carried me out of the party over his shoulders like a rag doll. Luckily, he was walking past the bathroom just as I stumbled out with my tiny beaded purse stuffed to overflowing with those big lemon mints. "I love these," I said, before tumbling into his arms, sending the candies skittering across the floor. "Hey, wait," I called in vain. "I wanna dance some more."

I also hadn't told Annie that he'd sat up with me all night as I sobbed and puked, certain that death was imminent.

Maybe it was the memory of that night that got me in trouble later in the evening. Or maybe it was the fact that Pete was really late, and I didn't eat until he showed up. But it was probably because Annie, who had straightened her normally curly hair and was wearing a silvery sheath that made her look like a movie star, rushed out of the cab and into the arms of the short, homely girl from Ellie's wedding, the one who'd refused to say hello to me. "It's so great to see you," cooed shortie; her name was Liesel. The blond with the long legs stood next to her. She, too, knew Annie.

I stood behind them. "Do you know my friend Mimi?" Annie asked, stepping back. Liesel showed off her pedigree with an empty smile.

"Of course, nice to see you. I hope you're going to lead us all in the hustle again?" She exchanged looks with the blond; they both giggled.

I didn't feel the need to respond. I pulled on Annie's arm and marched us away, offering my own stiff smile. "Can you believe the way those two are dressed? Those beaded gowns—it's like they're forty already," I hissed. Annie had no idea that battle lines had been drawn, and she was in my regiment.

The party was at the exclusive Bohemian Club, a San Francisco landmark best known for its summer camps for the nation's rulers and privileged. It's also rumored to be a haven of Republican conspiracy. But inside, decorated for the wedding, the place was a fairytale: pink, yellow, and white poppies covered the ten dozen tables; twirling silk ribbons hung from the ceiling. And I swear there were blue butterflies flitting about on flowered topiaries.

The cake was covered with lavender roses, and what looked to be a vintage pearl necklace draped down the five tiers. The groom's cake was chocolate buttercream and shaved gold, sculpted into the shape of an open book, telling the story of their courtship. I noticed they left out the part when she used to date his roommate.

The room was packed. I scanned for worthy single men for glamorous Annie, but she insisted she wasn't looking tonight. Jane and her new fiancé, Dave, waved us over to a table they had claimed next to the dance floor. Were they taunting me? Annie and I scooted over. "I'll get some pupus; you guys save my seat."

As I stood in line for sushi, Liesel, of all people, sidled up behind me. "Are you going to treat us to some dancing tonight?" she sneered.

Thank goodness Peter showed up. I brought over our sushi. We had a great view of the dance floor. It was a perfect spot for dishing. "Someone please help that poor Liesel—she's embarrassing herself," I whispered loudly to Peter. "I think that's what they call the white girl's overbite."

The waiters refilled our glasses yet again. Liesel finally sat down. And then, Aretha tempted me to the dark side. The wine dissolved my resolve to resist the beat. I couldn't sit any longer. I dragged Annie and Pete out there with me. I nailed my Madonna impression of "Material Girl" (thank god, they didn't play "Like a Virgin"). Once "We Are Family" got into its repetitive chorus, I was riding high.

Then I noticed the bright lights of the video camera. It was a calling

I couldn't ignore. I went toward the light like a moth. My *Flashdance* moment was about to shine. And then, without warning, I was covered in a huge mosquito net, flailing blindly to untangle myself from the flounces that had wrapped themselves around my knees.

Once I got free from Lauren's long veil, and Peter helped the bride's father regain his balance, Peter took me off the dance floor, apologizing to everyone we passed. I later learned that luck was with me that night. Since I came up from behind the bride, I was never captured on film. I've heard it looks like she was being attacked by something just offscreen, and then it goes blank. Like in *The Blair Witch Project*.

Months later, I promised to behave at Jane's wedding. I got a ride there with Annie and her new boyfriend. Peter was going to be late again. He was taking his CFA exam forty miles away, but I figured he would arrive well before dinner.

Annie was concerned.

"I won't try to set you up with anyone," I announced, "if that's what you're worried about." I rearranged my linen dress to prevent wrinkles and watched the rolling golden hills dotted with oak trees rush past my window.

"That's not what's worrying me," Annie said.

I had been playing dumb. "Okay, if you see me getting close to the dance floor, just stop me, please."

"And no tackling the bride?" Annie asked. "Or her father?"

"Definitely no tackling. Of anyone in the bridal party."

I did not want to embarrass myself in front of Jane's family. This was going to be an utterly elegant event, and I was planning on being an utterly gracious guest. The Moores were a perfect family, with four beautiful children, a gorgeous mother who had a quick sense of humor, and a quiet, thoughtful father who ran a publishing company famous for books on interior design, cooking, and gardening. He was also my boss.

I had wanted to work in Mr. Moore's company ever since college, and the fact that Jane was a good friend always made me feel a bit insecure about how I'd landed a job in his marketing department. Did he feel like he had to hire me? But since I hardly saw him at the office, this was my chance to make a good impression on him and his family.

I only had one glass of champagne after the ceremony, held in a private club in a redwood forest. After that, I drank sparkling water and congratulated myself on my maturity. The sun was intense and sent some fairer guests seeking shelter, but I was prepared under the cute hat I had bought for the occasion.

I drifted from group to group smoothly; conversations flowed. I even approached some of the relatives who I sensed felt out of place. I spoke with Aunt Marge about the delightful charms of her nephew, Dave. I spoke with a mechanic from Minnesota about the virtues of Click and Clack, the Tappet Brothers, on NPR—even lying to him about loving the show. I spoke with Jane's mom about how beautiful Jane and her sister looked that day. I was doing great. My skin was clear, my dress fit well with no visible sweat marks, and I was happy.

But the night wore on and Peter didn't show up. It got later, and I was still dateless. I had a glass of wine as I took my seat at dinner. And that was when I noticed an entire table of single men I recognized from the high school I'd attended after my family moved to California. They'd been on the water polo team together and, despite a few extra pounds here and there, they all looked great. How had I not noticed this group earlier?

I prayed they wouldn't notice me. I'd been the girl who showed up at their games. Every game. Eventually, I'd dated a couple of them.

"Mimi, is that you?" said Allen. I could have lied. Or adopted Liesel's blank look. But, instead, I nodded. I smiled big. "Oh my gosh, Allen, it's so great to see you!" I sashayed over to the table. "And Eric. And, Dave, Tyler . . . What a small world."

When I sat back down, I poured myself a fresh glass of wine.

This is when I stopped monitoring my alcohol intake. By the time Pete showed up, exhausted, as we were being served dessert, I was not a sympathetic or supportive girlfriend. I was a drunk girlfriend. I probably forgot to even ask how his test went. I was too far gone. Besides, the toasts had just begun. Jane's adorable younger brother, Paul, took the microphone.

"I would like to refute the rumors," he said. "Despite what my parents might say behind my back, I'm not gay—not that there's a problem with being gay—but I'm not, so please stop setting me up with your sons and brothers."

Everyone laughed, because he was very pretty indeed. There was much speculation as to why he was eternally single.

Over the years I'd known him, I'd always thought Paul was

funny. But tonight up on stage, he had star quality. The crowd loved his speech. They shouted back at him. *How dare these drunkards taunt that sweet boy,* I thought.

Then the dancing began. Jane and Dave had learned the dance Uma Thurman and John Travolta did in *Pulp Fiction* and pulled it off perfectly. I just want to state for the record that *everyone* was motivated by their performance, not just me. As I headed out to the dance floor, I held fast to Pete; I couldn't get into trouble as long as I stuck with him. We started innocently, it seemed. But then the twirling, spinning, and boogying blurred together. The rest of the night passed in a whirlwind of motion.

"That was fun, honey," I collapsed into the passenger seat of Pete's Bronchito. I yawned sloppily. I was weary. I rambled. "You know there were some water polo players there from high school, I should have introduced you . . ."

My mind shut down, maxed out from wine and dance. I slept peacefully on the long drive home—dreaming of my friends Michael, Tina, Elton, and Madonna.

Lying on the couch late the next morning, the sky outside as foggy as my head felt inside, I was grateful to Pete for bringing me a huge bowl of restorative tofu chow fun.

"Uh, that was fun last night," I said. "Wasn't it?"

"Which part was the most fun?" Pete smiled at me. A little smugly.

"The dancing?" I slurped down some food. "I think?"

"Do you remember The Commodores?"

I nodded. The music would take me back. "You were there, right?"

"Until MC Hammer and 'U Can't Touch This.'"

There was something about the way he said *MC Hammer* that made me think I didn't want to know. "When you pulled Paul out onto the dance floor?" he prodded.

It was coming back to me. Slowly.

"Even though he didn't want to go?"

And painfully.

"And wouldn't let him stop?"

I put my fork down.

"Does the term pelvic thrust bring back anything? Dirty dancing?"

The tofu was settling into my stomach like a gut bomb.

"Bump and grind?"

He sighed. "The good news is your water polo friends had already left. Though they were cheering earlier in the night."

I was too humiliated to protest that he seemed to be enjoying himself.

"The bad news is, all your dancing was caught on film."

I went to work on Monday with terror in my heart. I slithered into my cubicle, keeping my head down. I turned on my computer—and was stung by the lack of email support. No *Great seeing you* or *What a great party* notes. I stared at my computer screen.

I heard his footsteps first. They were distinctively self-assured.

"You're quite a dancer," said Mr. Moore.

"Really?"

"You seemed to be enjoying yourself."

I looked up at him. "I hoped nobody noticed," I said. "And if it weren't for that video camera, I'd claim that I wasn't even at the wedding." I breathed out a laugh, as if this were funny.

He raised his eyebrows.

There was no way to talk my way out of this, no one to blame, no bad mixture of cold medicine and liquor, nothing.

"You see there is this thing that happens to me when I'm dancing, I guess I always wanted to be on that show . . . you know, *Solid Gold?*"

I looked for a flicker of recognition, a bit of a smile. But his eyes were cold steel gray.

"I guess it's just something I need to work through," I babbled.

I waited for him to say, "Oh don't worry about it, we were all having fun." But he didn't.

"I don't think people will think Paul is gay anymore," Mr. Moore announced. "Though in the future he may shy away from older women."

Dry humping my boss's son at his daughter's wedding was as low as it got for me. I bottomed out. I realized that I had to grow up and learn from these experiences or else become the joke of every wedding.

So far, so good. In the ten years since, I've been to more than twenty weddings with relative composure. I even recently found myself on the dance floor with an old friend from college in a room full of former classmates (a recipe for disaster). But I stayed in control— not one pelvic thrust.

When it came time for our wedding, I was deep into control mode; I was not going to become Le Freak at my own event. There were plenty of appetizers, forced upon people if necessary—bad breath be damned. The wine and drinks were never refilled automatically. I put bottles of wine on the tables, forcing guests to reach over one another to get more, shaming them into keeping track of how much they were drinking. I had learned my lessons well and I applied them religiously to my own reception. After all, I certainly didn't want some drunken twit ending up on my video.

My Cousins
the Kennedys

Jennifer Ruskin

⌒ Growing up, I was well aware that my brother and I had the misfortune of being cousins of true chosen people. Even today, my mom's brother, Ronnie, and his five children are all tall, good-looking, good-natured, and charismatic. All five are marathon runners; three are triathletes. Two are doctors; the other three are in the family actuary business. All but one live within a couple of miles of one another in their Californian Camelot: Newport Beach. My stepfather calls them the Kennedys. It is sometimes difficult to believe we are related.

The Ruskins are not marathon runners, nor doctors, nor

particularly good-natured. Our side of the family is more of the passionate, moody, intellectual variety. As kids, my brother, Josh, and I resembled Dickensian waifs: tiny, dark, and seemingly undernourished.

At family gatherings, when Josh and I compared ourselves to the Kennedy cousins, the differences were glaring. They were from Southern California, land of leggy blonds and shopping malls. We were from Northern California, home to the Grateful Dead and banana slugs. They were well-off; we were no-brand-name-cereal middle class, products of a teacher mother and social worker father. Our messy house was full of yelling, pot smoking, and heated political discussions. We went to therapy. We ate weird foods like chicken feet and gizzards even though we could afford not to.

The Kennedys were like something out of a magazine. Uncle Ronnie's wife, my lovely Aunt Sandy, was your quintessential shiksa. Their house was a sparkling new ranch-style compound with a glittering pool that seemed to reflect the children and the traits of their pretty, blond, Catholic mother, with her sweet smile and willingness to drive them anywhere and do anything they wanted. Swimming at the Y? Sure. Drive-thru McDonald's? Absolutely. A ride to the mall? You bet. It was like gentile fantasy camp.

Unfortunately, I couldn't even be jealous of these creatures, my cousins, because they were so . . . what do you call it? Nice. While I list all the ways in which we were and are different, I am certain it would never occur to any of them to do the same. They just accepted these small, dark creatures with hand-patched cords as their family and offered us microwave bagels with margarine and cans of Tab cola.

But while the rest of the Newport crowd was postcard-perfect, my uncle seemed a little hard to read. It wasn't just the difficulty of reconciling the stories my mom told me about his hooligan past with the man I associated with handball courts and Good Earth Restaurants, it was because he, like the bookmaking Kobrinskis before him, kept his cards close to his chest. He would never commit to having a strong opinion or feeling much of anything. One of his favorite expressions was "not that I'm judging," as in, "He wanted to go to UC Santa Barbara instead of Harvard, not that I'm judging." My mom, the younger sister, was always seeking her big brother's approval. She would get excited about projects or upcoming trips, but she could never elicit the same enthusiasm from Ronnie.

"We're going to Hawaii for a month!" she would sing.

"Ah," he would answer, distracted. "Have fun."

He was even-keeled and reserved, which seemed foreign and odd in our family. As my mom put it, she could "never get a rise out of him."

His daughter, Joni, however, was like my flaxen-haired, aerobically hardened, outgoing alter ego. She was three years older and was, for many years, my dream girl. She turned me on to The Go-Go's a full two years before they made their way four hundred miles north to the Bay Area. She introduced me to miniskirts and leg warmers and even let me try on her clothes. She had a way of saying my name, "Jennifer," with a slight Valley Girl twang that managed to be both affectionate and teasing. She was the only girl in the Camelot brood, and we acted as surrogate sisters for one another. It was bad enough that I should have one brother—especially one who once infamously told a Johnny-Fucker-Faster joke in front of our grandparents—but she had four of them.

When our family made our twice-a-year pilgrimage to Southern California, Joni and I would pass our time swimming, visiting our grandparents, and shopping at the mall. When we were apart, we wrote each other letters, pining for the time we could once again be together.

When our grandparents died, first our grandfather when I was eight, then our grandmother three years later, the families got together less often. And even though I went south for college, I never saw her. My mom would send me the occasional photo for my album that showed how far apart our lives had drifted. There was Joni in residency in Colorado, wearing her scrubs after she completed her first surgery. There was me, drunk at a San Diego State fraternity party posing with a man wearing muttonchop sideburns and gold medallions and known only as "The Disco Stranger."

I had been invited to two previous Kennedy cousin weddings, but had neither the airfare nor the emotional energy to deal with the anticipated conversations they would require of me. "Yeah, I'm waitressing," I would have to say. "You know, just until I figure out what I want to do. No, I'm not seeing anyone special—though there's this musician I really like. So, anyway, how'd the Boston Marathon go this year? It must be really difficult for you to get away from the ER."

By the time I received Joni's wedding invitation, when I was thirty-two, I hadn't seen my cousins in many years, but I finally felt ready. I had a career as a middle school English teacher, and although I was neither married nor participating in any competitive sports, I was starting to feel more comfortable in my own skin. I was ready to see them and meet their children. A little nostalgic pang flared up; Joni and I had once been so close. I decided I would be there for her. And I was looking forward to a long-overdue family reunion.

My mother and stepfather rented a hotel suite in Irvine, less than five miles from where the wedding was to take place. The details were a bit fuzzy to me. All I knew was that it was taking place on a bay cruise and that the groom was several years younger than Joni. She was an anesthesiologist and he was a technician at the same hospital. Not necessarily a Jewish match made in heaven, not that anyone was judging. I was certainly in no position to judge—I was lucky if the guys I dated had jobs.

Although Joni was following along in the Kobrine (they dropped the "ski" when they dropped the bookmaking business) tradition by not marrying a Jew, she also was distinguishing herself by being the first in at least a generation to have her wedding performed by a rabbi. By my family's standards, this was practically Orthodox. Rabbi Mel was my uncle's closest childhood friend, someone who grew up in the old Boyle Heights neighborhood, knew my grandparents, went to school with Ronnie, and could dance the hora like nobody's business. Although my uncle had been characteristically cool and nonjudgmental when his first three children had married non-Jews, he was clearly thrilled that his only daughter had chosen to be married by a rabbi, even if her husband-to-be was named Shannon.

On the morning of the wedding Uncle Ronnie came over to visit us at our hotel around noon looking glum. The wedding was set for four that afternoon, and there had been a "terrible misunderstanding" between the wedding couple and Mel, he said.

"So what happened?" my mom asked, as she finished applying some blush.

"I'm not sure exactly," Uncle Ronnie said, distractedly rearranging the magazines on the coffee table. "Joni said they reached an impasse. She and Shannon wanted to keep the ceremony short—no more than fifteen minutes—but Mel didn't feel comfortable being limited like that. It all fell apart a few days ago, but they just told me today. The other rabbi wouldn't marry them because Shannon isn't a Jew, and nobody wanted a priest running the show. I'm not sure what they're going to do. I guess they'll just have to be married by the captain of the ship," he said.

I was half listening, half reading my *People* magazine from the other room when I heard my mom say, "Jennifer is a minister. Maybe she could do it."

"Really?" Ronnie asked, with the beginning of what sounded like excitement creeping into his voice. "Do you think she would?"

"Of course she would! She'd be perfect! And I know she'd do anything for Joni."

"I'll call Joni right now!" Ronnie said with more excitement than I'd ever seen him express. It never occurred to either one of them to actually ask me if I wanted to do it.

Strangely, what my mom had said was true; I was an actual minister. For $15 and ten minutes of my time, I had received my "certification" from the Universal Life Church. It had taken me twice as long to sign up for an online Spanish course at the local community college. I had become "ministered" to officiate the ceremony between one of my oldest childhood friends, Sarah, and her betrothed, David. We had spent many hours together writing the vows and planning the ceremony. I had co-officiated with David's nephew, Luke, who was wearing a kilt with Converse sneakers. And then yes, there had been a second time, a fluke really. Sarah and David's neighbors had been rejected by their Christian church because of his prior marriage; but as the Universal Life Church does not judge or condemn, phone calls were made, prices were agreed upon (fifty bucks), and I showed up to link two Christian bikers in holy matrimony. My officiant résumé doubled just like that.

When Ronnie got off the phone, he walked over to me, embracing me awkwardly. "They said they would love it! They would be thrilled if you would perform the ceremony."

I was ready to kill my mom. I had come to Newport ready to be a bit player, a part I felt comfortable with. A cousin at a wedding, who could be less important? Now I would be standing in front of a hundred and fifty people officiating a wedding for a couple I hardly even knew. To further complicate matters, my dress, an A-line, purple, spaghetti-strap thing, now seemed all wrong. There was way too much cleavage going on, for one thing. I'm no prude. Sexy is fine if you're a guest. It just maybe isn't the most appropriate quality in a minister, even one from an online church.

As I got dressed I had the strange sensation of looking into my life as if it were a movie and of not being able to stop what was happening. I had asked Ronnie what they had planned for the ceremony, but he had been characteristically vague. "I'm not sure exactly, I think they printed something off the Internet." It seemed the Internet was proving very useful for this wedding. If the vows were as thoughtful as my ministerial application, we might be in trouble. Still, this was my favorite cousin, my sweet Joni, my one-time surrogate sister, and if she was going to trust me with the job then I would just need to rise to the occasion. I pulled my curly hair into a modest bun and cursed the Ramada Inn for not having a minibar.

We arrived at the dock an hour before the boat was scheduled to leave. I was shuffled off to the bride's room where all Joni's friends were fussing over her, bringing her water, and trying to get her to eat something. She looked beautiful in her wedding dress and very, very thin. "Jennifer, it's so great that you can do the wedding," she said. Her voice was unnaturally high.

"I'm honored," I said, half meaning it. I was honored to be a part of the ceremony, but I was also focused on finding a way to cover my exposed cleavage and stop my palms from sweating. It was less than an hour until the wedding, and I had no idea what I would be saying. "Hey, Joni, does anyone have the vows?"

One of Joni's bridesmaids handed me a short stack of papers on a clipboard. I looked them over with apprehension. The vows were clearly from somewhere like genericweddings.com with blank lines where Joni and Shannon's names should be. There was even a poem in the middle, appropriately titled "Poem," that could have been written by any fourth-grader with a rhyming dictionary. It was a far cry from the carefully crafted personalized vows to which I had grown accustomed during my years as an officiant. But I had an important job to do and it wasn't to grade the creativity of the vows (D-). Truthfully, at this point I was just grateful to have a script to follow.

The wedding guests started boarding the boat, and I caught sight of a few of my other cousins. They all looked fabulously handsome in their matching dark suits and ties. My oldest cousin, David, who never had much to say to me, was sending me his sly easy grin. "Hey Jennifer, I hear you're performing the wedding. That's cool." Another cousin, Steve, gave me a high-five and said, "So, you're a minister." I started to correct him, but I was too thrilled. My Kennedy cousins were flashing me grins and high-fiving me? I had come to Newport as a somewhat estranged family member, and now suddenly I was someone important, holy even. And by a technicality, Uncle Ronnie would still get his wish; Joni would be married by a Jew, even if said Jew was a diminutive, curly-haired cousin from the Universal Life Church showing entirely too much skin.

Just as I was beginning to enjoy my glamorous role as the save-the-day minister, reality started to set in, in the form of Shannon, the groom. This was our first meeting, and no doubt he had heard as little about me as I had of him. But now, he was standing at my side, pestering me for directions. *How should we do this? Where are we going to stand? Who goes first?* I wanted to help. I really did. But didn't he realize that they hadn't actually hired me for this job? Was he hallucinating some sort of rehearsal at which I'd been present? Did he actually think I was a full-time minister? Didn't he know that I hadn't seen any of my cousins for years, and that I just got this gig a couple of hours ago and didn't know anything? Shouldn't he be more, I don't know, *Kennedy*-esque?

As the boat pushed away from the harbor, it dawned on me that it didn't matter whether they had practiced this moment or not. It was their wedding day. They were supposed to be nervous, for god's sake. They were pledging their union until death do they part in front of a hundred and fifty people, and it was too far to swim to shore. I had been behind the scenes at enough weddings; I knew that they could make otherwise-reasonable people more than a little crazy. It was a little like the first day of sixth grade when what was needed was for someone to take charge. Somebody needed to step up to the plate around here. I went into Ms. Ruskin mode.

"Shannon," I said a little too sternly, as if he were one of my students who'd asked what the homework was for the fourth time. "Joni's going to walk down the aisle and stand to my left," I said, motioning to the empty space beside me. "You're going to stand to my right. Then when I say 'Repeat after me,' you're going to repeat exactly what I say. I'm going to give you your line, and then you're going to repeat it. Got it?" Shannon nodded as if he understood, but didn't seem completely convinced. I looked him in the eye and said, "Everything is going to be fine, I promise. You just leave it to me."

It came time for me to march down the aisle. I looked into the crowd of mostly unfamiliar faces, took a deep breath, and wrapped my borrowed gold silk scarf around my shoulders. I assumed my position and clutched my script. I stepped up to the microphone and improvised, "I'm Jennifer, Joni's cousin, and it is my great honor to be here today to perform this ceremony." I scanned the crowd. Their expressions all looked approving, as if this had been planned all along, as if it were the most natural thing in the world that I was in front of them. They were fooled. Good. Using my best teacher voice I mostly stuck to the Internet script until I surreptitiously omitted the dreaded "Poem." At some point during the ceremony, both Shannon and Joni gained back some color in their faces and even started to look like they were enjoying themselves.

And then, in less than ten minutes, it was over. They were married. I walked back down the aisle while my cousins grinned at me, and my mom and stepdad gave me the thumbs-up. Even Rabbi Mel winked. I felt, I don't know . . . triumphant? I had saved the day, and I had done a pretty bang-up job.

I made my way to the bar for a little congratulatory glass of bubbly and found my uncle talking to my mom. He looked at her with tears in his eyes and said, "Just imagine how proud Mom and Dad would be if they were here watching those girls." I felt my throat tighten. I had gotten a rise out of Ronnie. For the first time in my life, on a yacht cruising the bay, watching the sun setting into the ocean, I felt like one of the chosen people.

Later, after the last of the chicken had been eaten, the toasts had been made, and only the diehards were still dancing to "Y.M.C.A." on the tilting parquet, Joni wandered over to me, just the slightest bit tipsy.

"That was great, Jennifer," she said, smiling her Pepsodent smile.

"I had a great time," I said, still drunk with my power to bring the family together. We clinked glasses and drank.

Then Joni looked off into middle distance, a slight puzzle forming between her perfectly arched brows. "I was just wondering one thing."

"Yeah?"

"What happened to the poem?"

The Canadian Question

PATRICIA SMITH

  TYPE THE WORDS "wedding planner" into amazon.com and you can peruse over one thousand books on the topic. Google those same words, and you get more than a million hits. Change it to "wedding etiquette" and you narrow your choices to just over seven hundred thousand. "Wedding websites" brings it back up to two million plus. There is help out there for the bride-to-be, the mother of the bride, the maid of honor, the mother of the groom. There is advice about working out a budget, about choosing the right kind of invitations, about destination weddings, about writing your vows. You can design your cake

---

online, figure out what the bridesmaids should wear, plan your ideal honeymoon. But in none of those books and websites do you find out what to do if real disaster strikes on the day itself. My mother could have used such advice.

"I can't believe it," my mother said after she hung up the phone. It was early on an August morning, the day of my brother's wedding, and it was already steamy. My sister and I sat around the table at my mother's house, the box fan blowing hot air. I'd just driven back to Massachusetts from Middlebury, Vermont, where I was spending the summer studying for my master's degree in French. My younger sister, a recent law school graduate and a bridesmaid in our older brother's wedding, was living at home. The ceremony was scheduled for five o'clock that afternoon, and we all hoped, above everything else, that it would cool down—my sister imagining sweat stains on her bridesmaid's dress and I, the sleek, satin African outfit I bought especially for the wedding and now had to insert myself into. Getting dressed, I could already see, would be like pulling on a wet bathing suit or worse, a sports bra over moist skin.

My mother shook her head. "I can't believe it," she said again. My sister and I waited for her to elaborate. We wondered if the fresh flowers had wilted or the cake was in ruins—perhaps the icing roses wouldn't hold or the whole thing had collapsed into a drippy mess at the bakery. Worse, we thought maybe the fans in the church—St. Mary of the Hills, our hometown parish—weren't working, a possibility we couldn't consider for very long, neither of us able to tolerate the thought of dampened panty hose in a sweltering Catholic Mass. As it was, my sister and I would have been all for postponing the wedding, at least the ceremony part. I'd been back from Senegal for nine months but here I was, sweating like I'd never left.

Who knew what other wedding details might have gone wrong and had our mother pacing the kitchen? We hadn't yet been through my sister's wedding—for which I would be the maid of honor—or my own nontraditional Unitarian Universalist "wedding" to my partner, and so we couldn't yet personally imagine all the *minutiae* one must consider when planning the proverbial Big Day. My mother had fretted about finding the right mother-of-the-groom dress. There might have been some talk about numbers of invitations, some back and forth about who could be invited from each of the families, but my brother and sister-in-law are down-to-earth, easygoing people, so up until that moment there hadn't been much wedding drama. But here it was the Day Of, T minus several hours to departure time for the church. My mother paced. "I don't know what to do," she said. The fan whirred; my sister and I sweated.

"Cousin Aubrey died," my mother said finally. "Over at the hotel. He had a heart attack in his sleep." The two of us sat there, stunned.

Aubrey was one of the Canadians—my mother's cousins who lived in Moncton, New Brunswick, where my grandfather had grown up. Aubrey had driven to Massachusetts with his wife, Rita, and her sister, Anne, and her brother, Edwin, and Edwin's new wife, Marguerite, to attend my brother's wedding. My mother put them up in the Holiday Inn, just next door to the reception site, a ten-minute drive from our house in Milton.

The Canadians had crossed the border several other times to visit us, more frequently in the years when my grandfather was still alive. But their visits always resulted in some kind of disaster. Once, when I was nine or ten, they were accompanied by my grandfather's sister, Cetie, who landed in the hospital after she choked on a chicken bone in my mother's kitchen. A nun, Sister Cetie wore the full habit. I watched in awe as she sat in a captain's chair in my mother's kitchen looking exotic and out of place. I was familiar enough with nuns from having attended catechism, but to have one up close and choking in our kitchen both thrilled and appalled me. For a regular person you could do the Heimlich maneuver, but what did you do for a nun? We brought her to the emergency room where they removed the offending bone and admitted her overnight for observation.

During another visit, when I was just out of college and living in France, Rita, Aubrey, Edwin, and his first wife, Mary, visited my mother, again for a wedding. The night before the ceremony—and just days before my mother was scheduled to fly to France to visit me—somebody burned down our garage with Edwin's prized Ford inside, the trunk full of oranges from their recent trip to Florida. Edwin swore he'd never visit my mother again after that, but here he was for my brother's wedding, and now Aubrey was dead.

No one knew what to do. My mother still had to get her hair done; my sister had to have her picture taken with the other bridesmaids; there were manicures to be had, flowers to pick up; and there was Aubrey, dead at the Holiday Inn. Luckily, Anne worked for Air Canada and was able to make arrangements to fly "the body" (as we were already referring to Aubrey) back to New Brunswick. The staff at the

Holiday Inn graciously offered Rita a new hotel room. But beyond that, we were at a loss. Could you postpone a wedding with mere hours to go? Did you make an announcement during the ceremony? Should we be somber? Wear black ribbons? My mother wondered if she should at least *offer* to postpone, but as soon as she stepped into their new room in the Holiday Inn, the Canadians insisted on attending the wedding.

"Now, we drove all this way," Rita said. "We're coming."

"Are you sure?" my mother asked. "Everyone would understand."

"We drove here for a wedding. We're *coming* to the wedding." Rita was firm. She drew herself up to her full five feet. "Don't say another word about it," she said. And she meant it. Not a word to anyone, she made my mother promise. "And don't you dare tell Kevin and Joanne," Rita warned. "Now shoo. We've got to get ready."

My mother relayed all this to my sister and me later at the house. By then her hair had been styled and her nails painted red. My sister and I were stretched out on our childhood beds, waiting until the last possible moment to put on our clothes.

"Won't people wonder where Aubrey is?" my sister asked. "I mean, he was at the rehearsal dinner last night."

"Just say he's not feeling well," my mother said.

Which was, after all, the truth.

My sister *had* to tell her boyfriend. Tim was driving to the church with us. But first he was meeting us at the house, and the Canadians would be there, too. We couldn't expect Tim to walk into *that* scenario unarmed.

"And they're *coming* to the wedding?" Tim asked when we told him.

"I know," I nodded. "I'm with you on that one."

No one wanted to answer the doorbell when they arrived. None of us wanted to play hostess to our relatives, who, though we knew them well enough, seemed like foreign people to us right then.

"Well, you can't stick Tim in with them alone," my sister warned.

"They're *your* cousins," I said to my mother. "*You* hang out with them." I felt like I was twelve. I felt like I was being asked to socialize with people I didn't especially like, which wasn't the case at all. But what did you *say* to a person whose husband had just *died,* whose brother-in-law's body was en route to being embalmed in Canada while everyone else primped and prepared for the wedding?

I *wanted* to say something about Aubrey. I think we all did. But instead we stood around in the living room—Rita, her white hair stiff with hairspray, in her floral dress and pumps; Edwin, in his dark suit and striped tie; Anne, a younger version of her sister, purse clutched tightly. Only Edwin's wife, Marguerite, looked pale and stricken. This was her first visit to our house, her first time meeting the American cousins. I wondered if she wanted to grab Tim and warn him—*Get out while it's still safe*. You could almost see her thinking: *Run!*

My mother was the second person to let it slip. She *had* to tell her best friend. Who *had* to tell someone else.

"See that woman over there?" My mother's best friend, Mary,

nudged Claire at the reception. Mary couldn't resist, just the way my mother couldn't resist when Mary first approached my mother at the back of the church to compliment her on her dress and to see how she was holding up. "Oh fine," my mother said. "Except you'll never guess what happened this morning . . ." Mary kept the secret through the ceremony and ten minutes into the reception. The receiving line was still snaking its way through the ballroom when Mary pointed out Rita to Claire. "That woman's husband died, just this morning," Mary whispered. "They left him there, at the Holiday Inn." This was technically no longer true, but Mary couldn't resist.

"Couldn't have been a happy marriage," Claire growled in her scratchy smoker's voice, "for her to leave him like that."

Later, when my mother's friends all wondered how big the wedding was, how many people my brother and sister-in-law had to feed at the reception, someone said with authority, "One sixty." Claire jumped in. "Nah," she said. "Only one-fifty-nine."

But the rest of us kept mum. The rest of us kept the Big Secret. We dismissed inquiries about Aubrey—*How sick was he exactly?* We watched in awe as the Canadians, short by one, shuffled along in the receiving line to shake hands with the bride and groom and kiss their cheeks. We bit our tongues when, at the Canadian table, there was, of course, an empty chair and Aubrey's sister-in-law, Anne, of all people, said out loud in her stupor, forgetting completely, "I wonder who couldn't make it?"

Then a certain cousin insisted on walking over to the Holiday Inn and visiting with Aubrey himself. The reception was almost over and the Canadians had gone back to their hotel. By then, only a few people remained dancing, shoeless on the makeshift wooden floor.

"But I just want to *see* him," Danny insisted, waving his glass of bourbon.

"You can't," my mother said.

"Why not?"

"He isn't there."

"Where *is* he?"

"By now, he's back in Canada."

My mother had to confess. She had to tell Danny that Aubrey had died.

"What?" Danny said, the glass of bourbon tipping dangerously.

"I know it," my mother said. "But Rita insisted on coming anyway." They stood there, my mother and her only remaining first cousin, the party winding down behind them.

"He's *dead?*" Danny said. "But he was at your house—he seemed *fine.*"

My mother shrugged. "He died in his sleep. He came all this way, saw all of the family, and then he died. Maybe it was the best thing." You'd think that if Aubrey had any control over it, he would have waited until the wedding was over. But what my mother said was also true—he'd driven to Massachusetts, seen everyone in his family, and then checked out.

It wasn't until we met my brother and sister-in-law at the airport after their honeymoon that we told them what happened.

Back from a week in California, they walked off the plane looking fresh, rested, happy. "So what's new?" they wanted to know. "What did we miss while we were gone?"

"Well," we said, "something happened before you even left." And then we told them the story. We said it the way we still tell it now—laughing at the oddness of it all, shaking our heads at the thought of yet another visit from the Canadians gone terribly wrong. We told them how our mother sighed when she got off the phone, as if the caterer had called with a miscount, but how it had been Rita, and instead of a catering problem, it had been a dead-relative problem. We said it wasn't funny, but somehow it was, and there we were, walking out of Logan Airport, laughing again, all of us.

"You know, during the receiving line, I wondered where Aubrey was," Kevin said afterward. "I sort of noticed he wasn't there." But in the chaos that is a wedding, he wondered only for an instant and then forgot completely.

It didn't occur to me, not at the wedding itself and not there at the airport with my brother—a newlywed, a married man, a husband—what a terrible irony for Rita to lose Aubrey at a wedding, what it must have felt like for her to watch my brother say his vows, her husband of many years dead of a failed heart in the Massachusetts heat.

Just recently, on the phone to my mother, Rita mentioned something about my brother's tenth wedding anniversary. "You've got a good memory," my mother told her, never thinking why it might be that Rita could remember the exact day my brother got married.

My Freckles Are Constellations Above Billowing Clouds of White Satin

ANGIE SUCHY MARSH

   I AM CARVED into my dress like the frosting in peaks and valleys sculpted on our wedding cake, so I nearly taste its buttery feel.

I wrote this line as a joke, to entertain a coworker. August was a particularly slow time in our college communications office near Portland, Oregon, since students, teachers, and most administrators had vacated the campus. This left my coworker JJ, a photographer, and me, a news writer, with lots of downtime in the office. On one extended lunch break, after reading everything in the newspaper from gubernatorial election news to goats-for-sale ads, JJ squealed at the sight of a call

---

for entries in a Harlequin Romance contest. She dared me—dared me—to write an opener for the contest, "Why a Harlequin Wedding Dress Would Make My Wedding Day Special." The prize was both the dress and a honeymoon on Maui.

"Harlequin?" I scoffed.

JJ planted herself in my office guest chair, where she began filing her nails. "So," she said. Never a good beginning. "When are you getting married?"

My boyfriend, Mike, and I had talked of marriage, but it was always something we'd get around to in the future, if at all—much like changing our car's oil. "I can't even commit to a cell phone plan."

JJ fluttered her hands and sighed. Her belief in the "every girl's dream" cultural norm of marriage could not be shaken—nor could her closet addiction to Harlequin Romances. I knew JJ hid them in the depths of her bookshelves; that she could burn through (in more ways than one) a paperback littered with "heaving bosoms," "long embraces," and "quickening pulses" in one sweaty hour. The problem was, JJ was all caught up on her reading; she needed more material. She knew I was a poor prospect; I didn't like to dress up for any occasion and complained each time I wore nylons to work.

That afternoon, the call for submissions, clipped from the paper, appeared in my in-box. WRITE AN ESSAY, WIN A TRIP declared the headline. It sounded so cause-and-effect. A note from JJ was attached: "Just try it—and I'll take you out to lunch in return."

Free lunch? I thought. Even better than a measly dare. I got to work—er, got to messing around at work.

Family and friends can drink in the beauty of the dress, toasting its timeless bell shape.

Ha! I was cracking myself up. I downed four cups of coffee in a half hour. Caffeine and the continuous rotation of Liz Phair's "Polyester Bride" (". . . do you wanna hang your head and die?" she crooned) on my headphones opened tacky gold-embellished doors in my vocabulary that I didn't even know existed. As I typed, my fingers became possessed by a wicked Harlequin tart. Her shtick was that this gown transformed her in both appearance and mental outlook. I was mocking the genre just enough to star in a parody that was believable.

The gown allows me to forget that I prefer pants to dresses, plain to fancy, and helps me remember how satin feels against skin. This is my moment.

In my mind's eye, this imagined dress contained every garish element that kept me from donning a wedding gown—the puffed-up sleeves, the bustier that creates a shelf of cleavage, bejeweled whiteness, the A-line so extreme that the bride could sink to the ground doing splits without anyone realizing.

Jewels of the dress throw starry glimmers, like dozens of photo flashes.

I peppered my essay with as many Harlequinisms as I could eke out. I parlayed my journalism training into romance writing, concentrating on the images and senses within the pages of the grocery store paperbacks of yesteryear.

I feel whole in its elegant short sleeves and the way it dips in front and back, as if the freckles dotting my skin are constellations above billowing clouds of white satin.

At 8:00 AM the next Monday, JJ came into my office, hard copy in one hand, the other hand covering her heart. She inhaled deeply and blurted out, "Ohmygodthisisthebest." To make this a true Harlequin moment, she collapsed, teary-eyed, in the guest chair. Wiping her face, she left a smear of black mascara.

"This is how you picture your wedding?" She wanted to believe.

I snatched the paper from her hand. "It's a parody, JJ. I wrote it as entertainment."

Her sniveling ceased. "It's as good as I've seen," she said, meeting my eye. "This . . . this is *classy* Harlequin." She swept out of the room. I was left to ponder whether I felt complimented or insulted.

She joined forces with the department secretary, and they cornered me in my office at noon.

"That essay of yours is something," Barbara said, leaning over my desk, her eyebrows arched above her glasses for effect. "Even I was moved by it—and I'm no sucker."

"It's time to go out to lunch, my treat as promised," JJ said, rattling her keys, getting on with her mission. JJ didn't deny her suckerdom.

"To the Thai restaurant?" I knew I was pushing my luck, getting them to agree to what they'd previously declared "weird" and "spicy" food.

"Sure—on one condition: You have to mail in your essay," JJ said.

"And waste thirty-seven cents?"

"Listen, the contest has no entry fee and there are all kinds of prizes," she said as she pulled a stamp from her big purse. "Besides, you'll have to eat an iceberg lettuce salad with stale croutons from the cafeteria if you don't."

She knew how to bargain with me.

The entry was mailed. Just the three of us knew. I sank deep into thought: yellow or Panang curry? Noodles or the rice bowl? So much to consider . . .

The only lingering connection I had to the contest was a desire to go to Hawaii. But I would do so on my own terms. That summer I began saving for a week of tropical holiday. All my life, Christmas had been cold and kitschy—all drafty homes and tinsel trees. Thoughts of trading evergreen for palm trees and the blustery gray downpours of the Pacific Northwest for lengthy sunlit Hawaiian skies kept me focused.

In December, we headed to Maui. There we were: my boyfriend and me . . . and my mom, dad, brother, and his girlfriend. No one said it would be a *romantic* trip. Besides, I couldn't really save *that* much on my communications writer's salary—it was a lot easier to pay for lodging with the family splitting the bill. But in the ocean, there was plenty of room for all of us. Though the concept of breathing through a plastic tube while navigating the waves intimidated me, by day four I practically had gills.

On the day before our departure, my boyfriend, Mike, showed me a page he'd dog-eared about a swimming hole in a travel book of "hidden treasures."

"If this is so hidden, how come it's published in a book?"

He shrugged.

My brother wandered over and glanced at the book's photo. "Nice. Can I go?"

Mike was arranging the snorkels into a pack. "Uh . . ." He stopped, straightened up, and looked at me. "I, uh, guess so."

When we began hiking on the ancient lava, my flip-flops rebelled. "Damn pumice," I muttered behind Mike as my plastic footwear slid from formation to formation. It was nearly impossible to keep my footing on the sharp lava in my slip-and-slide sandals. The "path" was a chalk line over coral-like humps.

"This is not what I pictured with the description of a brief hike," I muttered at Mike.

He actually hung his head.

"This adventure seeking is wrecking my feet. And where's the sunscreen?" I pointed at my reddening shoulders.

"Your brother interrupted the packing. Sorry, I forgot."

I wanted to turn around. My feet hurt. But Mike talked me into continuing. We made it to the apt-named Fishbowl. While Mike rummaged through the backpack, I hopped in the water. My brother motioned underwater to a stingray. I popped my head out of the water.

"Mike, check out this ray," I shrieked. He was still digging through that damn pack. My brother pointed at an eel. I called out to Mike, "There's something that looks like a slippery tube sock, too."

About fifteen minutes later, Mike swam over, grabbed my hand, and started pulling me back to shore. He swam fast. I couldn't keep up. We surfaced. I coughed out water. "I'm not coordinated enough to hold your hand *and* keep snorkeling. I'm going back to see that creepy eel."

He followed. He kept trying to grab me. We surfaced. *"What? Are you stalking me?"* I asked, trying to wiggle my eyebrows from beneath the mask.

"You *have* to see something," he said. "Follow me." He dove beneath the surface. I, however, can't dive. I swam above him. He pointed below.

Sunlight caught the glint of a palm-size treasure chest nestled in the sand on the ocean floor.

The dress—in all its glory—will become a backdrop as its illumination spotlights my flushed cheeks, like a moon highlighting a red horizon.

Mike pulled the treasure chest up to the surface, pried it open, and pulled out a ring. "Wa you nabby ne?" he said through his snorkel mouthpiece. I gasped—as a wave broke over me. I sucked down mouthfuls of salty water.

The mask magnified his green eyes, staring large and wide at me. I snorted, coughed, and flinched as I tried to pull off my own mask. Its elastic band was too tangled in my hair. I let it dangle from my head and tried to tread water with some composure.

"Yes." I bobbed, and coughed the word out. I thrashed my arms and legs in the water to stay afloat. Water splashed in my face. "Hell, yes!"

The neon stripes and pink fins swirling around me could as well have been electric currents, I was so shocked. I had a revelation: *He just proposed while I was wearing a bathing suit.* That could be the "Number one sign he loves you" on a tacky women's magazine list.

Just as the eel had simultaneously frightened and awed me, so had this question. Not just any question: *the* question. I was overcome with, well, mouthfuls of saltwater. But I just spit, snorted, and readjusted my mask. As I did so, I readjusted my vision through the mask of my life as well, focusing on myself as a polyester bride of sorts.

Back home I sifted through the accumulated piles of mail and unearthed midstack a FedEx letter addressed to me from Nebraska.

"FedEx sends letters?" I remarked to my now-fiancé. I wondered if it was a new marketing scheme, to send a solicitation in an envelope that looked official and important. I pulled out the letter. "You are a finalist in the Harlequin 'Walk Down the Aisle to Maui' essay contest, 'Why a Harlequin Wedding Dress Would Make My Wedding Day Special.'"

I screamed. It was the sort of scream that's part horror, part elation—like something Phoebe would do on *Friends*.

"You have ten days to respond with a notarized statement that you are the sole, original author of your essay entry. Harlequin requests that you also fill out the attached biography sheet and mail this, along with a current photo of yourself, via this prepaid FedEx system."

By now my fiancé was congratulating himself on popping the question at the perfect time, thereby increasing our chances of heading back to our new favorite island. How was it that I stood here with an engagement ring on my finger and a potential dress and honeymoon in my hand?

I sent Harlequin all my vitals and included a photo my dad took specifically for the occasion. He had offered to help me respond, fearing that I might blow this off and "miss an important opportunity," he explained, naming the website address of the Hawaiian hotel where the winner would stay for free. He'd done some research.

Before coming over for the photo shoot, he'd instructed me to "wear a nice blouse."

"What constitutes a nice blouse?" I'd asked, smiling at his antiquated terminology. "Does it have to be rayon? Should it tie at the neck?"

I figured I should do as Dad said, if only to make him happy. So I found a silk shirt that I'd worn to a wedding and extracted my hair dryer from the bowels of my closet. My hair got big. It looked a full inch shorter due to the newfound body on top of my head. It seemed to have gone into shock. Dad approved. Because my living room window was covered in what looked like plastic wrap to retain heat, he positioned me there for the photo. "We're going for a 'classy but needy' look," he explained, snapping from all angles.

I couldn't conjure up a vision of myself in a wedding dress. That night I dreamed that my mom resurrected my prom dress and re-covered it with white taffeta—much like re-covering a chair—and fastened safety pins to harness the puffy sleeves. In the dream I received a letter from Harlequin stating their approval of this dress, and their requirement that I wear it in my wedding in order to receive a cash prize. I awoke with my arms crossed in front of me and my hands gripping the sides of my arms, leaving nail marks. Wearing a Harlequin dress had become a polyester-bride nightmare.

The drama that was now my life continued when I returned to work. JJ was in my office first thing.

"Soooo, how were the tropics? You didn't miss—is that a *ring?*"

My hands were hovering above my keyboard, my antique ring hugging its new home around my finger.

"Oh, at last!" She grabbed my arm, her eyeball suddenly pressed up against the stone. She squealed.

"I knew Mike would conquer his commitment fears. Hawaii is the perfect place for that," she said.

"*I'm* the commitment-phobe."

"I knew this would happen." And it was almost too much when I told her about the contest. "I knew it! I knew it." She repeated herself like that all day.

She popped into my office hourly to ask about the wedding ceremony, location, flowers, and, most of all, dresses.

A few days later, she came in with a paperback. It said *SuperRomance* across the top. "Look!"

"If you think I'm going to start reading those, let me tell you . . ."

"No, *look*," she commanded.

On the cover the "S" was in loopy large script, like a spazzed-out signature, but the image was a body shot of a woman in a wedding dress gazing off in the distance.

"That dress is uglier than ugly," I said.

It looked like the woman was wearing a flotation device made of shredded toilet tissue around her midsection. And there was a large bow at her back. Below the tissue roll was a shaggy, afghan-esque material that splayed out into a tulip skirt. Above it, the boned, beaded, strapless top was stuck to the model as if it were spray foam. A bird's nest—or what looked like one—sat perched atop the woman's head, with a multitiered veil shooting out from underneath it. The angles made her head appear as if it were lodged in a miniature gazebo. Six white feathers poked out from the nest area. I sensed a theme. The final, wide tier of the veil reached the floor—and trailed slightly behind. To top it off, the woman was wearing gloves up to her armpits.

"You'd better get used to it," JJ said. "That's the dress you'll be wearing if you win."

For once I was speechless. I could not imagine this dress in the flesh—and wearing it? That was, truly, my nightmare. Just what I wanted around my hips—an attention-getting, faux-toilet-tissue life preserver. I could hear the attendees now: *She could float if need be! The safety-first bride!*

"It's not *that* bad," JJ said, and then paused before laughing—and laughing. She caught her breath. "Don't you find feathers inspiring?"

"It's a walking disaster," I said.

And then, smugly, JJ pulled out the contest rules: "The grand prizewinner of the contest will be the first to wear this special gown on her wedding day."

Shortly afterward, I heard JJ's scanner buzzing. She sent me a photo. She'd used Photoshop to superimpose my face onto the model.

"That's as close as I'll ever get to that dress," I yelled.

Weeks went by and I imagined I might make the runner-up category for my essay. I wondered if the contest judges glimpsed a wedding-ring-size nugget of truth in my prose.

What I truly expose is my happiness: This is the day I marry the only man I've ever loved.

There was truth to certain lines.

Wedding planning, however, was making me want to elope. Wedding-site venues promised "outdoor wonders" on their fancy brochures and websites. Maybe the muddy places I'd been trudging through would transform into verdant paradises in the summer, but dead ferns and rickety wood arch structures with hefty rental price tags hardly seemed ideal. At each site, Mike and I were given a full price sheet at the tour's conclusion. Our wedding had become a "package deal."

One location included a fee for a valet for the day, though the parking lot was adjacent to the site. Another required a contract whereby we would agree to "clear out all guests"—like cattle—on the hour to make room for a late-night reception slot.

When I spotted some fine print for one site that assessed a $1,000 "table linen usage fee," I drew a devil's face on the photo in its brochure—bridal disillusionment at its finest.

And so many places were already booked through the summer. I started considering a carriage in Vegas. We'd ride to a drive-thru chapel and exchange vows in minutes, for cheap. Or just walk to the courthouse one afternoon.

I was starting to feel like giving up my hunt for a wedding location when, one chilly January afternoon at work, my fiancé called. He didn't bother to say hello.

"There was a FedEx letter on our doorstep for you."

"And?"

"Haaaaaaaaaaaaaahhhhhhh," he wailed. "It says: 'Congratulations! We are pleased to announce that you are the Grand Prizewinner in the Walk Down the Aisle to Maui Contest.'"

He read the prize details:

. . . six-day honeymoon trip to Maui, Hawaii . . .

. . . includes airfare . . .

. . . and a sunset honeymoon sailboat ride . . .

I screamed. Barbara and JJ ran into my office, thinking I was dying. Until this moment, the most dramatic action I'd taken at work was kicking a jammed copy machine.

"I won!"

Barbara fox-trotted around my office, her head bobbing and heels clacking. JJ turned pink and began bowing in my direction. "You did it—you are the chosen romance writer." My boss muttered congratulations and slithered away, scared by the female shrieks that echoed down our office space out of some primal, high-pitched bridal frenzy. I couldn't catch my breath.

"You are also the chosen dress wearer," JJ cried.

The prospect of returning to paradise for free was invigorating. "You know, I'll do it," I announced.

They applauded.

"Let me finish," I continued. "I'll wear the dress *after* I take a sharp pair of scissors to it and make it my own."

Within days, JJ had spread the news. People I barely knew congratulated me in the halls on winning a Harlequin modeling contest.

An instructor called. "You're going to be on a Harlequin Romance book cover?"

I had to defend my reputation as a serious writer. Just after I shut my door for some quiet plotting, the phone rang. I picked up.

"Did you get my email?" JJ blurted.

"Why are you calling me from twenty feet away?"

"It's important," she paused, then giggled.

I clicked it open. It was a photo of a model in a sequined American flag dress.

"I'm hanging up on you."

An hour later, my phone rang again. I glared at it.

"Hello."

"Is this Angie?"

"Yessss," I played along.

"I'm calling from Harlequin . . ."

"Wha?" JJ was disguising her voice well, I thought.

"Did you receive the good news?"

This person was too polite to be JJ, I realized, and noticed that the red illuminated square on my phone indicated that this was an outside line.

"Yes, and thank you, this is such a remarkable opportunity for me to travel to the exact place I want to for my once-in-a-lifetime honeymoon," I said. I truly was thankful to this woman; being bankrolled in any fashion is a godsend. As I babbled on praising the contest and the good people at Harlequin, my brain was sending my mouth a telegram: Do. Not. Mention. Dress.

"I've been in your area to ski—do you ski?"

"All the time." Even though I'm a bona fide snowboarder. Even though I'd argued for years that skiing is for old married people. But I would even switch to skiing if that was somehow a requirement in the contest.

She explained that information would be arriving in the mail. Then came the clincher.

"Do you plan on wearing the Harlequin original dress?"

"Ahhhh," I breathed out.

"Our one-of-a-kind dress is a size 6."

"Oh dear. With my height . . ." my voice trailed. This polite Canadian woman cracked an audible smile. Did she loathe the dress too? Did she have to promote the hell out of it, despite her own philosophical opposition to bird's nest clothing? And perhaps even general good sense?

My arm went numb. I looked down and found that I had coiled the entire phone cord up to my armpit. I thought of the gloves on the book-cover bride. What was I doing?

"Would you like the cash equivalent?" she asked, matter-of-factly.

My heart sped up. "Hmm." I forced a deep breath in and out, as if I were considering. "Cash equivalent, instead of wearing the Harlequin dress? Well, I certainly wouldn't do justice to the dress if it was all out of proportion. And this is the *big day,* right? So my aim is to get everything—dress and all—near perfect. I guess I'll just have to take the cash."

Hell, yes.

When I received the check, I didn't even know how to sign for certified mail. I went dress shopping, but nothing looked right. Though I had espoused the wonders of the wedding dress in my essay, when I actually tried one on for the first time, I felt confined. The spaghetti straps—which were all the rage that spring—looked like they were tying off my suddenly sausagelike arms. Trying on so many yards of stark whiteness made my teeth suddenly seem a sorry yellow. I'd had enough of staring at my futile reflection. I felt defeated. The repurposed prom dress might be my best hope.

While posting a kayak for sale in the miscellaneous category on the craigslist website, I noticed a posting for a wedding dress—in my size. It was simple, no boning and no splayed-out tulle in the skirt. The dress didn't seem cursed, either; the woman wore it for a total of three hours before changing, and she had moved into her husband's studio (hello, honey!) and didn't have an extra inch in their shared closet for storage.

When she came over, I opened the door to a mirror image of myself; she was my height, my shape, and my age. I even liked her outfit. We both admired the dress when I put it on. It was satin with a slimming empire waist and a straight, simple skirt. Its tank style, dotted with iridescent miniature pearls, was tasteful; and no medieval undergarments were required.

Everything feels right. With this gown, I become a woman whose movements reflect poise and pride.

I gave her $325 cash—a fraction of the price on her original receipt. I stashed my remaining prize money away for what would become part of a down payment on a house. I put on the gown again when she left.

Together we become a magnificent work of art on display.

I hid the dress until the day of.

What a day it was: perfect eighty-degree weather, guests clustering beside a lake rimmed with poppies, snapdragons, lupine, and crocosmias in full bloom. Though the cake's fresh flower toppers were accidentally left behind in a refrigerator forty miles away, my mom and aunt clipped a few fern fronds from the lakeside for decoration—and the biggest "disaster" of the day was averted. One bridesmaid put the finishing touch on her sandals by giving them a last-minute coat of silver spray paint. The rest of us had finished spraying our inexpensive sandals the week before, so she was the one whose wedding souvenir was a silver crisscross pattern on both feet.

As I slid on my dress—Craig I called it, for the website that brought us together—I flashed back to the doctored image of myself in the Harlequin original. My mom got teary when I stepped out of the cabinlike dressing room in my dress, and I did, too: I was relieved that I didn't have to be a bird's nest polyester bride.

The groomsmen paddled a boat across the lake, delivering Mike to our sturdy arch. Our guests, everyone I knew, stood in the grass, smiling. I was flanked by my parents.

I see the bright green eyes of my husband-to-be widen, meeting my gaze with every step I take down the aisle, welcoming me into the rest of our life.

What I didn't anticipate is the way in which sunlight reflected on the water, and the fluttering of the butterflies by the poppies. Mike slipped a memento onto my finger, and I onto his. I didn't know I would be so elated, so grateful, so at ease at my own wedding. I melted into Harlequinism; it was as if the jewels of the dress—and of my being—actually threw those starry glimmers.

My face tells the story of our six-year courtship, our love, our lifelong marriage; the gown holds me, nestles me, helps me breathe out, "I do."

Acknowledgments

~ ANY ANTHOLOGY IS a collaborative work. It starts with the editor's vision and then is filled out and completed by the voices of the contributing writers. I want to thank all of the writers included here for their talent, patience, and willingness to work with us to create a single whole out of all their individual pieces.

A huge thank you to everyone at Seal Press, especially the most enthusiastic publicist anywhere, Krista Rafanello; copy editor Elizabeth Woodman and proofreader Elizabeth Mathews for excellent catches; and our editor extraordinaire, Marisa Solís. Marisa not only offered us immeasurable help by editing this book, she caved under our incessant urging and wrote us an essay.

Thank you to my agent, Nina Collins, for her excellent (and free) advice.

Friends and family have contributed with support, encouragement, and tons of hilarious wedding stories. Thank you Kate Chynoweth, Tara Bray Smith, Chris Weldon, LeeAnne Ramsey, Mark Fiore, Connie Biewald, Brooks Phillips, Laura Brown, Caroline Berry, and Wayne Schoech. And, always, always, always to my husband Pete, who is the best person I know and who drove in silence for eight hours while I read essays in the seat next to him.

Finally, thank you doesn't even begin to cover it for Lisa Taggart. This book was her idea, and she generously invited me to coedit. It's been a hilarious pleasure every step of the way.

—SAMANTHA SCHOECH

I would like to thank the funny and smart women in this anthology for sharing their stories; it has been a pleasure working with all of you. Many thanks also to Alison Aves, Lisa Vollmer, Erika Ehmsen, and Abigail Peterson, whose coffee break conversation was the seed for this book; Katie Tamony for approving my extracurricular effort; Seal Press's Marisa Solís for thoughtfully and gracefully shepherding the book along; Krista Rafanello, for super-duper energy; Mary O'Connell, for being the Lady of Perpetual High-larity; Karminder Brown, for having both stellar hair and a disastrous wedding; Fiona Fox, who's a perfect pal with perfect hair; Kate Chynoweth, for friendship that can survive any rocky road trip; Peter Fish, for wise writing advice and general role-model-dom; my sister, Jennifer, for being more fabulous even than her fabulous hair, and also for wearing a hat to my wedding; my mother, for, among the first million things, making that delicious cake; my dad and Karen, for showing up; Trent Stewart, for brilliance, inspiration, encouragement, and the salad days past and future; my coeditor Samantha, who is all-around kick-ass and superb, and whose smart editing and total hilarity made this project infinitely better as well as a joy; and Jimbo, for being as good at telling the joke as being the joke, and with whom I'm profoundly delighted to be committed to a lifetime of laughs.

—LISA TAGGART

About the Contributors

ℜ— SARA BERKELEY grew up in Dublin, Ireland, and now lives in a rural community north of San Francisco. She has published four collections of poetry *(Penn, Home-Movie Nights, Facts About Water,* and *Strawberry Thief)*, a collection of short stories *(The Swimmer in the Deep Blue Dream)*, and a novel *(Shadowing Hannah)*. This wedding, her second, was even more fun than her first, but she thinks she is done.

ℜ— HEATHER BRYANT has published nonfiction and fiction in *City Limits* magazine, the *San Francisco Chronicle, Grecourt Review,* and *Speak Up*. She won the Gertrude Posner Spencer Prize for fiction writing from Smith College. An MFA candidate in fiction writing at Vermont College, she lives in Brooklyn, New York.

⌒ Patricia Bunin (patriciabunin@sbcglobal.net) is a freelance writer and PR consultant who lives in Altadena, California. She writes features for the *Pasadena Star-News* and has published in *Chicken Soup for the Soul, Cosmopolitan,* Oprah.com, and numerous other publications. She is the author of *Do You Think We Could Have Made It?* (a book of poems for the separated and divorced) and was founding editor of *RUFUS* poetry magazine under a grant from the National Endowment for the Arts. She writes and speaks extensively on breast cancer and is working on a humorous book about her personal experience with it.

⌒ Jennifer Carsen is a freelance writer and editor who lives in the Chicago area with her husband and cat. She specializes in the areas of fitness, food, relationships, and travel writing, and her work has appeared in *Chicago Health & Beauty* magazine and other publications. A former attorney, she has written two nonfiction books on legal topics—one of which, ironically, is a do-it-yourself divorce guide. She has ghostwritten a novel and is currently at work on a novel of her own. Most of the time, when she's not dealing with Bridezilla, she loves weddings.

⌒ Danielle deLeon, former cartoonist and current ice hockey goalie, is busily establishing herself as an up-and-coming memoirist. In 2004, her essay "You Got Beat by a Girl" appeared in the anthology

A Cup of Comfort for Courage (Adams Media) and received one of the four cover blurbs. In addition to developing her memoirs, she writes feature articles for the Stanford University School of Medicine. She lives in Redwood City, California, with an annoying parrot that is still alive merely because he is so cute. She is 99 percent romantically compatible with Ray Bradbury. Find out more about her wildly eclectic life at www.leapintothe.net.

⌒ SARAH GAMBITO is the author of *Matadora*. Her poems have appeared or are forthcoming in the *Iowa Review, Antioch Review, New Republic,* and *FIELD*. She holds degrees from the University of Virginia and the Creative Writing Program at Brown University.

⌒ CAREN GUSSOFF (www.spitkitten.com) is the author of the novel *Homecoming* and *The Wave and Other Stories*. Her work has appeared in *Strictly Casual, Inappropriate Random,* the *Gotham Writers' Workshop Guide to Writing Fiction,* and she was a nominee for the 2001 *Village Voice*'s "Writers on the Verge." She and Chris were hitched last year in Seattle's historic and dizzying Smith Tower. Their best friend was the officiant, only desserts were served at the reception, and Caren wore knee-high combat boots with her perfect dress.

⌒ SARAH K. INMAN moved from Rhode Island to New Orleans in 1995. Despite a spontaneous sabbatical, thanks to Hurricane Katrina, she, her husband, and cats still reside in New Orleans. Her publications include a novel *(Finishing Skills)* and a nonfiction narrative in the forthcoming anthology *Do You Know What It Means to Miss*

New Orleans? Her fiction has also appeared in the *Melic Review, Fell Swoop, Rogue, Washington Square Review,* and *Cups: the Café Culture Magazine.* She is the fiction editor of *Rive Gauche.*

⌒ When she was five, ANNE JOHNSON married her golden retriever, Ajax, in a quiet ceremony in her back yard. Today she is a clinical social worker whose previous writing has appeared in *Health* magazine. She works at the San Francisco VA Medical Center, where she specializes in care of the elderly. To her knowledge, none of her patients has ever owned a bed-and-breakfast inn. She lives in San Francisco with her husband, Peter; son, Joseph; and current retriever, Della; and their house has a view of the ocean (from the roof).

⌒ STACEY LUFTIG is a playwright, lyricist, and editor living in New York City. Her work was featured in the long-running off-Broadway musical revue *That's Life!* and she is currently writing book and lyrics for *Understood Betsy,* a family musical. Her books include *The Joni Mitchell Companion* and *The Paul Simon Companion.* Stacey is grateful to her husband and favorite collaborator, Daniel Jussim, for his invaluable ideas and edits on this essay, and for putting up with the wedding *mishegas.* She has not yet told him that she is planning her own bat mitzvah.

⌒ ANGIE SUCHY MARSH works in communications. Her articles, essays, and short stories have been published in *World's Best Shortest Stories, Oregon Quarterly,* and *Oregon Restaurant Association*

Magazine, as well as in websites and newspapers. Her writing quest is to top her newspaper story, "Local Man's Chickens Come out Clucking in National Competition."

᧐— MARY O'CONNELL is the author of the short story collection *Living with Saints.* She lives in Lawrence, Kansas, with her family.

᧐— SOPHIA RADAY lives in Berkeley, California, with her husband, their four-year-old boy, two bipartisan dogs, and assorted firearms. Their ongoing exploits as a couple are chronicled in Sophia's regular column, Mommy Athens, Daddy Sparta (MADS), from which "Shotgun Wedding" is adapted. Mommy Athens, Daddy Sparta appears bimonthly in the online literary journal *Literary Mama* (www .literarymama.com). *Forbes* recently listed *Literary Mama* in its "Best of the Web" listings, mentioning a MADS column specifically. Sophia's writing has also appeared in the online magazine *Books and Babies,* in *Stanford* magazine, and in the anthology *Using Our Words: Moms & Dads on Raising Kids in the Modern Neighborhood.*

᧐— An award-winning journalist, SUZ REDFEARN sits at home in her jammies freelancing full-time for the likes of the *Washington Post, Salon, Slate, Men's Health,* and *Child.* Her travel essays have appeared in the books *Whose Panties Are These?* and *The Best Travel Writing 2005,* and she has done commentary for NPR's "All Things Considered." Sired in South Florida and seasoned in Louisiana, Redfearn now dwells in the Center of the Free World (Washington, D.C.) with her husband, Marty; two dogs; and 1.5 cats. Continuing in a no-frills theme, Redfearn and her husband don't exchange presents when their wedding anniversary rolls around, nor do they even go out for an overpriced dinner, since those are just digested and discarded in a matter of twenty-four hours. Instead, they travel, doing their best to create indelible images in their heads.

〜 JENNIFER RUSKIN has taught English, social studies, and drama to middle school students for eleven years. Her superpowers include handling hard-to-open jars, noticing even the most subtle of haircuts, and making a mean matzo ball soup. She has officiated three weddings and is available for hire for the months June through August. She both summers and winters in San Francisco. She'd like to thank her incredibly supportive family and David, a real mensch. This is her first time in print.

〜 JENNIFER LI SHOTZ is a happily married writer living and working in Brooklyn. She earned an MFA in creative nonfiction from Columbia University. Her work has appeared on *Salon* and in *Budget Living,* and she is working on a nonfiction book. Even her parents were in agreement that her wedding band rocked.

〜 PATRICIA SMITH'S work has been published in places such as *So to speak: a feminist journal of literature and the arts, The Tusculum Review,* and *One Teacher in 10: Gay and Lesbian Educators Tell Their Stories.* She received an MFA from Virginia Commonwealth University, where she teaches writing and coordinates the VCU First Novelist Award. She hasn't seen her Canadian relatives in a few years, as they have stopped crossing the border to come visit her family.

⌐ Marisa Solís has been writing vicariously for the past six years, four of them as an editor of travel guidebooks and two as the managing editor of numerous parenting, women's studies, and travel literature titles. Aside from regularly being published in *Juxtapoz* magazine on assignment, this is her first time writing for pleasure since college, which she realizes is *long* overdue. She lives and plays in Oakland, California, with her husband of almost-nine years whose definition of getting dressed up is putting on a clean shirt without skulls on it.

⌐ Mimi Towle currently enjoys watching her two daughters, Grace and Natalie, in their Tiny Toes dance classes every week. She is an editor at *Marin Magazine,* and has been published in *Self, Parenting, Shape, Fit Pregnancy,* eHow.com, and eve.com, among others. As a working mother she was inspired to write the book *Bilingual Babycare*. She lives with her husband, Peter, and daughters in Mill Valley, California.

© CAROLINE BERRY

About the Editors

﹏ LISA TAGGART works as a staff travel writer for *Sunset Magazine*, where she has covered camel racing, frog counting, amateur ballet dancing, dune boarding, and scenic cemetery walks. She is a graduate of Harvard University and the Iowa Writers' Workshop. She lives with the man of her dreams in Santa Clara, California; their house is, conveniently, a short walk from the hair stylist of her dreams.

﹏ SAMANTHA SCHOECH'S fiction has appeared in many magazines, including *Seventeen, Gettysburg Review, The Sun,* and *Glimmer Train.* Her travel pieces, fashion copy, and lifestyle articles appear in books and magazines here and there, most often in *Marin Magazine,* where she is an editor. She has also worked as a waitress, a very bad secretary, and a worse daycare provider. She recently starred in her first and only TV commercial. She lives in San Francisco with her husband, Pete.

﹏ TO READ MORE more funny wedding stories, and to view photos, visit www.tiedinknots.com.

Selected Titles from Seal Press

For more than twenty-five years, Seal Press has published groundbreaking books. By women. For women. Visit our website at www.sealpress.com.

IT'S A GIRL: WOMEN WRITERS ON RAISING DAUGHTERS edited by Andrea J. Buchanan. $14.95. 1-58005-147-2. The companion title to *It's a Boy*, this anthology describes what it's like—and why it's a unique experience—to mother girls.

CONFESSIONS OF A NAUGHTY MOMMY: HOW I FOUND MY LOST LIBIDO by Heidi Raykeil. $14.95. 1-58005-157-X. The Naughty Mommy shares her bedroom woes and woo-hoos with other mamas who are rediscovering their sex lives after baby and are ready to think about it, talk about it, and *do* it.

MEXICO, A LOVE STORY: WOMEN WRITE ABOUT THE MEXICAN EXPERIENCE edited by Camille Cusumano. $15.95. 1-58005-156-1. In this rich anthology, two dozen women describe the country they love and why they have fallen under its spell.

ABOVE US ONLY SKY: A WOMAN LOOKS BACK, AHEAD, AND INTO THE MIRROR by Marion Winik. $14.95. 1-58005-144-8. A witty and engaging book from NPR commentator Marion Winik reveals what it's like facing midlife without getting tangled up in the past or hung up in the future.

RECKLESS: THE OUTRAGEOUS LIVES OF NINE KICK-ASS WOMEN by Gloria Mattioni. $14.95. 1-58005-148-0. From Lisa Distefano who captains a pirate vessel on her quest to protect sea life, to Libby Riddles, the first woman to win the legendary Iditarod, this collection of profiles explores the lives of nine women who took unconventional life paths to achieve extraordinary results.

THE RISKS OF SUNBATHING TOPLESS: AND OTHER FUNNY STORIES FROM THE ROAD edited by Kate Chynoweth. $15.95. 1-58005-141-3. From Kandahar to Baja to Moscow, these wry, amusing essays capture the comic essence of bad travel, and the female experience on the road.